State of Mind

The Success Secrets of 50 South Australian Entrepreneurs

State of Mind

The success secrets of 50 South Australian entrepreneurs

CHRIS DOUDLE AND KAREN BALDWIN

Wakefield Press

1 The Parade West

Kent Town

South Australia 5067

www.wakefieldpress.com.au

First published 2005

Photography by Peter Hoare
Designed by Liz Nicholson, Design Bite
Colour reproduction by Graphic Print Group, Adelaide
Printed in China at Everbest Printing Co Ltd

ISBN 1 86254 684 3

Chris Doudle is the founder and Managing Director of one of South Australia's leading corporate communications firms, Strategic Public Relations.

He is a member and former South Australian President of the global Young Entrepreneurs Organisation and a former Board Member of the South Australian Enterprise Workshop entrepreneur development program.

Karen Baldwin is Strategic Public Relations' General Manager. She is a graduate of the Governor's Leadership Foundation and a Trustee of business facilitator vivasa (formerly Business Vision 2010).

Both former journalists, Chris and Karen jointly have almost 40 years' communications and image management experience.

Their work in public and media relations has focused heavily on fast-growth businesses in the family and corporate sector, and they have had the good fortune to work closely with many hundreds of entrepreneurial businesses and inspiring individuals.

Contents

Introduction

Bravo for entrepreneurs. Hooray for the risk-takers. Three cheers for those who break the mould, do things differently and are willing to embrace innovation as they build their businesses.

The *Macquarie Dictionary* defines an entrepreneur as 'one who organises and manages any enterprise, especially one involving considerable risk'.

South Australia has many hundreds of individuals who fit this description. Our intention with this book is to bring you some valuable business insights from a small selection of them.

This book is not a list of South Australia's 'best known' entrepreneurs. While some of those featured enjoy a high profile, others are virtually unknown beyond their own client base – the classic 'quiet achievers'.

Nor is it a catalogue of those entrepreneurial companies that are 'the largest', have 'the highest turnover' or are 'the most profitable', although there are some significant businesses – and larger than life personalities – featured within these pages.

Instead, we have chosen to present a broad cross-section of risk-takers and innovators from a diverse range of industries, showcasing 'the good, the bad and the ugly' of their path to business success.

As you would expect, common issues emerge and others overlap. Staffing, budgeting and strategic planning are just a few.

Where possible however, we have chosen to profile individuals whose stories demonstrate starkly different business scenarios and the lessons that can be drawn from the entrepreneur's own experience.

We are extremely grateful to all those who participated and for their openness in discussions with us. Many were happy to bare their soul about mistakes they had made, in the knowledge that this book was intended as a learning tool for others.

We believe the wide range of individuals and companies that we have chosen helps canvass experiences and lessons that may never have been uncovered if we had interviewed only the '50 largest' companies, or used some other arbitrary yardstick.

Not all the individuals profiled invented their own 'widget' or launched their own company. Our belief is that entrepreneurship and innovation are attitudes that can shape the success of any company, not just a start-up.

In fact, some of our profiles focus on second or third-generation companies, demonstrating that a new and innovative approach can reinvigorate a decades-old business.

This is why we have titled the book *State of Mind*, as self-belief, independent thinking and willingness to make bold decisions are at the core of the entrepreneurial spirit.

Some of the case studies featured are friends and associates. Some are clients. Many are drawn from the ranks of the South Australian chapter of the Young Entrepreneurs Organisation (YEO), the Young Presidents Organisation (YPO) and The Executive Connection (TEC), all extremely well-respected peer-to-peer networking and learning organisations.

All those profiled are relevant to the theme of this book and have been included because of the insights they bring to building businesses in an entrepreneurial fashion.

This book is not meant to be the most in-depth analysis of the companies involved or the economic environment in which they operate. It doesn't include any charts or graphs. Often it does not even provide turnover or profit figures.

It is simply aimed at letting entrepreneurs relate their stories about what worked and what didn't work during their climb to the top.

The international Global Entrepreneurship Monitor (GEM) report – prepared by leading scholars from Babson College and the London Business School, with support from the Kauffman Center for Entrepreneurial Leadership in the US – is one of the key ongoing studies into worldwide entrepreneurial activity.

GEM analysis shows that those who believe they have the skills to pursue a new venture are six times more likely to be active entrepreneurially than those who do not think they have the skills. The findings of GEM consistently show that knowledge of entrepreneurs and their modus operandi encourages others to 'have a go', take risks and build better businesses. This, in turn, drives the development of an economy.

It is interesting to note that, unprompted, many of the participants talked about why they chose to establish and/or retain their business base in South Australia. Where appropriate we have included these comments, as it helps paint a picture of the economic and lifestyle elements that make the State attractive to people and business.

Perhaps this will help provide some reference point for politicians and other decision-makers as they chart South Australia's future direction.

As communications professionals, both of us are fortunate to hear many inspiring business success stories in the course of our everyday careers. Wherever possible we have applied lessons learnt from others to assist us in our own business and personal development.

Hopefully, this book will help other individuals and businesses with strategies for survival and growth.

We hope you and your business are among them.

Chris Doudle   Karen Baldwin

Stefan Ahrens

Stefan Ahrens admits that the diverse activities of his company, Ahrens Engineering, can at times be mind-boggling.

From chicken sheds and seed bins, grain silos and mine sites, to large industrial buildings and warehouses, wineries, aircraft hangers, commercial buildings, material handling, and even the roof of the Telstra Stadium in Sydney, Ahrens Engineering has carved a 'can do' reputation as a design, fabrication and construction company that thrives on a challenge.

The diversity and complexity of Ahrens Engineering's projects have helped win the company a loyal customer base and transformed a small regional blacksmith shop into an $80 million construction group.

Ahrens Engineering was established by Stefan Ahrens' great-grandfather Johann in 1906 at Sheaoak Log in South Australia's Barossa Valley. For two generations it ran as a one-man operation serving local farmers.

In the mid-1960s Stefan's father, Bob, widened the company's product base to include grain silos, rural and chicken sheds, stone and land rollers, and the construction of general industrial buildings in the Barossa.

Stefan joined in 1990 and has spearheaded a bold new era for Ahrens Engineering, moulding the company into a design and construction powerhouse. He was appointed Managing Director in 1996.

With more than 230 staff nationally, Ahrens Engineering is now a leading supplier of industrial buildings, grain silos, structural steel and domestic and rural buildings.

The Ahrens Engineering group includes Ahrens Construction (with operations in South Australia, New South Wales and Queensland), Sherwell Ahrens (in South Australia, Victoria and Tasmania) and M&S Steel Buildings and Silos (in Queensland). The group has undertaken projects in every Australian state and territory, as well as overseas in locations ranging from New Zealand, the Solomon Islands and Hawaii to Libya and France.

The Telstra Stadium in Sydney shows the scale of some Ahrens projects. The company designed and constructed the north and south grandstand roofing in a $9.5 million contract that involved fabricating and erecting the structural steel trusses for the roof along with the polycarbonate roof sheeting and stainless steel guttering.

The steel was processed at Ahrens' massive facility at Sheaoak Log and transported to Sydney where it was assembled on-site and lifted into place. It was a huge logistical exercise but a major feather in the cap for the company.

Other major projects in recent years have included a Westpac Call Centre building in Queensland; the Amcor glass bottle facility in South Australia; a huge chicken feedmill for Inghams in New Zealand; steelwork at a gold mine in the Northern Territory; a waste recycling facility in New South Wales; a Tiger helicopter factory in Queensland; and a wine processing facility in the Loire Valley of France.

If you can help make money for your clients then they're certain to come back.

When Stefan joined the company, the rural recession was threatening the future of the small enterprise. He pulled Ahrens out of the grain silo market to focus on structural steel platework and industrial buildings, with a particular focus on the wine industry.

It was a shrewd move. The wine sector was growing rapidly and wine companies were frantically constructing new facilities.

Stefan soon realised that other sectors also required large industrial facilities that could be constructed by Ahrens. The company began building larger silos for the grain industry, as well as designing and constructing industrial buildings and warehouse/office complexes.

Ultimately, Stefan re-entered the farm field bin and silo market through the acquisition of Sherwell Silos. With Ahrens buying metal in bulk and undertaking large-scale manufacturing the bins were much more profitable, and the company now makes more than 1600 field bins and silos each year for Australian farmers.

Ahrens Engineering has a national reputation as a company that thrives on difficult or challenging projects.

A significant portion of the Ahrens work is in the design and construction of large industrial buildings and warehouses.

The company has developed a niche in this market based on a high level of experience and the capability to offer a 'one-stop shop' from design through to complete fit-out of the building.

'We are willing to look at projects others will shy away from. A good example is a project in Brisbane that involved building a 70-metre high round tower on top of a 260-metre high building. The logistics of that were extremely difficult but we were able to provide the whole design and construct package.'

This approach is a major marketing advantage and wins a great deal of work for Ahrens Engineering.

'Our aim is to give our clients a complete solution. If somebody wants something built – for instance, a large grain complex – we are able to do the lot. They can say to us that they want to store 10,000 tonnes of grain, conveyor it to the silo at 100 tonnes an hour and outload it at 200 tonnes an hour. We can come up with a complete design solution.

'With our farm products, a farmer can come to Ahrens to buy a silo to put their grain in or a field bin to store it in the paddock. Then they can buy one of our implement sheds or hay sheds, or even a garage for their car. It's the same one-stop philosophy, just different projects.'

Ahrens Engineering's 'start to finish' capability has proven a huge competitive advantage.

'For some clients on large jobs the alternative to using us would be to contract a project management company – but then that company would have to engage separate designers and steel fabricators which creates a double margin. Because we can do it all we wipe out that double margin and make it more attractive for people to use us.'

Stefan has always set strict targets for himself as he goes about winning work nationally. Under Stefan's stewardship Ahrens Engineering is always 'punching above our weight'.

'I would plan a trip to Darwin for instance and say, OK, I have to win a million dollars worth of work while I'm there or it's not worth going. I'd get there and go flat out to win that business. I find that you need to set goals like that to keep moving forward.'

In 1996 Stefan won a $9.3 million infrastructure project at the Mount Todd Gold Mine in the Northern Territory. At the time, Ahrens Engineering's entire turnover was just $12 million and there was plenty of discussion around the dinner table as Stefan and Bob debated the risks and merits of such rapid growth.

'I told Dad I had won the job and he was a bit negative about it so I told him the best thing he could do was get an airline ticket and go on holiday. In the long run we made a very solid profit on that job and it was a real turning point.

'It gave us the confidence we needed to stretch ourselves and go for bigger jobs.'

The specialised nature of Ahrens Engineering's work means that once the company wins a customer it tends to keep them for subsequent projects. For example, after constructing a complex feed mill for the giant Inghams chicken group a few years ago, Ahrens has been engaged for additional Inghams projects throughout Australia.

'After a while we end up doing all the work for some clients because we have a really good relationship and they know the job will be done extremely well.'

Stefan's team also likes to add value to client projects.

'We built a barrel store for a winery and the wall panelling required to maintain the constant temperature for wine was going to be very expensive. We came up with a different system that used cladding inside and out, along with insulation, and that saved the client $400,000 just by redesigning the cladding system.

'If you can give your clients that sort of service it's gold to them. If you can help make money for your clients then they're certain to come back.'

Client loyalty is reciprocated. Stefan will take his team anywhere to undertake a project for a loyal client. One recent project for Inghams involved building a feed mill in New Zealand.

'Once a client can see that you have the capability and the willingness to basically do work anywhere for them, more work comes. We did a small material handling job for a cement company recently and they said they had been looking for a company with our kind of flexibility, as they have similar projects in the next 12 months. So we look to strengthen those ties by doing the right thing by our customer.'

Lessons Learnt:

* Talk to your customers about how you can improve your product – and then make sure you actually make the required changes.
* Know your business, analyse all the information and take advice from others when making major decisions – but make sure you go with your own gut feel. Just because others have advice to offer doesn't mean you should always take that advice. If you know your business well enough you will be able to make the right decision yourself.
* Learn from your mistakes but be passionate and go for it! Don't be in a position where you look back and say: 'I wish I had done that'.

Advice to Others:

* One of Stefan's favourite lines is 'work hard and play hard'. Put another way: 'You have to make sure that you stop and celebrate your successes and major milestones with the people who helped get you there.'

Simon Brown

Kermit the Frog once said: 'It's not easy being green.' Resourceco's Simon Brown would probably agree, but it's certainly getting easier.

Simon founded his business in 1992 at the age of 22 and has since built Resourceco into a $25 million, leading-edge resource recovery business.

Along the way he has worked hand-in-hand with government authorities and the construction sector to reshape community attitudes to the disposal of demolition waste. He has also helped create a number of new and innovative recycled products that are now standard materials for road bases and other construction purposes.

Resourceco began when Simon Brown and David McMahon (a shareholder and director), built a mobile plant for crushing demolition waste. Simon had been working with David's company in the demolition business and recognised the cost and environmental benefits of being able to crush demolition waste on-site for immediate re-use as a sub-base, reducing the cost of transportation to landfill.

From its South Australian base, the company – then known as Mobile Reclaimers – expanded into Victoria and New South Wales, adding earthworks and the recycling of asphalt and other construction materials to its menu of services.

In 1995, Simon saw more value in centralising the company's operations to a fixed site, so he established a Resource Recovery Depot at Wingfield, north of Adelaide. Concrete, asphalt, green waste and mixed loads could now be accepted in exchange for a small dumping fee. These materials were recycled into construction materials, garden mulch and compost.

Production was further enhanced in 1998 when a $1.2 million crushing plant was commissioned, capable of processing 1200 tonnes of concrete a day. Since then, more than $8 million of additional investment has transformed the company into one of the most modern resource recovery operations in the world.

Renamed as Resourceco in July 1999, the company now has more than 800 customers diverting their waste from landfills to the company's recycling centre. These customers – including state and local government authorities, as well as companies from the civil contract construction and demolition industries – are then encouraged to re-use the recycled products in their civil and building works.

More than one million tonnes of waste go through Resourceco's facility each year.

Resourceco was founded on Simon Brown's belief that environmental awareness should become a way of life encouraged by political leaders, the business sector and the community in general.

Noble sentiments, but is there any money in it?

'Not in the early days. I probably spent five years standing on a crushing plant sucking in dust and asking myself: "What am I doing?" But we knew where it was going and the trends overseas, and we knew we just had to stick to it.'

Simon recognised the gradual global change in attitudes to the dumping of waste, and believed he could create a business based on providing a sustainable alternative to the traditional method of sending virtually all demolition waste to landfill.

'In the old days, if someone was pulling down a building most of the bricks, concrete, timber, steel and garden waste would normally be sent straight to landfill. It was crazy because all of these things can be used for other purposes.

'Our facility is now able to transform these materials into useful and usable products such as road bases, asphalt, alternative fuel and construction material. As a result, the amount of landfill is substantially reduced, further improving the sustainability of our environment.

You have to be passionate about what you are doing. You've got to really enjoy it. I think if you're just in a business to make money, I don't think you'll find it easy to make that money.

'We could see what was happening and we knew where the market was heading but the early days were a bit of a struggle. It wasn't an easy message to get across. Back then what we were doing was probably considered a bit "out there" for the South Australian market.'

Initially, Resourceco found itself competing head-on with the major quarries in the provision of road pavement materials. Eventually, though, Simon joined forces to supply recycled products to CSR Readymix, one of Australia's largest construction materials providers.

'It made sense for us to join forces. We were banging our heads together in the market and eventually it just made more sense for us to work together.

'They actually closed one of their quarries and we are doing about 600,000 tonnes a year for CSR Readymix at the moment. They are well positioned to take our product to a number of locations in each state. Everyone wins.'

Competition is fierce in the provision of construction materials and Simon admits that the price difference between his products and those of other suppliers is negligible – however the end price has not been a major factor in building his business.

Resourceco's major market advantage is that its materials are recycled, which means the company benefits directly from the ever-increasing push for government authorities and the construction industry to focus on the environmental benefits of their activities.

Many government authorities now stipulate in construction contracts that a proportion of recycled pavement materials must be used. In some cases, Resourceco is the only supplier of these products, virtually guaranteeing the company a secure and growing market.

'Everyone in government and the construction sector is starting to get an environmental conscience. If a recycled product performs as well as any other product and yet is seen as environmental, people increasingly want to use it.

'With some of the larger companies there is an increasing emphasis on triple bottom line reporting, so they are paying a lot more attention to our activities and our products. We are a preferred supplier.'

There are other advantages to being a recycler. For instance, Resourceco's 'green' credentials enable it to avoid the $10-a-tonne South Australian levy on waste sent to landfill.

'That gives us a big advantage over our competitors,' says Simon.

Partnerships are a core focus for Resourceco. Other than the CSR Readymix alliance, Resourceco has also built business links with Adelaide Brighton Cement and South Australia's road transport authority, Transport SA.

Adelaide Brighton, a large consumer of gas, has formed a new company with Resourceco called the Alternative Fuel Company to process more than 100,000 tonnes of reclaimed material into alternative fuel.

Meanwhile, Resourceco has partnered with the technical department of Transport SA to create new road pavement materials from waste asphalt, concrete and brick. These products are already being specified for major new roadworks such as the Port River Expressway, creating additional large supply contracts for Resourceco.

'That entire freeway has been built out of recycled product, which is a fantastic result. It's very exciting to see that level of commitment by the Government.'

While Simon says Resourceco was a 'quiet achiever' that struggled for credibility in its early days, the company's profile took a significant leap forward when it entered and won the 2002 Telstra South Australian Small Business of the Year Award.

He says the award win definitely opened doors, something that surprised him but which he has been quick to utilise to Resourceco's benefit. The award logo was swiftly emblazoned on the company's website, newsletters, letterhead and profile documentation.

'Winning the Telstra Small Business Award was just amazing in terms of building our credibility with the Government and some of the companies we work with.

'It also gave us the ability to pick up the phone and speak to heads of government departments and other senior government people who may not have paid too much attention to us previously. It gave us more access to those sorts of people, and that was very helpful in making them understand more about our business.'

Persistence and passion are at the core of Simon's business philosophies.

'You have to be passionate about what you are doing. You've got to really enjoy it. I think if you're just in a business to make money, I don't think you'll find it easy to make that money.

'You've got to be prepared to put in the hard yards. All the successful people I have met stick to things for a long period of time and don't keep swapping and changing into other jobs, other companies or other areas.

'Resourceco's journey has been very satisfying for me. With all of the waste streams that we recycle, we are now responsible for diverting about a million tonnes of waste that would have gone straight into landfill 10 years ago. That's a great feeling.'

Lessons Learnt:

- Enter your business into appropriate award competitions. It generally involves some time and effort in preparing the award entry but the right kind of award win can open doors for your business and your people. It also helps raise your profile in the eyes of government and other businesses.
- Rather than going head-to-head with strong competitors, is there a way of exploring partnerships with mutual benefits? You'll never know if you don't ask.
- Be involved closely with those setting the agenda for your industry. Resourceco has worked alongside Transport SA and the Environment Protection Authority (EPA) in driving industry standards and promoting the benefits of recycling to government and the private sector.

Advice to Others:

- Enjoy your work and be passionate about it. It is hard to make money from something you hate doing.

Cashflow MANAGER GOLD
Cashflow MANAGER
The practical tool for recording, planning and controlling business cashflow
Cash Reconciliation
Payments
Employers!
Save amazing amounts of time on pay days, and protect yourself from the Tax Office!
Rent MANAGER
Managing your Rental Property Has Never Been Simpler!
Another simple record keeping tool from CASHFLOW MANAGER
CASHFLOW MANAGER™
THE PRACTICAL TOOL FOR RECORDING, PLANNING & CONTROLLING BUSINESS CASHFLOW
CASHFLOW MANAGER
The Practical Tool for Record
and Controlling Business

Wayne Burgan

Wayne Burgan is as much a marketer as he is an accountant.

While some may find the combination unusual, Wayne's strong entrepreneurial flair has seen him turn a very good, simple idea into business success throughout Australia and overseas.

His company, Cashflow Manager, and the easy-to-use bookkeeping program of the same name, saves small business owners from countless frustrating hours using complex programs to do their accounts.

Rather than the traditional double-entry accounting system, Cashflow Manager uses a simple single-entry column system where the user can see where their receipts are coming from and their payments are going, allowing them to manage their cashflow.

The idea for Cashflow Manager came about in the 1980s when Wayne had his own accounting practice, Burgan and Associates, providing services to small businesses.

His early career was spent in various accounting positions with John Martins and the Public Trustee before he joined the Australian Tax Office (ATO) and worked in assessing, audit, business tax and Pay As You Earn (PAYE) roles.

'Working at the ATO gave me an insight into the difficulties that small business people face.

'Cashflow Manager was born out of wanting to help clients in the small business area because they were the ones that I felt needed the most help in the most cost-effective way.'

During his career, Wayne soon discovered that while most small business people had extensive knowledge in their chosen fields, they had little understanding of accounting.

Success can often come from the simplest of ideas, but people haven't seen or grasped it. I am still surprised by the simplicity of the idea and its success.

He initially began drafting step-by-step instructions and examples to help his clients prepare their records, eventually leading to the creation of Cashflow Manager.

'From the outset of my accounting practice, I really enjoyed the marketing side and promoted myself through public speaking and writing articles. I wrote an article that someone at the Government's Small Business Centre was impressed with, and they started referring clients to me.

'One of the things I did when I started my accounting practice was to get together with a group of about half a dozen other accountants – most of whom I used to work with at the ATO – so we could bounce ideas off each other and discuss the issues that we and our clients were facing.

'I took the Cashflow Manager concept to this group and they assisted me with feedback on ways to improve it. They all had clients who were facing the same issues that mine were, and they were keen to use it.

'I could see there was an enormous need for a product like this.

'A friend of mine worked for a stationery wholesaler and I showed the original manual system concept to him. He told me not to waste my time because these things just didn't sell. But I knew the accountants wanted it so we decided to take it direct to them.'

Two thousand copies of the first edition were self-published in 1990 and distributed to small business clients through Wayne's own practice and those of other accountants.

The manuals were personalised with the names of the accounting firms on the front cover, so they could use them as a marketing tool for their own practices.

Buoyed by the initial enthusiastic response to the book and following subsequent print runs, Wayne started selling the book into New Zealand in 1992 and the United Kingdom in 1994.

Such was the success and demands of Cashflow Manager, Wayne then made the decision to sell his accounting practice to focus full-time on publishing, recognising there was considerable scope to further develop and expand the product.

The first software version was released in 1996.

Cashflow Manager is primarily marketed to businesses that are reporting on the cash basis (generally businesses with a turnover of less than $1 million), use the Simplified Tax System or don't understand double-entry accounting, depreciation and journal entries.

Users of the product include plumbers, electricians, lawyers, doctors, dentists, retailers, restaurants, farmers, consultants and even accountants for their own records.

Cashflow Manager continues to be sold through accountants and business advisers such as banks and business associations that have a focus on assisting small businesses. More than 200,000 manual systems have been sold and software system sales have topped 95,000.

In addition to Australia, the product is sold in the UK, the United States and Canada.

The original Cashflow Manager has been expanded into a suite of products in recent years based on feedback from users and ongoing changing legislative requirements.

These include Invoice Manager, which prepares invoices and controls money owing from clients and customers, and to suppliers; Wages Manager, which helps pay employees and complies with all ATO rules about superannuation; and Rent Manager, for owners of rental properties.

After 14 years selling the product only through accountants, early in 2005 Wayne made the move into selling Cashflow Manager through retail channels. The product is now sold through small to medium-sized computer hardware and software retail outlets. Wayne is carefully monitoring the success of this move before considering the possibility of selling to larger retailers.

While a natural progression for the company, the move into retail had to be carefully handled to ensure that accountants – particularly those who had been loyal to Cashflow Manager for so many years – didn't feel alienated by the development.

'We are still the small player up against two huge brand names in MYOB and Quicken. In working with the smaller retailers we can still be somewhat of a referred product rather than being an "off-the-shelf, pick up the box and compare" type product.

'At the same time as moving into retail, we have gone to great lengths to further strengthen our relationship with accountants and ensure that they are not threatened by the move. I call it the trusted adviser strategy as we focus on helping the accountants meet their goals.'

This strategy has been reflected in an added value approach, after research by Wayne found that only about 5 per cent of the accountants who distributed Cashflow Manager had a website to promote their services.

Wayne's team has developed software infrastructure that allows accountants to quickly and easily develop a website enabling them to increase their exposure and provide additional services to their client base.

The website service is offered as part of the Cashflow Manager Professional Partner Services provided to accountants.

'We had been thinking about the move into retail for some time but we wanted to make sure the transition strategy worked.

'While we have experienced growth of about 10 per cent per annum in recent years, I wasn't really happy with that as there is still so much more possible growth in Australia. In fact, an article in the *Australian* in November 2004 described Cashflow Manager as "one of Australia's best-kept secrets" so we knew we had to make this move.

'My research indicates that the move into retail will actually help us to build our sales with accountants because there is even greater confidence in the program when people see that it is available as a retail product.

'But we will continue to focus on the accounting marketplace as the central part of our Australian marketing strategy.'

Overseas markets – particularly network marketing companies in the US and Canada, and the product developed for them – are a key platform in Cashflow Manager's future success.

As a result of requests from these companies, a new online web product, distinct from the stand-alone software product, has been developed.

While presenting an excellent opportunity for the company, it has also proved to be a major challenge, requiring a redesign of the Cashflow Manager system for the web.

French and Spanish versions have also been designed, which will open up opportunities in much of French-speaking Canada, as well as with the large Hispanic community in the US.

The move to an online version has enormous benefits for Wayne's company, with users paying a monthly fee to access the program – rather than a once-off purchase price – providing an ongoing income stream.

Like many good ideas, Wayne believes the beauty of Cashflow Manager is in its simplicity.

'I wouldn't mind a dollar for every time someone said to me, "what are you going overseas for, surely they've already got something like this?"

'Well, we went overseas, and there wasn't anything like it. Success can often come from the simplest of ideas, but people haven't seen or grasped it. I am still surprised by the simplicity of the idea and its success.

'Every other product available assumed people knew what they were doing. The only thing I did differently was hold people's hands with simple step-by-step instructions – I certainly don't think I'm a genius or anything like that.'

Lessons Learnt:

* Challenge 'but this is the way we've always done it' thinking. You can create a very successful business by finding a better – and simpler – way to do something.
* Look for opportunities to network with your professional associates and peers – chances are many of you are facing the same issues and may be able to come up with better solutions together.
* Look beyond your core operations and explore new ways of using your skills. What starts out as an 'add on' may one day become your main business.

Advice to Others:

* The 'trusted adviser' approach can have enormous value to your business – chances are your business will grow as you help others to grow theirs.

Simon Chappel

Some people might think it was a brave move in such a 'blokey' industry – others foolish. Either way, Simon Chappel's radical decision to paint his truck pink was the foundation for his now thriving building company.

Such was the importance of that old Morris truck to Simon's business success, the pink truck (PT) even spawned the company's name – PT Building Services.

Simon has turned his original $200 investment in that pink truck into a diverse, $15 million-a-year building company. Not bad for someone who, by his own admission, wasn't really focusing all his attention on that company until recent years.

In 1978 Simon was studying planning and architecture after spending several years working as a draftsman. Needing to replace the regular income he had earned drafting he bought the old Morris truck on a whim from a friend who was moving interstate.

After undergoing the now infamous paint job, the truck was originally used for a few weekend household clean-up and transporting jobs.

Then, one day while Simon was enjoying a drink in the Torrens Arms Hotel, a representative of the Housing Trust spotted the truck out the front and offered Simon maintenance work on teacher houses in South Australia's country areas. Simon employed a couple of people to carry out the work while he continued studying. Over the next few years, more contracts were secured and the business's revenue and staff numbers steadily grew.

For Simon, the experience was a valuable lesson in the importance of standing out from the crowd.

'I didn't have any money to spend on advertising, so I was looking for some sort of a gimmick – we were remembered that's for sure. I am certain I wouldn't have been in the business very long if I hadn't painted the truck pink.'

PT Building Services bubbled along for a further 15 years, all the time still being a very secondary focus for Simon as he dabbled in a string of other business opportunities in true entrepreneurial style.

These included everything from a hot dog business, a bike hire outlet in Elder Park, and fashion and shoe shops, to buying and selling houses. Other business experiences included working with a large lawn-mowing franchise to expand their services interstate, and running a serviced office, along with various marketing and advertising roles.

'I was always exploring new opportunities to create a business and PT was ticking away in the background just growing slowly and running itself to a certain extent, with some minimal input from me.

'Throughout this time I was still looking for something different to do. I was never really satisfied that this was a business I was going to devote the rest of my life to. I just saw it as an income earner while I continued to pursue other opportunities.

'It wasn't until about the mid 1990s that I decided that I would really give it a serious push, ignore all the other things that I had been dabbling in for years and concentrate on the business that I had owned for a long time.

'I think I finally realised that the grass is not necessarily greener in another business. You sometimes think there might be better things that you could be doing and easier businesses to run, and I was looking for that.

'I enjoyed starting up new businesses, forming partnerships, exploring opportunities and I also learnt a lot along the way. Over time, the businesses that I had been involved with had given me experience in all sorts of business disciplines – corporate, property, retail and marketing.

'I pulled all of those skills together over 15 years of doing different things and it gave me a wealth of experience that not too many people have. I think I understood that I had gained all that experience and now needed a business to put that into. I already owned PT Building Services so it made sense that I concentrate on that business.'

Having committed to focusing on PT Building Services, Simon then turned his attention to further growing the business.

The main aspect of PT Building Services' operations at that stage was building demolition. With only a limited amount of demolition work in Adelaide in 1997, the decision was made to expand interstate into Melbourne and Canberra.

The idea was that the three cities would form a 'nice neat triangle', allowing the sharing of plant and equipment supported by the administrative facilities already established in Adelaide. While it sounded like a very logical plan at the time, Simon now believes the move was company's 'biggest disaster'.

In hindsight, the greatest lesson for Simon was the need to be hands-on in order to run the business's operations effectively – a difficult feat for one person to achieve over three states.

While the company won plenty of work (despite the reluctance of the building industries in the two cities to use interstate contractors), the high cost of labour and constant union problems meant PT lost money on many of its largest jobs.

After 18 months of effort that nearly sent the company broke, Simon withdrew from Canberra and Melbourne, regrouped and decided that trying to create a national demolition operation was not an option for PT.

While seeing it as a 'terrible mistake', Simon takes the philosophical view that it was a valuable – if costly – learning experience and 'you'll never know until you try'.

The secret to being successful in business is never giving up. It is tempting to look for an easy way out or a solution to the problem which involves sacrificing something you have worked hard for, but it's not worth it.

Having determined that interstate expansion wasn't necessarily the best approach, in 1999 Simon decided to diversify the company's operations into civil works – site preparation, excavation, underpinning piling, minor concrete works, curbing, bitumen and paving – to complement the existing business.

While the work involved in the demolition and civil works was quite different, there were considerable synergies between the two. Much of the machinery used was interchangeable and many of PT's clients required both services. In 99 per cent of cases the structure was demolished and activity commenced immediately on the civil works to prepare the site for major construction.

A Civil Manager was employed at that time and the company started tendering for civil work. The move proved a huge success for the company. Approximately 70 per cent of PT Building Services' turnover is now in civil works and the company has created a competitive advantage for itself in being able to offer clients the two services, reducing the often complicated interface between demolition and civil.

The third linchpin in the business has been the establishment of a building materials recycling business, Perpetual Products. Fifty per cent of that business was recently sold to publicly listed Waste Management New Zealand, in line with Simon's belief in finding and linking with the best possible strategic business partners.

Two Perpetual Products facilities in Adelaide, at Wingfield and Lonsdale, recycle demolition material for PT and numerous other companies. The material is 100 per cent recycled back into quarry product, which is then used in the civil business.

In recent years, Simon has also turned his hand to property development. In partnership with local real estate agent David Smallacombe, Simon is involved with the redevelopment of the former Coopers Brewery site at Leabrook into a retirement village.

Simon is also involved with the Flinders Link development in the Adelaide CBD, a $120 million project on the old YMCA site in Flinders Street featuring an 800-space car park, a 12,000 square metre multi-storey office building and two apartment buildings.

'I generally have plenty on my plate in a business sense. Dabbling in lots of different things has given me a great deal of experience which I'm now utilising. It's also given me an appreciation of the challenges of business.

'You imagine that the business you are running is the toughest business in the world and there are easier ones that you could go out and explore. But every business has stress and they all have their own difficulties. That takes a long time to recognise.

'If you want to be self-employed you have to be prepared to deal with the ups and downs of business. That is something I have learned through being involved in a number of different businesses and finding that they are all relatively similar.

'The secret to being successful in business is never giving up. It is tempting to look for an easy way out or a solution to the problem which involves sacrificing something you have worked hard for, but it's not worth it.

'However, the single biggest mistake that I see in business is empire building. People looking to build an empire and who make decisions just on ego, in my mind, don't get there. Those who succeed are generally people who build a business because they enjoy it and not because they want to promote themselves.'

Lessons Learnt:

* Stand out from the crowd. Simon Chappel wouldn't have been able to build a business if it hadn't been for his pink truck and the cheap – but extremely effective – advertising it provided in a very 'blokey' industry.
* Interstate expansion looks attractive, but sometimes it's not the best move for a company. If it doesn't work, don't be afraid to admit defeat and re-focus on your local market. Persevering in a difficult trading environment could cripple the company in the long run.
* Look for opportunities to diversify into complementary activities. Expansion into civil works enabled PT to use much of the same machinery it had used in demolition on the next stage of works.

Advice to Others:

* Be in business for the right reasons. Do it because you enjoy it, not because you want to stroke your ego.

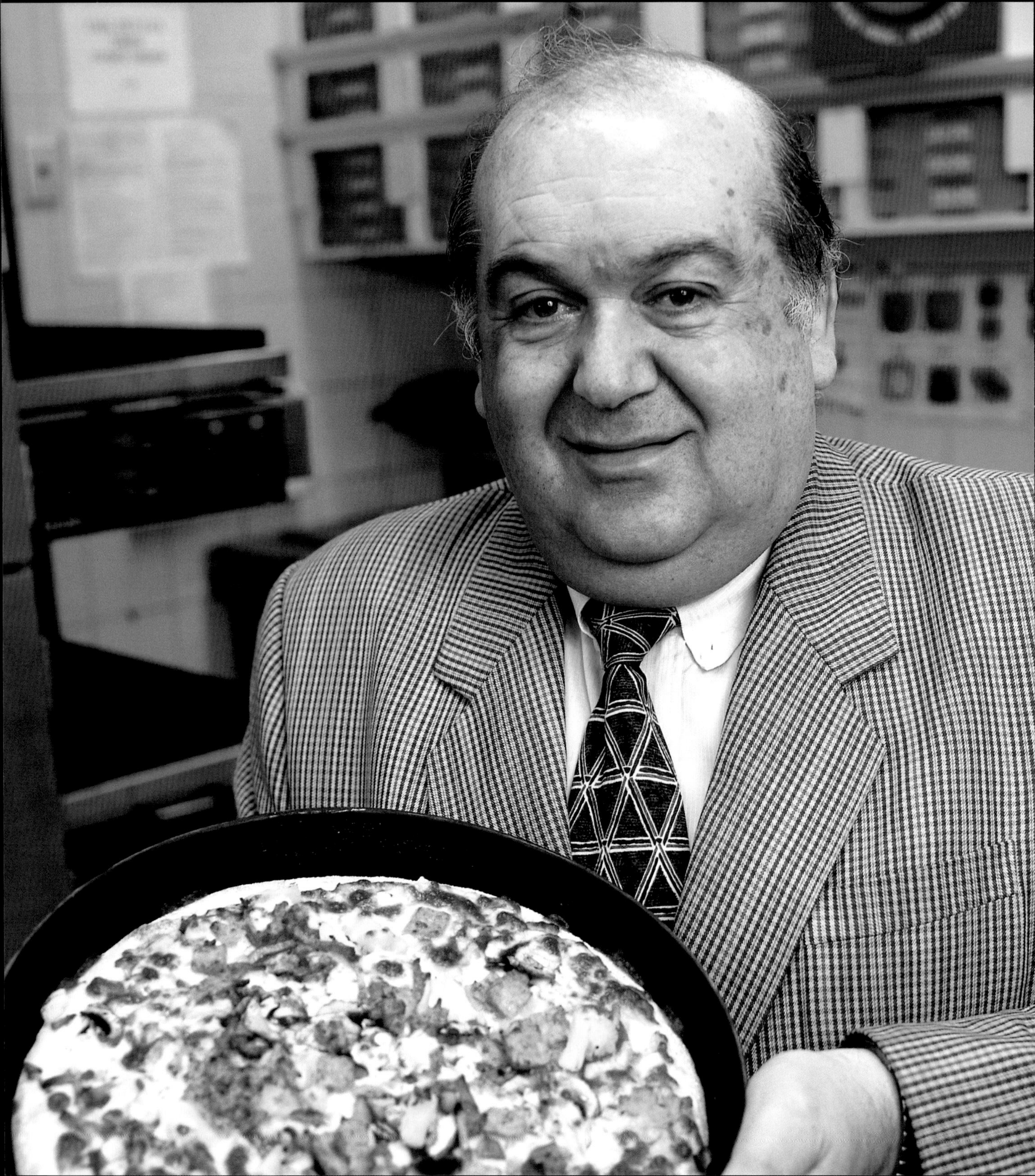

Evan Christou

A strong family background where working hard and working together came naturally has delivered one of Australia's greatest fast food success stories for the Christou brothers.

As founders of the high-profile Pizza Haven franchise chain, the four brothers – Evan, Louis, Bill and Gabriel – have not only adapted to ever-changing consumer trends, more often than not they have driven them.

The Christou family – mum, dad, grandma and the four boys – came to Australia from Cyprus in 1964. From the moment they arrived, they wanted to improve their family situation and started a fish and chip shop in the Adelaide suburb of Marion, working hard while looking for new opportunities. Other business ventures followed.

In 1984 an empty restaurant at Glenelg came to the attention of the family. Recognising the enormous growth in the popularity of pizza in cities such as Melbourne, the decision was made to establish a pizza restaurant.

The four brothers took out a $24,000 mortgage over their parents' home to open the restaurant and all worked long hours taking turns to make and serve the pizzas and clean at that first Pizza Haven restaurant.

'From the very outset, we opened the restaurant with a view to expanding. It was never our intention to open just one restaurant.

'We always said, "let's open something that we can develop further".'

That initial goal has been exceeded far beyond the expectations of the Christous. Pizza Haven is now one of the largest pizza chains in the Australasian region.

Working up to 15-hour days, the brothers put their energies into developing the 'perfect dough' and tasty toppings.

While the restaurant did well in the first few months, companies such as Dial A Dino's and Pizza Express were starting to offer Adelaide residents home delivery for the first time. The establishment of Pizza Haven's own delivery service less than a year after first opening was the turning point for the Christous.

It was a novelty and, never having had access to anything like it before, consumers embraced the concept. A Pizza Haven driver would make a delivery to a house, with the neighbours seeing the branded delivery car and ordering pizza as well. The driver could suddenly find himself making four of five trips to the same neighbourhood in the one night.

Soon afterwards, the Christous were ready to open their second store, with the doors to Pizza Haven at Christies Downs opening in October 1985. Stores number three to six quickly followed and the Christou brothers decided it was time to turn to franchising. Store seven, the first franchise, opened at Enfield in 1986.

'At that time we didn't plan to go to Melbourne or Sydney or anything big like that. 'We wanted to make sure we did everything possible to establish ourselves here, from menus to equipment.

'We learnt how to monitor our franchises and work through any problems. It was another three years before we were satisfied and felt ready to expand again.'

Pizza Haven opened its first interstate stores in Melbourne in 1990, followed by Sydney in 1992. Family was again the key to success during interstate expansion, with two brothers, Gabriel and Bill, temporarily moving to Melbourne and then Sydney to oversee growth of the business. Meanwhile, Evan and Louis kept operations running smoothly from the company's South Australian headquarters.

'Having the family establish Pizza Haven interstate rather than relying on others who might not have had the same focus helped us to move quickly and grow the way we wanted it to. It was a real hands-on expansion.

'In an industry which is primarily dominated by large multinationals, we've benefited from being an Australian, family-founded company. We're very proud of being Australian and South Australian and I think that does still mean something to a lot of people.'

While establishing franchises throughout Australia and New Zealand, the Christou brothers were also working to ensure Pizza Haven was at the forefront of pizza developments. Pizza Haven pioneered many of the innovations that are commonplace in the pizza industry today, such as cheesy crusts, large pizza as standard and '2-for-1' meals.

While enormously successful, Pizza Haven has faced two major challenges during the past 20 years, the first being the shift from delivery to pick-up.

'When we started our sales would have been 90 per cent delivery, but that has now switched to 80 per cent pick-up, Therefore, the business has changed from almost pure delivery to pure takeaway.

'While that didn't slow us down at all, it did impact on turnover.

'The prices of our products obviously had to be reduced to reflect the removal of the delivery costs. While it didn't affect profit, it did see turnover come down.

'The changing trend did have an enormous impact on our shop fronts though. When the majority of our sales were through deliveries, our stores were pretty much just pizza kitchens with a couple of parking bays for the drivers' cars.

'Because our customers weren't originally coming to our stores, we could position ourselves in locations that were the most convenient for our drivers to get in and out.

'When the focus moved to primarily takeaway, we had to spend a lot more time thinking about not only the configuration of our stores, but their location. We suddenly needed to be in areas that had heavy foot traffic.

'We had to cater for that vast influx of pick-up customers by making our stores an enjoyable place to visit. We did this by establishing large open plan areas at the front of our stores for customer comfort, and by installing high production equipment for efficient service.

We try to be different in everything that we do – whether it's visible or not. That's simply the way we do business.

'Externally, we introduced floodlit signage and more car parking spaces. The end result was an even greater focus on customer service.'

This change has also required an increase in Pizza Haven store numbers. When most pizzas were being delivered, each store could service about 20,000 to 25,000 households. With the emphasis now on pick-up, the optimum number of households for each store is about 10,000.

The second major challenge has been remaining at the cutting edge of the pizza industry despite the large number of competitors that have entered the market. For Pizza Haven, the secret has been to focus on pizza quality rather than price alone.

'The best pizzas are made by what you put in them, the amount of toppings, the sauce, the base.

'It's about taking the time to find pineapple that won't make your Hawaiian pizzas soggy or trialing different flours to get the fluffiest pizza base.

'We only use the best products to make sure our pizzas have the least fat in them, and are always conscious to produce the healthiest pizzas without affecting the taste.

'That attention to detail has paid off – we're selling more pizza than ever before. To the connoisseur, Pizza Haven pizza is the best quality in the market.'

At times when competitors would be offering large pizzas for only $2.95 each, this quality approach has been integral to Pizza Haven not only surviving these challenges, but continuing to grow.

Having come this far, Pizza Haven is not content to rest on its laurels. The Christou brothers remain ahead of the industry by introducing new products such as fish bites, chicken chunkies, burger pizza and the frozen Pizza Haven range available in supermarkets.

'The moment you become rigid in your ideas and your way of doing business, you stop.

'The flow of information, the flow of ideas between the family members and the franchisees adds enormous value to what we do.

'It's all about keeping it fresh and we've always differentiated Pizza Haven by offering something that people don't get elsewhere.

'We try to be different in everything that we do – whether it's visible or not. That's simply the way we do business.'

Lessons Learnt:

* Never underestimate the power of a family business. For the Christou family, their combined drive, commitment and hard work has seen them achieve enormous success together.
* Even in a highly competitive market like fast food, ensure your focus is always on quality, rather than price alone.
* No matter how big you become, don't take your hands off the wheel too much. Get expert advice when you need it, but don't become too detached.

Advice to Others:

* Don't fear changing trends and the damage that these may do to your business. Instead, make sure you're at the forefront and put the pressure back on your competitors to play 'catch-up' with you.

Paul Crawford

Paul Crawford's father Jim had a saying: 'If you can't stand in Rundle Mall and shout about something you are thinking of doing, then don't do it.'

It's a credo Paul has worked hard to infuse into all elements of the giant CMV Group, one of Australia's largest commercial motor vehicle companies.

Founded by Paul's grandfather Sidney in 1934, CMV now has around 700 staff and a turnover in excess of $520 million – about $1.4 million a day. It sells approximately 7000 new and used commercial and passenger vehicles a year.

In the early days, CMV distributed Leyland and Diamond T trucks before acquiring the sought-after Case tractor distributorship in 1935 and Commer in 1938. After a period of steady growth, in 1963 the company's Commercial Motor Industries (CMI) division was awarded the South Australian distributorship for Toyota commercial vehicles, and sales skyrocketed.

In 1968 and 1969, the company secured dealership arrangements with Kenworth and Volvo, enabling CMV to offer the widest range of commercial vehicles to the local market.

> People like to have targets. It's important to get really good people and give them confidence in their own ability.

While the company was already strong when Paul and his brother Michael took the reins in 1987, their entrepreneurial approach, vigour and determination have turned CMV into a commercial vehicle powerhouse in Australia.

The entrepreneurial spirit in family companies is something Paul Crawford believes few people genuinely appreciate.

'It's one of the difficult legacies of a family company. As soon as people find out that you're in a family business it's pretty much assumed that you won't have an entrepreneurial spirit. They think it's been knocked out of you because you haven't really had to struggle. That's something I find ironic because we have had some significant struggles.

'In fact, we pride ourselves on our entrepreneurial approach. We managed to leverage the existing strength and capital of the family company to take some fairly high risk opportunities. That way, rather than just sit on a $100 million revenue company and become absentee landlords, we have taken CMV to a much higher level.'

In the late 1980s, Paul and Michael spearheaded CMV's aggressive expansion strategy into the eastern states, buying vehicle dealerships in Wagga and Griffith before eventually acquiring two Volvo truck dealerships in Melbourne. Numerous other acquisitions followed, including a Kenworth dealership in Hallam, and now more than 30 per cent of CMV's business is in Victoria.

'In the early 1980s we were highly dependent on the South Australian economy. We knew we had to diversify geographically.

'What we did was a bit unusual. Most owner-operators tend to be quite big in one market and stick with that market with many franchises. We took another view that interstate expansion was shaping the company for the future. We took the franchises we had into a different market.'

It was hard going. CMV bore the full brunt of cost-cutting and other competitive manoeuvres by Victorian dealers keen to maintain market share and fend off the 'outsider'.

'We took some heavy losses for a few years but we did some fairly innovative things and it started to turn around as we built a mirror image of the truck franchises that we had in Adelaide.

'Our approach to staff and customers was very different to what the Melbourne market had been experiencing. We had a fairly open approach to trading and that presented us with a number of opportunities. We proved to the market that we were a fairly straight-shooting business. If a customer got into trouble we tried our best to help them rather than be a "hit and run" merchant.'

One of CMV's greatest successes has been winning the right to handle so many competing truck dealerships. For instance, CMV has secured dealerships for Fuso, Kenworth, Volvo, Hino and DAF, many of which go head-to-head for sales. Paul says CMV's watertight approach to segregating the business units along with its integrity-based management model have enabled the group to win the confidence of competing truck manufacturers.

'Transparency and fair trading are crucial. It's not the truck "game" these days, it's the truck "business" – and it's a serious business. To have a common dealer for Volvo, Kenworth and DAF, for instance, is quite rare. We have worked hard to maintain this segregation and the truck companies have put their trust in us to make it work. Our solid stance on this gave us the chance to grow with those franchises.'

Diversification is important to Paul. CMV has numerous other interests including almond growing and packing, vineyard development, pistachio production and, more recently, furniture manufacturing and sales. All of the agribusiness comes under the direct control of another brother, David Crawford, who has spent more than 25 years growing this side of the business.

The move into furniture sales came about almost by accident. Paul had negotiated the purchase of the Keen Office Furniture warehouse for CMV's future expansion.

'We hadn't actually been looking at the business, just the property, but we took it on. Anyway, it turned out to be a very good business with some great people. We started taking more of an interest and getting more involved. Now it's going really well and it's just had a record year.

'A little while back I gave the staff a challenge. I asked if they could come up with an orthopaedic chair that we could sell for under $100 that would suit the student or home office market. The manager's eyes lit up and he said: "I reckon we could do it." I don't think anyone had ever given him a challenge like that before. His response was fantastic.

'People like to have targets. It's important to get really good people and give them confidence in their own ability.'

Paul is a strong believer that successful entrepreneurs don't just think up great ideas – they actually do something to make them happen. He says action should be the catchcry. Anything else is procrastination.

'My experience is that if you have an idea and then just sit on it, it ends up on the weekly review list and nothing happens. But if you actually do it then it's amazing what will happen.

'Yes, fast actions can get you into trouble because sometimes you move too quickly. But that still produces more results than doing nothing. In our situation, maybe eight out of 10 actions are positive and only two out of 10 would be negative. Those are pretty good odds for me.'

CMV's culture is to embrace staff and involve them at every turn. CMV has an open-book policy with management where profitability and all elements of budgeting are readily discussed.

Paul also has in place a staff shareholder system – something of a rarity in family companies.

'We now have about 200 staff who have invested in the company. We wanted to give them a sense that they were indeed part of the company, and it's worked well. The share price is indexed to the appreciation of the company's net equity. We also pay a dividend on those shares and that's ranged from 7 per cent to 10 per cent in the past few years.'

Paul's business style involves 'management by walking around'. He believes owners must spend plenty of time on the shop floor and be directly involved in solving major issues.

'One of my business techniques is what I call "commando raids". For example, if there is a customer bad debt, rather than just looking at the last transaction I may go back and ask for the credit application form and the credit references that supported it. I'll check the history and what work was done when we gave the customer a credit limit, rather than castigate the person who gave the credit on the last transaction.

'I would rather spend time looking very deeply at one specific problem than superficially at a number of things. You can drill down to fine-tune the procedures and processes that safeguard the company.

'Also, it shows staff that you are not looking for a scapegoat or somebody to yell at. You're actually looking to solve the problem.

'One of the things with our culture is that we deal fairly with employees who have a problem or make a mistake. There are always going to be cases that disappoint you but we try not to dwell on those. Instead we make sure that the processes and mechanisms are there to support and help people.'

This sense of 'family' is reflected in the CMV Foundation, which now holds about 14 per cent of the company's ordinary stock and donates a substantial amount annually to worthy causes. Strategically, it also acts as a conduit and filter for all charity requests to the group's many offices nationally.

'Our staff can take a great deal of pride from projects that the CMV Foundation has undertaken. Just by working for CMV they're helping the community.'

Lessons Learnt:

* Use your balance sheet to take calculated risks and open up new markets – and don't be afraid to explore opportunities outside your traditional market boundaries, even if it means short-term pain.
* Take a forgiving approach to mistakes – and never make assumptions. As Paul says: 'Assumptions are the mother of all stuff-ups.' Investigate the circumstances of a mistake or problem and improve your processes based on the results. Don't just point the finger.
* Settle legal disputes quickly. Don't pursue a principle through the courts 'at all costs' because it can be a bottomless pit. 'Sometimes you just have to bite the bullet and settle.'
* Think carefully about what you say before you say it. 'Sometimes in the cut and thrust of a fast-moving transactional business you say something inappropriate in the heat of the moment. But you can't "un-say" something and an ill-considered comment can do significant damage, especially in a family company.'

Advice to Others:

* Be confident. Take action. Procrastination creates nothing. A bad decision can still be better than no decision at all – and you'll learn from your mistakes. Make even poor decisions work by follow-through and determination.
* Always keep key people in your business informed – for instance, staff, bankers, financiers, partners, franchisors and shareholders. Work on a 'no surprises' policy. Make the call rather than take the call.

Geoff Davis

Wendy's Supa Sundaes is one of Australia's best-known franchise success stories – but throughout his company's 25-year history, Geoff Davis has had to reinvent the business twice.

Changing consumer tastes, a maturing market and a focus on new target customers has seen Wendy's evolve into a very different business from the one Geoff co-founded in 1979.

Geoff was involved in fast food franchising from his early days in business. Having spent a few years in South Africa running a bakery with wife Kathy, friend and business partner Phil Rogers and Phil's wife Diane, the two families returned to Adelaide in 1971. Together they established the first Wimpy Bar franchise in Adelaide.

Eventually one of 70 stores Australia-wide, the Hindley Street business became the most successful Wimpy Bar in the country.

Just four years later, under pressure from rival McDonalds, the British-based Wimpy withdrew from Australia, leaving the business – minus the trading name – to Geoff and Phil. They renamed it the Feed Bag and continued to build it into a thriving fast-food outlet.

In late 1978 Geoff saw a potential opportunity in the first ever food courts that were being established in Adelaide shopping malls at that time.

He was keen to open a Feed Bag store in the new Gallerie Shopping Centre in the CBD, but to his dismay the food court was almost fully leased and did not have enough space for a full-menu restaurant. The location was too good to miss though, so Geoff and Phil snapped up the lease to a small corner of the centre and set up an outlet selling only items from the Feed Bag's ice cream dessert menu.

With the involvement of two new partners, Geoff and Phil were also keen to explore other opportunities for Wendy's outlets. Geoff, known for his persistence, pounded the pavement talking to shopping centre leasing managers and working hard to convince them that a Wendy's store would be a great addition to their centres.

'Shopping centres were being developed throughout Adelaide at this time and we wanted to be part of these malls from the outset. We saw huge potential for these centres as a hub for shoppers and we didn't want to miss out getting in on the ground floor.

'The problem was, we didn't have any concepts or visuals of how the stores would look. However, we did have pictures of the different products that we thought we could sell. We had displayed big, colorful product photographs above the counter in both the Wimpy Bar and the Feed Bag – at that stage we were the first business to do anything like it.

'We kept on visiting the leasing managers and talking with them about what we thought we could do. I think they ended up signing leases with us just so we'd leave them alone.'

Geoff secured additional locations for Wendy's stores in the Colonnades, Marion and City Cross centres. All proved enormously successful from the first day.

Opportunities soon arose in Melbourne and two stores were established there soon afterwards.

I'm a very persistent person. You could hit me 20 times and I will get up the 21st time. I would encourage people to persist if they are ambitious in life.

As the Wendy's chain was rolled out around Australia under a franchising model, the focus was on young consumers – five to 12-year-old children and the 13 to 19-year-old teenage market. It was a huge success and Wendy's grew rapidly.

In the early 1980s decorated cones were the mainstay of the business, with the stores decorated in hot pink and featuring bright, coloured transparencies of the various products. This was the focus of the business through until the late 1980s. By this time Wendy's had more than 100 stores – but then sales started to falter.

'There was an obvious flattening in our sales figures at this time and so we closely worked with our advertising agency and undertook considerable market research to understand what was happening.

'I had always been a strong believer in research and listening to our customers. We were always prepared to listen.

'Our research highlighted to us that times and tastes were changing. The kids that we started serving in 1979 were now 10 years older. They were maturing and they were looking for other products from us.'

As a result of that research, a new product range was developed and introduced – decorated milkshakes, including the Mega Choc Shake and the Flake Shake.

Wanting to protect the company's key points of difference, trademarks and patents were registered for many of Wendy's products with exclusive product names (such as the Hedgehog Cone and the shakes), and vigorously defended in the courts if necessary.

'In 1983 we developed a unique cone wrap and we put a patent on that. We were quick to slap a legal action on anyone who attempted to make a similar cone wrap because we had the exclusive design.

'We forced competitors to shred millions of cone wraps because they just ignored us and didn't think we'd kick up a fuss, so we responded with an injunction.'

Sales rose strongly on the back of this new strategy, and store numbers continued to climb. Then, in the early 1990s, sales once again began to stagnate.

At about this time, McDonald's introduced its 30 cent soft serve cone as a loss leader, selling about 70 million cones in the first year. Wendy's – the ice cream specialist – sold just 13 million that same year.

Facing such enormous challenges, Geoff realised the business would have to be reinvented once more. Market research again came to the fore as Wendy's gauged how to maintain its position.

'When we started doing research again the mothers were telling us that they only bought a cheap soft serve from McDonald's to keep the kids quiet, whereas they saw a scoop of quality ice cream as something they would prefer themselves.

'We realised that there was a huge opportunity for us with 20 to 40-year-old women, who represent about 65 per cent of consumers. They had a passion for indulgent ice cream, perceiving it as a treat and a reward.

'We bought a five-star ice cream manufacturing facility in 1995 and experimented for about a year. Then, based entirely on research, we rolled out a new range of high-quality ice cream.

'By now we had gone through two eras – decorated cones and decorated shakes – and this was our next re-invention as our store numbers hit 300. It was like starting the business for the third time. We re-focused our business from concentrating solely on kids and teenagers – who only ever represented 10 per cent of mall traffic – and put more attention on the ice cream habits of the adult female.

'We went after that market with a vengeance and invented a new store concept called "Family Image", featuring images of soft pink hearts, a new menu system and new heart logo, and products such as Chocollo, a no-fat chocolate soft serve with low sugar.'

The first Family Image store was opened in 1997 at Westfield Marion and immediately doubled that same store's previous best turnover.

Two of the original partners left the business much earlier in its development in 1984, but 1997 saw Geoff and Phil go their separate ways. While the split was amicable, Geoff says it was difficult because formal exit strategies and partner buy-out structures were not in place.

'These days they teach you about exit strategies as part of modern business principles, but we had been partners for two decades and had no formal agreements in place to fall back on.

'It was eventually resolved but it was a real lesson for me. I know so many people who are 55 years old and are wondering what their exit strategy is going to be. But how can you exit if your business isn't saleable to someone?

'A business with no corporate discipline lacks continuity. It has no goodwill. As a business owner, you have to be thinking about these issues early on.'

Wendy's now serves more than 750,000 customers each week with annual sales of about $114 million.

While Geoff's business has taken many forms over the years, two things have endured – his belief in what he was doing and his commitment in 'sticking to his values'.

'I'm a very persistent person. You could hit me 20 times and I will get up the 21st time. I think persistence is a great trait to have. I would encourage people to persist if they are ambitious in life.'

Lessons Learnt:

* Research is a valuable business tool. Listen to your customers and act on what you learn from them. Use whatever means are available to you to research what the market wants from your business.
* Be vigilant in protecting your company's points of difference. Legal action can be time consuming, expensive and distracting, but sometimes it's essential to keep your competition from stealing your ideas.
* Have a formal exit strategy in place well before you need it and ensure that everything that you do adds to the saleable value of your business.

Advice to Others:

* Continue listening to your customers, persist and innovate. Recruit the very best people around you.

Jeff Dominikovich

Helicopter drop-ins to remote locations. Abseiling off steep cliff faces. Hauling equipment through virtually impenetrable scrubland. It may sound like the stuff of army exercises, but in reality these are just some of the ways that Jeff Dominikovich wins business.

Jeff's business – Grounds & Gardens – is one of Australia's leading grounds maintenance businesses, with a reputation for being able to take on projects that others can't manage.

The company's ability to find solutions for logistically or horticulturally complex jobs is one of the factors that has set the business apart from the many 'backyarders' who typified the grounds maintenance sector until recent years.

Jeff has also pioneered a professional, systems-based approach to project management that has seen Grounds & Gardens create new efficiencies and change the shape of its industry.

Grounds & Gardens now turns over more than $15 million annually and has some of Australia's largest companies among its clientele, including Tempo, Stockland, Transfield, Spotless, Multiplex, Mirvac and Australand.

It provides professional horticultural services and management to corporate, government and statutory bodies, local government and private organisations. Services include project management, horticultural maintenance, landscape design and construction, sports turf services and herbicide/weed control. The company also services some of Australia's highest profile resort landscapes, including Hayman Island, Sanctuary Cove and Laguna Quays.

Jeff moved to Australia from New Zealand in the mid-1980s and travelled the country before finally settling in Adelaide to study. He and fellow student Craig Hosking began working together in a lawn-mowing round.

As the business grew, the duo took on a third partner and launched an aggressive expansion program. The company – by then known as Mr Clip – grew to about 30 franchises over the next eight years, with Jeff responsible for much of the organisation's business development.

One of the opportunities identified by Jeff was a project management role for the South Australian Housing Trust. While it was an excellent contract, it wasn't the right fit for the more domestically focused Mr Clip. As a result, Jeff sold out of Mr Clip and established Grounds & Gardens in 1995.

Jeff had already recognised the considerable client benefits of a more systems-based approach to horticultural services. The contract with the SA Housing Trust was an excellent proving ground for his new model.

'We weren't doing the hands-on grounds maintenance work. Ours was primarily a project management role. We were managing all of the Trust's contractors on site using the Trust's budget. Our goal was to improve the value of what they already had and also improve the services that the contractors were providing. We were very successful at doing that,' Jeff said.

'The project management approach was our strong point of difference. At that time there weren't any companies offering those services to the corporate or commercial market. While other contractors competed with us in our market, they were traditionally hiring out machines and people, whereas we were hiring out our management expertise to facilitate those projects and achieve the best value.'

With a heavy financial exposure to the SA Housing Trust contract – at that stage 75 per cent of Grounds & Gardens' turnover – Jeff began tendering for more traditional maintenance contracts to boost his client base.

'By winning these contracts however we then had to sub-contract out all that work. It was awkward because we were effectively sub-contracting to our competitors, which only helped build their businesses and make them a greater threat to us.

Our structure makes people feel part of a team. They are offered a career path with the company. They know that if they do their job well, the business will grow and everyone benefits.

'As a result, we made the decision to strengthen our position by taking those services in-house as well as sub-contracting as needed. That provided us with greater control over the quality and cost of the service.'

As part of this strategic change in focus, in 1998 Grounds & Gardens purchased its largest sub-contractor.

From operating with only five people out of a serviced office in Kent Town, Grounds & Gardens now needed a depot, warehouse and significantly more office space. Jeff bought and refurbished a former Transport SA depot at Clarence Gardens.

A major challenge for Jeff was managing the large number of staff who now worked for the business – as well as juggling the delicate relationships with sub-contractors.

'It was a big learning curve for us. We had to find the right people to hire, and someone to manage them. We had to make sure we knew everything about the range of services, be more competitive than others in the market and maintain a positive relationship with the sub-contractors because while we had hired people in, we still also needed subcontractors.

'To this day we'd be using probably 100 to 150 subcontractors on a regular basis while still doing a lot of the work ourselves with our own 140 staff. Our relationship with those subcontractors is still very strong because we treat them well, we pay them on time and yet we have that flexibility to be able to do the work ourselves too.

'The sub-contracting companies that we choose to work with these days are relatively small in comparison to Grounds & Gardens. That way they are not a threat to us and we can build a mutually beneficial relationship in an environment of trust and openness.'

Grounds & Gardens' expansion interstate – the company has offices in Victoria, New South Wales, Queensland, the Northern Territory and Western Australia – began when Jeff secured a contract with the giant Australian services group Tempo. Again, Jeff's systemised approach proved to be the catalyst.

Unlike his competitors, Jeff could provide Tempo with specially tailored information about Grounds & Gardens' services that could be easily built into Tempo's own tender documents. Jeff's company was effectively helping Tempo win major maintenance contracts. Then, when a contract was won by Tempo and sub-contracted to Grounds & Gardens, Jeff could provide Tempo with fully detailed reports and risk management documentation whenever required.

'That's what differentiated us from other contractors. We were self-managing. Tempo didn't have to hold our hand at any stage. We made it easy for them to do business with us. We did things and provided information that made Tempo look good in their clients' eyes.

'It was through our relationship with Tempo that we ended up securing jobs such as the maintenance of all of Telstra's sites in Victoria.'

Meanwhile, Grounds & Gardens was building a reputation for accepting projects that its competitors could not – or would not – undertake. Jeff's solutions have ranged from using boats and helicopters to service remote Telstra relay stations in Far North Queensland, through to abseiling down cliff faces to eradicate and remove hard-to-reach pest plants. Jeff's team even devised a special climbing system to trim the grass growing on the steep slopes of army ammunition mounds.

The company's philosophy of hiring employees or using sub-contractors with a broad range of skills means that there is 'no job too far away, too big or too complex'. If the company doesn't already have access to people who can do what is required, it will find them.

It isn't always easy, but Jeff says that once again comprehensive systems and procedures have helped Grounds & Gardens attract and keep exceptional employees in an industry known for its high staff turnover.

'Our structure makes people feel part of a team. They are offered a career path with the company. They know that if they do their job well, the business will grow and everyone benefits. There are plenty of career opportunities here and those who have done well have seen their salaries increase.

'Our business manages some of the largest and most challenging horticultural contracts in the country and we are very dependent on the people who manage and service these contracts. We work very hard to maintain a stable workforce to make sure our people are happy and meeting the client's needs while achieving the company's objectives. It pays to recognise and reward good performance.

'Almost three years ago we engaged HR support from an external consultancy. More recently we have appointed an internal HR manager and HR coordinator to further strengthen the development and management of our most important aspect – our people.

'This has provided many benefits, including greater scope for in-house promotion. At one stage we were growing so quickly we were focused on recruiting externally, but now we always look inside the company first to see if anyone has the skills and is ready for the promotion.'

While systems have an important role to play, Jeff is conscious of not allowing Grounds & Gardens to be 'over-administered'.

'There needs to be a balance between the administrative procedures and the core operations of the business. The operations side of the business is where we earn 100 per cent of our money. That's the area that determines whether we win or lose as a company.

'You have to free up people so they can do what you need them to do. If you have any administrative process in place that doesn't add significant value to your people on the ground, then you probably should scrap it.'

Lessons Learnt:

- Make it attractive for others to do business with you. The easier you can make it for them to use your services, the better.
- Don't be satisfied with 'the average Joe'. Get superstars onto your team and into positions where they can make the greatest impact.
- Communicate to your team the company's vision, strategies and critical success factors – and keep them informed about the organisation's progress.

Advice to Others:

- Improve efficiencies in your business through the introduction of systems and processes – but don't over-administer. Don't put obstacles in the way of people doing their job.

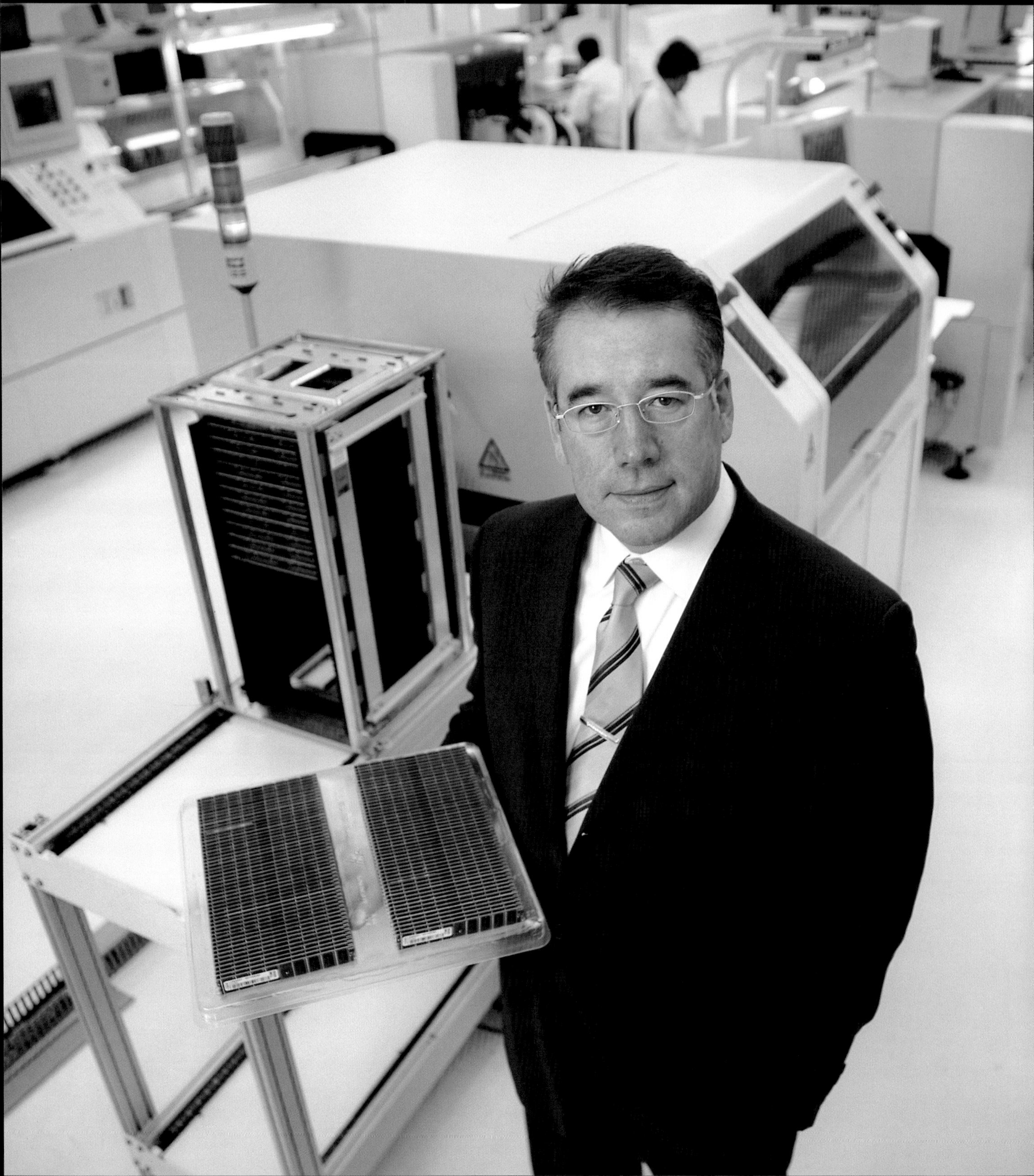

Bradley Dowe

Predicting and adapting to IT and business trends has enabled Bradley Dowe to take Legend Corporation from the kitchen table to a listing on the Australian Stock Exchange.

Bradley strongly believes it is Legend's ability to 'evolve' as required to meet new market demands that has enabled the innovative electronics engineering company to emerge as a global leader in new technologies with turnover in excess of $170 million a year.

Legend was established by Bradley, wife Louise and other family members around the family kitchen table in Melbourne in 1989, and initially started life as a computer software company.

However, Bradley could sense that the evolution of computers would see software overtaken by operating system function, and that computers would ultimately drop in price to become more of a commodity item – not much different to a toaster.

'If you go to buy a toaster nowadays, you tend to buy it for reasons that don't have much to do with the function of toasting bread. You may buy the toaster because you want a stainless steel toaster. It might be a retro toaster or a modern toaster. You tend to buy it for issues that ignore the fundamental function of the product.

'So looking at that and seeing the headlight of that train coming in the computer sector, we thought we should optimise our position rather than get run over.'

Bradley began analysing the various components of computers, with the intention that Legend would focus its 'meagre' resources on a product or a market segment robust enough to enable the company to survive and prosper.

'We thought manufacturing hardware was the direction in which we should head, rather than services or reselling an imported product which many others were doing at the time.

'In looking at hardware components we liked the possibilities that were available in the manufacture of memory. In a finished PC, memory is about 10 per cent of the sticker price and up to 17 per cent for a server. Memory is robust and easily transportable, allowing us to easily export it from Australia.

'We believed that investing in manufacturing and in channel development would have two-pronged benefits. On the component side it would provide good supplier lines, while on the client side it would allow us to have a personal relationship with a larger group of clients.

'It was our insurance against what we saw as an increasingly competitive world.'

At that time Legend was still a Melbourne-based company, but Bradley assessed other cities around Australia to determine the best location in which to establish the company's new manufacturing and administration infrastructure. This research identified Adelaide as the best spot because of its low cost to do business and its access to facilities. The company moved its entire operation to Adelaide and started manufacturing at its Edwardstown facility in January 1993.

Since that time the company has developed more than 9000 memory module products and related computer components and boasts an impressive clientele including Dell, Hewlett Packard, Acer, NEC, Intel and major Australian computer assemblers ASI and Optima.

Legend Corporation employs 130 staff in eight countries with operations extending throughout Australia, New Zealand, South Africa, Asia and Europe.

The company has developed a range of memory modules, CPUs, mainboards, display adaptors, digital technologies and storage devices which are essential components of any IT or electrical product.

Legend's memory modules are used in a vast array of PCs, notebook computers, servers, printers, photocopiers, routers and other applications, and the company currently releases 10 to 15 new products each month.

'We have optimised our impact on the market by producing technologies that are indispensable to the IT and electronics industry.

'Our job is to create synergy in product development by working with key IT companies to design the supporting infrastructure for new technologies and facilitate the timely release of complementary products.

'Our business is about growing sales for our clients and we see our product as being a fundamental key to our clients' business. We have targeted the type of customer that we want to develop and we seek means by which, as a partner, we can add value to their business.

'That's how we've marketed our product although we always saw it as an opportunity to bring better value to a wider group of people.'

Legend has also developed a range of branded consumer electronics products, which are distributed through key national and merchandising chains including Harvey Norman, Dick Smith Electronics, Kmart and Myer.

One of its most exciting new technologies is a special purpose computer which transfers the signal from a regular TV antenna and broadcasts it as a digital image onto the screen. It also enables users to record on multiple channels at digital quality for up to 35 hours using a regular VHS machine, and work is underway to extend this to a two-week capability.

As the company has expanded its operations to include consumer electronics, it has worked to make its products user-friendly. In order to maintain a competitive edge, Legend has set careful parameters to ensure that people who know nothing about computers or technology are able to take a product out of the carton, plug it in and use it without needing an instruction manual.

Our business is about growing sales for our clients and we see our product as being a fundamental key to our clients' business.

Legend's business growth as a result of these initiatives is even more impressive as much of it occurred during some very difficult years for the IT industry globally after the Y2K 'bug' scare.

In 1999 and early 2000 companies around the world invested huge sums in upgrading their IT systems as a result of concerns about what Y2K would do to their business.

Spending on IT then dried up after this time, exacerbated by slowdowns in most of the world's mature economies, the bursting of the Asian tech bubble, the decline of Japan's stock market, and the commencement of Australia's property boom which saw resources diverted elsewhere.

This 'recession' in the global IT market only ended in 2003 as economies recovered and companies looked to replace equipment that was now four years old.

'It was our expectation that with the return to positive growth there would be a large wave of re-equipping throughout the world, and that did prove to be the case.

'Recognising that, we felt a stock exchange listing would provide us with the capital to expand at a time when we would see major growth return to the IT market.'

Bradley ensured that procedures were put in place to take the company to an ASX listing well before the actual event.

'Listing the company had been a matter under review for several years. We put ourselves on that footing for at least three years before it happened in 2004.

'We saw corporatisation of our company and the lifting of our internal systems and standards as part of good governance. So once we listed there really were no champagne corks popping, it was just business as usual.

'We had in fact prepared ourselves for just about every eventuality associated with listing. Consequently, we were able to take up those funds and effectively utilise them much faster than our prospectus had indicated.

'Also, unlike some other stock exchange listings, our IPO (initial public offering) did not include a vendor sell-down, there were voluntary escrow periods and the amount of free float was actually extremely small. We weren't looking at the listing as an opportunity to get as much money as possible. We were only seeking as much money as we could profitably use so we could return some value to our shareholders.'

Having successfully made the transition to a listed company, Legend's focus is now on expanding further into Asia with the company opening offices in Hong Kong, Thailand, China, Malaysia, Vietnam, the Philippines, Indonesia and Singapore.

Having to adjust to both different cultural and business values and procedures, Bradley is keen to ensure that both the company and its systems can 'evolve' rapidly enough to actually meet the needs of these multiple new geographies, in much the same way as it has throughout its history.

As in the past, integral to future success will be tight management and administration structures that extend from the top to the bottom of the company.

'It's the science of business; thorough, accurate and timely accounting, management reporting, management practice – all of those things together.

'While it might not necessarily make you successful, it certainly preserves you from a great deal of pain.

'We operate in an industry which is fundamentally high revenue and low margin and with quite a significant risk profile.

'Our business is about mitigation of those risks and the time invested on strategic evaluation is one of those ways by which you don't get run over by the oncoming train.'

Lessons Learnt:

* Listing your company on the Australian Stock Exchange should be part of a strategic development plan – not 'cashing in'.
* Forecast what your market needs and plan accordingly. Legend saw the re-equipping of the computer market with the looming economic recovery and moved to take advantage of that.
* Systems at all levels of your business are essential, as they provide discipline for everyone in the company.

Advice to Others:

* Adding value to your customers' products provides an excellent opportunity to take your product to a wider market.

Andrew Downs

Frustration with external contractors was the spark that caused electrical engineer Andrew Downs to found SAGE Automation in 1994.

At the time Andrew, then aged 27, was running the electrical department for Bridgestone and regularly commissioning external automation companies to help with large projects – but he was constantly disappointed with the poor service he received.

'As someone who was trained in this field, I was often disappointed by the work that was done for me and the customer service I received,' said Andrew.

'Then I realised that there must have been many other people feeling exactly the way I did – there was a hole in the market.'

Andrew moved quickly to capitalise on the opportunity.

He negotiated to reduce his hours at Bridgestone and, with a friend, established SAGE Automation in a shed in his mum's backyard. From the very start, SAGE Automation was totally committed to excellent customer service.

'Because of my experience with the external consultants I decided that quality was everything.

'I knew that it had to be all about the customer. The customer comes above everything else. I knew that if I could supply the best quality and the best service, then the work would come.'

Andrew eventually parted ways – on good terms – with Bridgestone, who immediately engaged his new company's services.

Within a year SAGE Automation had six staff, $1 million in turnover and more work than the fledgling enterprise could handle.

'It was exciting. We kept winning work, we hired more people and everyone was motivated because we were moving forward. It was a great environment and a fantastic culture.'

Eventually, business was so brisk that the company had to move from its backyard shed to a dedicated manufacturing facility in nearby Melrose Park.

'The business continued to grow at a very high rate and I was able to attract the right calibre of people. They were, and still are, hard-working, loyal and love performing at a high level. Our reputation grew and so did our business.'

'We have always employed the right people – people who can drive the business. Our level of commitment to the customer can be very draining on the resources of a company, and that includes its people. We like to find and hire people who can inject passion into their work because, once again, that leads back to customer service excellence.'

Following a decade of remarkable growth, SAGE now employs more than 140 people and has a $24 million annual turnover.

The company is widely recognised as an Australian specialist in the design and integration of automated electrical control systems. Its key markets include the automotive, wine, food and beverage, water and manufacturing sectors.

It is also established internationally, having partnerships with companies in Korea, Germany, Spain, France, the US, and Canada.

However, like many companies, SAGE did experience growing pains.

'In our early years SAGE didn't have a Board and we had little direction other than to keep finding work. It was a steep learning curve.

'The need for cash was the single biggest hurdle in growing the business. Our ability to provide extra security was exhausted, so our bank couldn't increase the overdraft. Eventually I found a debtor finance facility which suited us as a high-growth business with limited capital backing.'

Andrew's financial predicament wasn't helped by poor accounting advice.

'I would have to say that getting a good accountant is paramount. You can survive bad business advice or bad marketing advice or bad employment advice, but bad financial advice will make your company disappear.

'But I've never been scared of getting advice and I've never been scared of learning.'

In fact, Andrew has enthusiastically embraced mentoring as he continues to build the business. He is an active member of The Executive Connection (TEC), a global peer support network for chief executives, and an avid reader of books on building a better business.

One tactic he has employed to help secure SAGE's longevity is to turn the business into a public unlisted company. Key personnel have already taken up shares in the firm and Andrew is now examining methods to extend share ownership to every employee.

'I have always felt the need to find the right reward mechanisms for people's hard work. I am also a firm believer that people should share in the upside – and that there is nothing wrong with an owner having a smaller slice of a larger pie.'

This commitment to finding and keeping the right people has paid off. Andrew knows that without the right people SAGE cannot continue to grow and improve.

'SAGE has a continuous improvement philosophy which is extremely well received by our clients and the people working here. We embrace the latest technology and continually investigate ways to do better.'

As part of this commitment, SAGE is now a systems-focused company. The financial accounts, purchasing, payroll and project management are all on the same platform.

Furthermore, Andrew recently invested in a specialist business intelligence software package to process post-project reviews and help improve every element of the business.

I've never been scared of getting advice and I've never been scared of learning.

'The introduction of this system will make us better at what we do into the future. We want exceptional service to be repeatable. We want to learn from every project, gathering information and feeding it back into our system so we are constantly improving.

'We can clearly identify if something went wrong, but just as importantly we can see what went right so we can do it again.

'Our innovation in the marketplace is to embrace the latest technology and investigate better ways of performing work. This continuous improvement philosophy has been extremely well received by our clients and the people working at SAGE.'

As an example of Andrew's desire for constant improvement, he once simply phoned the head of a major company similar to SAGE in the US and asked if he could visit their operation to see how they did business.

'Australian companies can be too closed, treating everyone as a competitor. In America, I think they are more open. I spoke to the company's management and they didn't see us as a threat and invited me in to look at the business.

'I visited the company and I was so impressed by its profitability and professionalism I negotiated a technical exchange agreement, so now we are introducing some of their systems, which will bring further improvements to our own operations.'

Thanks to the excellent results SAGE has provided to clients over the past 10 years, Andrew is in the enviable position of not having to chase every piece of work.

'We do our very best to be competitive, but quite simply we are not going to win every contract on price. We provide excellence and our customers should recognise that.'

Improving business is about working smarter. A key SAGE tenet is to avoid doing 'silly deals' to win work. Andrew is happy for his competitors to win work at prices that he knows must be hurting them.

Losing work to a lower-cost competitor can even become a marketing advantage.

On several occasions SAGE has been contracted to 'save' jobs that have foundered in the hands of competitors who won the work with a low bid.

'We have enough confidence in our business and our pricing that we won't cut our own throat to keep that work. You are better off letting it go to the company that has cut the price because then they have to deliver the product. That just makes them weaker.

'At the end of the day, whether it's their business or my business, you have to pay the people, get your materials, pay your overheads and make a margin – otherwise you are not going to be in business for very long.

'Our philosophy is that you've got to believe in what you do and draw a line in the sand.

'This is the point of difference I am most proud of. Everyone makes mistakes, but if SAGE takes on a job and we do something wrong we will not walk away. We will fix it even if it costs us money. We will not argue and fight. We will keep faith with our client and get the job done.

'That is why SAGE is flourishing, because we provide excellent customer service.'

Lessons Learnt:

* Don't be scared to ask for advice and don't be fearful of talking with others who you believe can help your business. It's amazing how much information some people will give you about their business – and how much of it you can use in your own enterprise.
* Invest in systems, processes and procedures to keep the company heading in the right direction. You can't do it all in your head.
* Consider share ownership for employees. It gives them a stake in the outcome.

Advice to Others:

* If finance is not your strong point, make sure you have strong financial advisers – and listen to them.

Roger Drake

A passion for customer service has made Roger Drake 'master' of his trade – supermarket retailing.

Now Australia's largest independent grocery retailer, a young Roger was told during a Woolworths job interview that he wasn't suited to a career in retailing. Forty years later, Drake Foodmarkets owns 41 stores throughout South Australia and Queensland, turning over approximately $450 million annually.

Ignoring the Woolworths feedback, Roger began his retailing career with the Coles Myer Group in 1965, learning all facets of the supermarket industry during the ensuing years. In 1974 he opened his first supermarket – Jack and Jill's, a three-lane supermarket in the Adelaide suburb of Mitcham employing four staff.

The original store was a success and within three years Roger opened his first large supermarket, at Torrensville. The company's chain of stores now includes 27 Foodland and three Timesavers supermarkets, six stores in Queensland, four newsagencies, a liquor store and a substantial property portfolio.

In South Australia, Drake Foodmarkets is the third-largest grocery retailer behind Coles and Woolworths.

'Life is about living with people. I passionately believe that if you can personalise your service to exceed customers expectations, you will succeed in business and in life.

'I was told at age 17 that I was unsuited to a retail career, but success isn't about being tailor-made to fit any one profession. It is understanding what makes people feel valued.'

Calculated risks – where the head and not the ego makes the decisions – have also been integral to Roger's business success.

'I decided very early on that if the business was going to grow, I had to be willing to take chances.

'It becomes a conscious effort to enlarge your thinking and dream bigger and better than anyone else.

> Humility is an integral part of being successful in business. When people ask me what I do, I say 'I'm just a grocer'.

'There's a risk factor in almost everything that you do. What we try to do is calculate it and make sure that we always have an exit plan. The bigger the business becomes the more responsibility you have to make sure that the decisions you make don't impact on the whole business.

'This also requires you to have your ego in check, otherwise it can interfere with good business decisions and distort perspective. So I believe humility is an integral part of being successful in business. When people ask me what I do, I say "I'm just a grocer".

'We've learnt some important lessons the hard way. We have bought a couple of stores which were marginal, but which we thought we could turn around. But sometimes you can't turn them around. I often say if it smells like a rat and looks like a rat, chances are it is a rat.

'So we've taken the ego aspect out of the equation and we put any prospective store purchases through a model that we've set up over the years that's been pretty successful. If the store we're considering doesn't stack up against the model we don't buy it.'

It is these types of expertise and systems that are being utilised in the company's consulting arm, Select Professional Retail Advice, which advises supermarkets, developers and banks locally, as well as throughout Australia and overseas.

Despite a series of national and international retail awards and being named Master Entrepreneur in the 2003 Ernst and Young Entrepreneur of the Year Awards, Roger's main focus is on finding ways to improve the business, believing there is still much to be done.

Roger and members of the management team travel overseas every one to two years to study retailing trends and innovations.

Roger benchmarks Drake Foodmarkets against an independent retail chain in the US called Wegman's, with the American company's coffee cup on his desk a constant reminder of the unfinished business of becoming the world's best.

The Drake Foodmarkets family – in addition to Roger's wife and three children who all work in the business and are committed to seeing it successfully pass to the next generation – also includes around 3200 South Australians.

'We've worked very hard to ensure that we've got enough people coming through to take this company to the next stage.

'I've always had the philosophy that you should help your understudy to do your job better than you can. That will ensure the long-term success of your business no matter what may happen to you.

'As growth has come we have worked very hard at ensuring that the reason for our business success – our absolute dedication to customer service – is embraced throughout. I'm constantly reinforcing that nothing should be too much trouble to meet the needs of our customers.'

While there are still some opportunities for the company in South Australia (including potential green fields sites as well as refurbishing and extending existing stores), the next obvious move for Roger is to look to interstate for future growth. Once again, he is taking on the might of Woolworths and Coles Myer.

Between August and October 2004, Drake Foodmarkets took the next exciting step in its growth by acquiring six stores in Queensland, located in metropolitan Brisbane and the Gold Coast. Roger is already planning to refit and upgrade the stores to the Drake corporate standards.

The next target is northern New South Wales, off the back of the steady immigration flow into that region, where Roger believes the bigger chains have had it too easy for too long due to the lack of independent competition.

As in South Australia, the focus is on acquiring existing, strong performing stores and those that have potential for significant expansion. It was this approach that saw the company double in size, turnover and employee numbers in just three years with the purchase of stores from both the Davids Group and the failed Franklins chain.

'Get big, get small or get out – that's always been my business philosophy.

'I've really stuck to that and I still believe that there is an opportunity for niche or boutique operators as well as those at the opposite end of the spectrum. I think anything in between is dangerous.

'Our growth has had to be very strategic in order to compete with larger retail chains, and we now have enough stores with enough different formats to maintain an edge against our competitors.'

Drake Foodmarkets is also investigating further opportunities in liquor retailing, following its foray into the sector with the purchase of a store in the South Australian country town of Wallaroo. Roger's belief is that Australian – particularly South Australian – food retailers should be increasing their focus on liquor retailing.

He believes this is logical for South Australia as the 'wine capital' of Australia and would emulate the success of retailers in Europe and America who offer alcohol as part of the food shopping experience.

'Again, it's all about service. Customers shouldn't have to do their entire food shopping in one location and then have to go to another store to buy their bottle of wine – it just doesn't make sense.'

While Roger recognises that technology will have a role to play in changing the long-term future of food retailing, he doesn't believe that it will be in the form of internet shopping as many predict.

'Everybody talks about food shopping being radically different in the future, but I don't think it will be.

'While there will be a place for internet shopping, it won't be the be all and end all. Food is the essence of life and the shopping experience we provide customers allows them to see it, feel it, touch it and smell it. Internet shopping might be okay on occasions, but I don't think people will want to do that every day.

'I'm more interested in our business using technology for customer identification, to find out what the customer likes, what they regularly do and don't buy, and then providing service and products that meet these specific needs and encourage them to buy more.

'If our systems show that Mrs Smith hasn't bought meat in our store in her last two shopping trips, we might offer her 20 per cent off meat on her next visit or we might tailor our advertising to promote our meat range.

'I'm sure technology will give us that advantage in the future, although it is still many years away.

'But I know our long-term business success won't come from technology. It will continue to be as a result of the customer service that we provide and the passion with which we run our business and deal with our customers.'

Lessons Learnt:

* Don't let ego get in the way of good business sense. Put models and systems in place to take the emotion out of making key decisions and ensure financial success.
* Decide early where you want to position yourself in the market, either as a niche operator or as a major player. 'Middle of the road' will see your business picked off by your competitors.
* Provide an environment where those coming up in the business have the opportunity to learn as much as possible – and then train them to be better than you.

Advice to Others:

* Know thy customer. Take the time to talk to them, learn the names of their children, and find out their likes and dislikes. The more you know about them the more passionate you will be about providing them with outstanding customer service.

Scott Elvish and Greg Mudie

When fire devastated the premises of plastic card manufacturer ScreenCheck Australia in late 2001, the owners, Scott Elvish and Greg Mudie, were facing business oblivion.

The blaze had destroyed 60 per cent of their plant and equipment and left their expansion plans in ashes. But this energetic duo refused to be beaten. Instead, they took a significant leap of faith, mortgaged themselves to the hilt and bought the latest state-of-the-art plastic card production equipment.

It was an expensive move at a time when both men were still uncertain of the true potential market for their products – but it turned out to be the right decision. Since then, ScreenCheck Australia has grown rapidly and cemented itself as one of the country's leading plastic card manufacturers.

'The fire was a tragedy, but it was also a turning point for the business. It prompted us to think hard and eventually we decided to buy all the equipment needed to significantly upgrade the quality of our production,' said Scott.

ScreenCheck Australia now makes approximately seven million cards annually from its Melrose Park location – and that number is rising rapidly. The company has about 35 staff nationally servicing clients ranging from retailers, fuel companies and gymnasiums, to nightclubs, football clubs, schools and libraries.

Most of ScreenCheck's cards are used for corporate identification, photo identification, credit cards, loyalty cards and membership cards.

Scott and Greg formed ScreenCheck Australia in 2001 after teaming up to buy a long-standing South Australian company, Plasticard Data Systems. Scott had recently sold a micrographics business and moved into photo identity production, while Greg was running another small business specialising in ID cards for schools.

In its first year of business under Greg and Scott's ownership the company sold about 500,000 cards.

Initially, Scott and Greg imported the cards, but as volumes increased the two realised that manufacturing their own cards would give them more control over their destiny in an extremely competitive market.

They quickly determined that their existing printing machinery was sub-standard and would not enable them to produce the top-quality cards they knew would give them a long-term marketing advantage.

Then the fire hit their premises, compounding their problems. While some of the machinery was insured, it only covered a fraction of the upgrade cost, which meant Scott and Greg had to dig deep to fund their expansion and purchase the required equipment.

That wasn't the only difficulty. At the time, no other company in South Australia was printing on laminated plastic cards, so Scott and Greg had little idea how to adapt the existing technology to give them the best results. And they certainly weren't going to get any help from their interstate competitors.

'We ended up tracking down a guy from Sydney who had specialist expertise in this area,' said Scott. 'He built the equipment and installed it, and then gave us some technical advice on how to make the cards using his equipment. We were able to kick it off from there.'

Scott remembers the early days as 'a nightmare'.

'We were in completely inappropriate premises about a third of the size that we really needed. Everyone had to suck their stomachs in to squeeze past the machines,' he said.

'Also, we made the classic mistake of skimping on the equipment that we bought initially. Of course, that backfired because we then had to reinvest down the track to buy production equipment with more capacity – which in hindsight is what we probably should have done in the first place.

'You don't know these things at the time though. We've been pleasantly surprised at how our market share has grown so quickly.'

Greg says that when he and Scott bought Plasticard Data Systems it had been the only card company in South Australia for 20 years, but its market share had slipped significantly in the period leading up to its sale.

People could see that we were excited about the business and its future. We won clients because they could see the energy in the company and they wanted to be part of that.

'A lot of Adelaide-based companies had gone from buying locally to buying their plastic cards from suppliers in Sydney and Melbourne,' he says. 'Fortunately we were able to reclaim much of the local business by reinforcing the fact that we were a local provider and could give them the personal service they wanted.

'We were also fresh faces with new ideas; new management for an older business. People could see that we were excited about the business and its future. We won clients because they could see the energy in the company and they wanted to be part of that.'

Scott says that while it would be easy to see plastic cards as simply a commodity to be purchased at the cheapest possible price, the card market is more complex than it appears.

'You have to remember that we are dealing with people's databases, some of which are quite confidential, so they need to be able to meet with you, know what kind of people you are, and that they can trust you with this sort of information,' he says.

'We have built our business on being able to give our customers peace of mind and fast turnaround with control of the project in Australia. It's very satisfying for us because we will often win business at a higher price than our competitors simply because we enjoy a strong and trusting relationship with our customers.'

ScreenCheck's mission is to provide a one-stop total solution to clients. While manufacturing is based in South Australia, the company has offices in Perth, Sydney and Brisbane. Customers can deal personally with ScreenCheck staff in each of those locations.

'You can't beat that sort of face-to-face personal contact. It certainly gives our clients the comfort that their interests are being looked after,' said Greg.

ScreenCheck Australia's name is based on that of Dutch company ScreenCheck, which globally markets a number of innovative photo ID software products. Greg and Scott's company was primarily a photo ID company when it started, so the trading alliance was a good fit.

Even though ScreenCheck Australia's focus is increasingly shifting to plastic card production, the strategic link with the Dutch company has been maintained.

'It's actually a great marketing advantage for us. It gives us a link with a very large and aggressive software development company that is leading the way with their products,' Scott said.

'They are the leaders in that field and that's been of tremendous benefit to us. It's certainly helped us lift our profile in Australia and it also means we can gain access to the Australian offices of global companies who have the potential to use our products.'

Scott says another significant advantage for ScreenCheck Australia is the fact that the company only makes one product.

'Of course there are many variations of that single product and none of them are alike, but if you look at us as a "widget" factory, we only make one widget.

'We're not like an engineering company, for instance, that has to put so many resources into just gearing up for the next project. We already have everything in place for the next job we win.

'That means we can focus all our energies into making sure that our sole product is the best of its kind. A client can brief us, we can make their card quickly, get it delivered, and then move on.

'Even a normal printing business will be doing different kinds of print jobs, with varying documents every day – but we do the same product every day.'

For Scott and Greg, growth over the next few years is being approached strategically and carefully.

'We are always careful to improve our processes to facilitate the further growth of the company,' said Greg. 'It's no good to keep on growing just for the sake of it without having the platform that enables you to move to that next level.

'It's important to stop and consolidate from time to time, preparing for the next big growth push.'

Said Scott: 'From my point of view, I also want some balance. Growth is important but when you've got a good business you should enjoy it for what it is. You need to put some of that energy into other parts of your life.'

Lessons Learnt:

* Having only one product can be a significant advantage, enabling you to focus all your energies on perfecting that product.
* Strategic links with a well-respected international company can help open doors for your business.
* Before buying expensive equipment, make sure it can meet your anticipated long-term production requirements – otherwise you may end up having to replace it with another expensive capital purchase sooner than expected.

Advice to Others:

* Approach everything you do with energy and enthusiasm. Both are contagious and can help you win clients who will be keen to work with such a vibrant company.

Marty Gauvin

While many entrepreneurs experience challenges along the path to business success, Marty Gauvin was introduced to the pressure cooker of corporate life from the outset.

His internet hosting company, Hostworks, was in fact created amid the turmoil of legal action against IT multinational, EDS.

Hostworks was spun out of the South Australian Government's Ngapartji IT centre in 1999 as a private company. During the process, EDS withdrew an important Microsoft contract – hosting the ninemsn website – which it had subcontracted to Ngapartji, taking half the Hostworks team and much of its intellectual property.

Despite the challenges already associated with getting his company off the ground, Marty wasn't going to take the move lying down and legal action was launched against EDS. The matter was quickly resolved out of court in Marty's favour and the Microsoft contract went to – and remains with – Hostworks.

While it was certainly a stressful experience, this 'baptism of fire' provided Marty with many valuable business lessons.

'I kept saying to my wife "it's about the journey, not the destination". If I wasn't able to think that way through our early difficulties I would have woken up and started every day thinking I was a failure. There were so many little battles along the way and there was a tremendous amount to learn and do through that whole process.

'It was an incredible learning experience. I actually got to sit in the room and effectively arbitrate between these two enormous companies, Microsoft and EDS. I learnt to understand their corporate cultures, understand their differences and similarities, and really get inside the thinking of both organisations. That provided a tremendous grounding.'

Marty says the experience taught him that small companies don't need to be afraid of 'the big end of town' – whether standing up to them in a stoush or just having the courage to ask for their business.

'When you're in those conflict situations, success is highly dependent on knowing which levers to push and what matters most to the various players. I think that can be difficult to understand if you haven't been in that kind of situation before.

'You also need to be clear about what you are risking. From my perspective it was unlikely that everything would have gone pear-shaped. If it did though, my company was barely off the ground, so if it fell over I could have quite easily just gone out and got another job. At that stage I didn't have a lot to lose by challenging the larger companies, and a good deal to win. Everything was upside.

'On the other hand, the risks for Microsoft and EDS were enormous in terms of goodwill and reputation. I think if you have a small company you need to be prepared to put it on the line if you are going to go up against the big guys.'

I think if you have a small company you need to be prepared to put it on the line if you are going to go up against the big guys.

Having survived that early experience, Hostworks has gone from strength to strength, with Marty viewing any subsequent business challenges as 'a breeze'.

The company is Australia's leading provider of critical internet and application hosting and is responsible for managing the availability, performance and critical on-line components of its customers' essential business applications.

Clients managed by Hostworks account for 15 per cent of all Australian website traffic with more than 300 e-commerce transactions hosted by Hostworks per second and data traffic throughput of more than 20 terabytes per month.

Hostworks' client base is becoming increasingly diversified and includes American Express, Sony, Ticketek, AAMI and the Compass Group, as well as ninemsn. No single client accounts for more than 20 per cent of revenue, with average individual client revenue of more than $20,000 per month.

Contracting those applications to Hostworks provides the company's clients with a strong win-win, saving them operating and capital expenditure while providing them with access to industry-leading expertise and breadth and depth of capability.

A number of canny investors saw the potential and bought into the company during its early days and Hostworks listed on the Australian Stock Exchange in 2001 through a merger with its largest shareholder.

Marty believes there are two key reasons for Hostworks' success.

'The first and most important reason is because of the company's culture. Hostworks was established from the very beginning as a mini-Microsoft. We had to fit culturally with the customer that we were trying to win work from, but I was also keen to capture what I saw as the positives of the way that organisation operates.

'There is a lot of informality at Hostworks. We're fairly much a meritocracy. People who have plenty of technical skill and capability are left to do their thing but are rewarded significantly.

'The second part of it was an understanding of what mattered in the internet, particularly when we started. People were still coming to grips with the limitations of the internet. It wasn't a terribly stable kind of system. It was not a computing environment that you could just "set and forget".

'We were setting internet reliability records every few months in terms of scale of operation and the types of things that our client was asking us to do. We had to invent the solutions as we went along.

'Rather than trying to spend potentially large amounts of money on building something that would work all the time, we embraced the daily challenge of "how are we going to make this work despite its unpredictable nature?"

'Our competitors made the mistake of approaching it on a traditional computing basis saying "pay us a fortune and we will build something that will never break". In the internet that was not realistic so they were promising what they couldn't deliver.'

In order to further expand his business skills, Marty has taken on several board positions that provide him with exposure to other companies as well as allow him to contribute to the business and IT communities. He is on the Board of the IT company incubator Playford Capital and on the IT Committee of the Federal Government's IR&D Board which provides research and development funding in Australia.

Both of these positions have provided him with the opportunity to view a large number of early stage companies and the various management, funding and operational issues that they experience. This includes the problems many entrepreneurs face when they shun advice and try to control every aspect of their business themselves, as well as the tensions that can arise when new investors come on board.

For Marty, this experience has reinforced the strength of Hostworks' own board, which has directors with a wide range of skills in operational issues, business start-up and growth, and mergers and acquisitions.

Marty believes all of these skills will be necessary as the company looks to move from its current position as a 'good, small listed company' to revenue of $50 million or more through acquisition, organic growth and the provision of additional services.

Recognising this, in the past few years the company has made what Marty calls 'practice acquisitions'. Interpath Australia was purchased in 2001 and Dimension Data Central in 2003.

'The two small acquisitions that we have done so far have taught us enormous amounts about integrating another company into our existing operation. Both have been financially very successful for the company and so we feel quite confident in being able to take Hostworks to the next step. But you need to be a tough negotiator and you don't want to fall in love with a company you are considering purchasing or you will pay too much.

'Acquisitions are like children; no two are alike. While these two have been almost like rehearsals, we know we can't say "we have that sorted, now we will do the next one and it will be the same". It won't be.'

Hostworks' continued success and expansion has reinforced for Marty how a great company can be founded on just one good idea.

'Lots of people come to me and say that no one is prepared to invest in their idea. Perhaps that says more about their idea than any perceived lack of funding.

'My experience has been that it is fairly tough to come up with a good, new idea for a business. It's been 20 years since I started my first company and Hostworks is probably my only seriously good idea for running a business.

'If you do have a good idea there is plenty of investment funding out there.'

Lessons Learnt:

* Don't be afraid of 'the big end of town'. Whether it's standing up to them in a stoush or just having the courage to ask for their business, you may be surprised at the result.
* Take relevant board positions. It's amazing what business skills you can pick up from observing other businesses in action, and which you can use in your own business.
* Don't believe you have to take on new challenges – including acquisitions – in one big leap. Dip your toe in the water and get a feel for the process before taking on 'the big one'.

Advice to Others:

* There's no shortage of money for good ideas, despite what many people may say. If you're finding it difficult to secure funding for your business, maybe you're looking at it from the wrong angle.

Martin Haese

The name for Martin Haese's company, Youthworks, came to him in a dream.

Since then, the innovative streetwear company has grown to become a national youth fashion phenomenon – and the dream continues.

Youthworks actually had its beginnings with an accessories and giftware stall Martin operated at the Brickworks Market in Adelaide in 1989.

The cut and thrust of trading in a bustling market environment honed Martin's early business skills and laid the foundations for what would evolve into one of Australia's most innovative clothing retailers.

'That store in the market was real coalface retailing. You don't learn any faster than trading in a market. It was great experience.'

Martin had a habit of leaving a dictaphone on his bedside table in case he had any good business ideas during the night. One morning in the early 1990s he woke and played back the tape, vaguely aware that somewhere in the middle of a fitful night's sleep he had woken from a dream and left a simple one-word message: 'Youthworks'.

'At first, I hated it. I thought it was a terrible name, but for some reason it kept coming back to me so I registered it and trademarked it – and then did nothing with it for two months.'

Eventually, convinced that he had discovered a yawning gap in the clothing market, Martin opened his first Youthworks store in Regent Arcade, off Adelaide's Rundle Mall.

'It was an eclectic mix of accessories – a bit of a carryover from the stuff at the market. The fashion component was relatively small. When the store first opened it wasn't a great success. It was only as I reduced the amount of accessories and increased the range of apparel that the business really took off.'

As they say in retail, timing is everything, and that certainly proved to be the case for Youthworks as young consumers hungry for something a little different flocked to the unique new store.

'At the time there was an increasing demand for streetwear and there weren't many people selling it. None of the retailers understood what it was all about. As we boosted the amount of clothing the store just erupted. It was a phenomenon.

'There was huge demand for product and not a lot of supply. We would have people queuing up on Friday nights and Saturdays to get in the door. It was amazing.'

The lack of supply turned out to be a revelation for Martin. Because some of the fashions were in short supply, young buyers were falling over themselves to purchase something that was seen as relatively 'exclusive'.

He has since built this into Youthworks' ongoing sales strategy. Many of the company's garment lines are available in strictly limited numbers, with some available only from particular stores.

'This high degree of tailoring is a challenge for the buying team, but one which we do extremely successfully. We even order some items in single units and put that item in the window for a week. It might sell in an afternoon or it might sell in a week, but it won't be repeated, so the customer can say "I bought this from Youthworks" and others will come in for it and we won't have it. That has done amazing things for our brand.'

Youthworks Group now has 17 stores and 85 staff in Adelaide and a similar number in Melbourne. The company has a turnover in excess of $24 million.

In 2003, Martin's growing enterprise caught the eye of Australian clothing legend Craig Kimberley, who turned Just Jeans into a 500-store retailing giant through the 70s and 80s. Craig has since taken a strategic shareholding in Youthworks and is working with Martin to build the business.

Martin says the Youthworks brand is about far more than just clothes – it's a youth culture shopping experience. For instance, popular local DJs mix the latest music live in-store and the company has its own biannual Youthworks Magazine.

Youthworks has won several store design awards for its funky layout, an international retail lighting award and numerous business awards.

Martin has gained more leverage for the Youthworks brand by establishing the Youthworks Infinity Card client loyalty program. With more than 15,000 active card members throughout Australia, the company is able to track the spending patterns of its best clients and better manage its inventory as a result.

Youthworks has also established cooperative marketing relations with high profile nightclubs and music retailers throughout the country.

'We have long held the philosophy that we can expand our business and offer more value to our clients by undertaking joint marketing initiatives with like-minded youth-orientated businesses. It creates a win-win situation whereby we open up our businesses to each other's client bases in a non-competing environment.'

In 2000 the company expanded laterally and has since opened several specialist footwear stores under the Soles Shoes banner – successfully diversifying while maintaining a focus on its core youth consumer.

Martin says the key to the group's growth has been its ability to remain innovative and versatile.

'We change frequently. We re-invent and we re-define. Being quick-footed is something I learnt from being a trader and merchant at the markets all those years ago. I also listen carefully to my clients and retail team who are at the coal-face.'

Martin talks with enthusiasm about the Youthworks 'offer' and how that has helped differentiate his stores from competitors.

'There is no shortage of competition in the rag trade. Having great product alone is not enough. You have to have a list of ingredients to add to your product to have a great business. Youthworks has a great offer. It's the product, the merchandising, the racking system, the team, the in-store music, the marketing, the signage, the window displays, the finishes, the flooring, the website – it's all part of the offer.

We change frequently. We re-invent and re-define. Being quick-footed is something I learnt from being a trader and merchant at the markets all those years ago.

'Placing clothes on a rack is just not enough. We are a lifestyle retailer of which clothing is just one element.'

As the company has grown, Martin's frontline sales team has become a vital conduit for the information he needs to gauge trends and make key decisions. So how does he keep good people in an industry renowned for its staff turnover?

'I think they stick around because I have managed to offer them a career in retail rather than a job in retail. It's also about communicating where the company is going and what their role is in taking it there.

'The payoff for them is partly monetary but it's more than that. It's ownership of the results, it's responsibility, it's recognition, it's praise – and it's also accountability.

'People who don't want to be accountable don't stay in our company because the culture of the company won't allow them to stay. The rest of our team will push them out the door if they are not prepared to be accountable for their actions, well before I have to think about pushing them out.

'I have a number of people who started off here as casuals and who now have great roles in the business with dozens of people reporting to them, in a company that in a few years will be twice the size it is now.'

So is Youthworks' growth driven by the fashions of the time? Or is Youthworks actually driving the fashions and thereby charting its own destiny?

'A retailer can't be so arrogant as to believe they are driving the market and creating the trends. That's actually a recipe for coming unstuck.

'The consumer is very educated. Our buying public are not primarily driven by price. They are driven by style, quality, fabric, trend, colour, design and a million different elements, including what the celebrities are wearing. When Kylie Minogue was photographed wearing military pants a few years ago that created huge demand for that particular item overnight.

'It's about being quick with those sorts of trends and making sure you are able to provide what the consumer wants.

'The three things that keep Youthworks where it is today are the product, service and people. It's a triangle you have to get consistently right week in and week out. There are probably a hundred other sub-categories but if you don't get those three right you've got nothing.'

Martin is a strong believer in peer-to-peer support and learning. He is a co-founder and Past President of the South Australian chapter of the Young Entrepreneurs Organisation, which is devoted to building the skills of business owners.

He also emphasises that any level of success he has achieved has come through persistence, self-belief and an ability to pick himself up after making an error.

'There is no road map. Whether you win or lose, experience is often the best teacher.'

Lessons Learnt:

* Think and move quickly – and don't be slow to admit mistakes. Martin's first store was not trading well until he switched his focus to apparel rather than the accessories that he originally thought would be the winning products.
* Go for win-win by pursuing mutually beneficial trading arrangements with people who are not your competitors. It's amazing what you can achieve.
* There is opportunity in disaster. Early problems sourcing enough product turned into a marketing bonanza for Youthworks as customers interpreted 'not available' as 'exclusive and limited'.

Advice to Others:

* Fine-tune your 'offer'. Whatever business you are in, it's not just about the product but all the other elements that go to make your company special to your customer.

Footnote: As this book was being published, Martin Haese contracted to sell the Youthworks and Sole Shoes businesses to two separate interstate-based retailers, creating a successful exit strategy for himself and launching the next phase of his business career.

Tom Hannah

Tom Hannah is as much a real estate developer as he is a successful publican.

The man behind many of Adelaide's icon dining and entertainment venues over the past 15 years, Tom has also built up a portfolio of prime inner suburban and coastal real estate in a strategy not dissimilar to that of fast food giant McDonald's.

'McDonald's is just as much about owning real estate as it is selling hamburgers. We've developed some great pubs over the years, but have sold off the businesses and moved on to other opportunities when the time was right. However, we've always hung onto the property,' Tom said.

'Every hotel that we've developed has deliberately been in a prime position. The rationale is that if the pubs ever disappeared, we still have a good townhouse site to develop.

'The challenges of having to deal with landlords in my early days in business taught me the importance of owning your own piece of dirt. I've only done business that way since and wouldn't do it any other way.'

Tom's hotel projects are just as impressive as his real estate holdings. He has owned and developed the Earl of Leicester, Seacliff Hotel and the Bombay Bicycle Club (Ovingham Hotel) in recent years. Other venues during his career have included the Alma Hotel, Gouger Hotel (now The Directors) and the Fish Manse restaurant.

His latest project is the $11 million redevelopment of the Kent Town Hotel, renamed the Tap Inn and embracing a golfing theme. In Tom's tradition of including a 'wow factor', the Tap Inn is believed to be the only hotel in the world to feature its own golf driving range.

Tom started working in hotels in his early 20s, despite 'not knowing one end of a beer keg from the other'. He worked 'part-time' – 40 hours a week on weekends and in the evenings – at the Leg Trap Hotel for two years while also holding down a full-time internal audit job for a government department.

At the age of 23 Tom sold his house, as did his mother and sister and brother-in-law, to raise the funds to buy the Gouger Hotel in Gouger Street. The family opened a disco in the hotel complex and hired a high-profile seafood chef to run the hotel's Crustacean Kingdom restaurant.

After more than four successful years in the Gouger Hotel, and having learnt an enormous amount about food quality and presentation, Tom bought the Fish Manse restaurant in North Adelaide – his first attempt at up-market dining at a time when the city was acquiring a taste for the cafe lifestyle.

Battling the popularity of much cheaper cafes and unable to buy the building in which the restaurant was housed, Tom returned to the hotel game after a couple of years. He purchased the Alma Hotel 'lock, stock and barrel' with a partner at a time when many Adelaide hotels were struggling to survive.

'The Alma was really where we first developed what we thought would be a winning hotel formula – a nice piece of real estate, the right demographics and a strong focus on food. Gaming was always a nice extra earner, but unlike many other hotels it has never been our main focus.

'The number one priority is always the real estate, the second is the right demographic. We make sure we target a very mixed crowd so we're not dependant on one type of person. What we do in the way of food and drink needs to appeal to a broad range of people.

'Another point of difference for us is that we only have one bar. We don't have a front bar, lounge bar and dining bar – it's one bar for everyone. If you're a bricklayer or a truckie you're welcome to come in, but change your shirt and watch your language to make sure you don't offend the many women that we always have in our pubs.

'We recognised a long time ago, and this is obvious now, the local pub is becoming the centre of the community again. People are visiting hotels to satisfy many of their entertainment and hospitality needs.'

Having put those foundations in place, Tom sold the Alma in the early 1990s and within a few months purchased the Earl of Leicester at Parkside. Many people questioned Tom's judgement, as the Earl had never made much money and was dogged by complaints from nearby residents.

The restaurant was substantially renovated and quality hotel food was introduced, while the bar was turned into the Liars Club, modelled on a similar concept in Melbourne giving patrons and staff the licence to tell lies. The changes and quirky atmosphere were immediately successful and the Earl of Leicester was soon an extremely popular venue.

Two years later the business was sold to fund the purchase of the Seacliff Hotel, on the Esplanade, which required a major renovation. At the Earl of Leicester, Tom had pioneered a distressed, half-renovated architectural look with exposed red brick, bluestone and timber – which was unique at that time but much copied now. A similar theme was introduced at the Seacliff, which went on to win major hotel and architecture awards.

The timing of the Seacliff Hotel development also proved perfect, as it coincided with a rising interest among Adelaide residents keen to live and socialise near the beach.

Three years later the Seacliff business was sold to fund the purchase of the Ovingham Hotel – another move that raised eyebrows in Adelaide hotel circles.

While it was very run down and in the 'wrong spot', Tom believed that the hotel's proximity to areas such as North Adelaide, Prospect, St Peters and Walkerville provided it with almost unlimited potential. He saw it as the perfect venue to develop a British Raj concept he had been considering for many years as an alternative to the Irish 'kit' pubs that were so popular at the time.

He called it the Bombay Bicycle Club, and interest in the concept surged well before the hotel's opening in mid-2002. With so much anticipation, the hotel was one of Adelaide's most popular from the outset.

'The momentum and the buzz around the project was just amazing and we had Australia-wide interest in the hotel. We had line-ups to get into the bar on Friday and Saturday nights. The restaurant became an Adelaide phenomenon – not a spare seat for the two years that we ran the hotel. Many tables were being re-set on most nights. I had old friends ringing me up to complain that they couldn't get a table, but I couldn't help them.

'One of the biggest compliments I received after the opening of the Bombay was, "It doesn't feel like you're in Adelaide. You could be anywhere." We knew we had achieved the highest level of point of difference that we look for.

'One of our main strengths is our attention to detail. Most hoteliers and publicans are looking for maybe a couple of points of difference. Our most recent development, the golf-themed project at Kent Town, has about 60 points of difference.

If you can create a whole new clientele of people that follow you, that's what it's all about.

'When I'm working on a project I like to be in control of it and my over-riding concern is always, "Will every corner work for the customer and for the business?"'

The Bombay Bicycle Club was sold in mid-2004 to allow Tom to focus on the Tap Inn. As well as the usual features that have served Tom so well, up to 14 patrons at a time will be able to use the 50-metre driving range. While golf is an all-important point of difference, Tom also sees it as a significant additional income earner.

'I'm always looking for ways to incorporate additional income streams into our businesses. That was the benefit that gaming provided to the hotel industry. It was a fresh income stream that complemented existing cashflows.

'The Tap Inn is an opportunity for us to introduce golf to a whole new group of people who perhaps wouldn't have had a go at it, while providing them with great food and drink and an excellent atmosphere.

'If you can look after the people who follow you in your new business endeavours, then that's one thing, but if you can create a whole new clientele of people who follow you, that's what it's all about.

'I also have to admit that another reason for this concept is that I love golf. Everyone said to me, "You've got great hotels full of excellent food and wine and beautiful women, what more could you ask for?" The answer was: "We need golf." So that's what we did.'

Lessons Learnt:

* Owning the real estate on which you operate your business can often be just as valuable as your core operations. It's also good insurance against fluctuating business conditions.
* Consider ways to incorporate additional income streams into your business.
* Don't rely on just one target market for your product. Cater to every demographic so you're not dependent on the whims of just one.
* Surround yourself with the right people. 'I have been blessed with an exceptional team of people who make me look good. Business partners Lara Roberts, Doug Goodfellow and chef Chris Sellars are all as much a part of my success as anything else.'

Advice to Others:

* Attention to detail is paramount. Don't just settle for a couple of points of difference to build an exceptional business. And remember: 'To get it perfect all the time is great, but to fix a problem with pizzazz is what people will talk about.'

Paul Haysman

From pipe fittings to stove cleaners – the change could not have been more stark for businessman Paul Haysman.

In 2002, having spent several years climbing the corporate ladder as Managing Director of Australian company Philmac, one of the world's leading pipe fittings manufacturers, Paul walked away from the opportunity of an international career to become a small business owner.

He purchased Hillmark, then a relatively low-profile manufacturer of cooktop and stainless steel cleaning products.

The move fulfilled Paul's dream of running his own business. What he didn't reckon on however was the amount of energy he would have to pour into the company in his first 18 months of ownership.

Early in his career at Philmac, Paul had promised himself a maximum of seven years in the Managing Director's chair. As that deadline loomed, he began considering his future career path.

'Most of the options involved doing the same thing in another possibly larger organisation. The alternative was to do something completely different.

Two years down the track the business is booming and in another two years our turnover will be double what it is now.

'What really attracted me was trying to do it myself with my own company – something that enabled me to draw on my portfolio of interests and that I could build as my own family business.'

Paul approached a number of business brokers and associates to help him find a suitable business that he could purchase and shape into an even bigger entity. Eventually, he learned through his brother that the owner of Hillmark, Robin Hill, was considering selling the business.

The two were introduced and spent the next 10 months getting to know each other and determining a realistic purchase price for the business.

Hillmark was founded in 1980. Its original products were stove hotplate element covers and a hotplate 'restoration' kit.

Gradually, Hillmark's lines evolved to meet the diverse needs of appliance technology. By the time Paul Haysman became involved, Hillmark's products included SteelKleen (for cleaning stainless steel appliances), Cerapol (a non-scratch cleaner for ceramic cooktops), a range of barbecue cleaning products and a gas conversion kit for barbecue kettles. The company had also become the exclusive Australian agent for Ezidri home food dehydrators.

After months of negotiation with Robin Hill, Paul took ownership in October 2002. By then he was itching to take Hillmark to the next level of its development.

From the day he started however, Paul realised that he would need to put his own stamp on the business.

'There was no consistency with regard to the corporate image, packaging, brochures and literature. Basically, it was all a bit piecemeal. Things were all over the place. On the day I arrived I said "OK, I need business cards", and the logo I had to use just didn't look right. I decided right then and there that we needed to start all over again.

'We needed an identity and we needed a consistent marketing message, so that was where I started.'

Paul began a major project to revise and standardise all Hillmark's marketing and packaging, ensuring a consistency of message and image throughout all the company's products and merchandising.

The more Paul scrutinised Hillmark's existing activities the more he knew that a 'clean sweep' approach was required for virtually every part of the business.

It began when Paul was trying to patch up some customer disputes simmering from the previous ownership. The cause of the problem was faulty nozzles on the plastic product containers. Paul changed the bottle style, but then the labels couldn't be printed onto the new bottle shape. That meant adhesive labels were required – but Paul realised that if he was going to go to that expense then he should bring forward proposed changes to all the logos and label designs. That meant immediate and significant additional costs in graphic design and printing.

One by one, various small issues began mounting up as Paul realised that every aspect of the company's operation was inextricably linked and that any minor change impacted on numerous other parts of the business.

'It was like a ball of string where you just pull the thread and the whole thing unravels. None of the issues were very big or insurmountable, but together they amounted to a great deal of work and significant expenditure – all at a time when I was still coping with the significant debt burden of buying the business in the first place.

'I could have left it all as it was but it wasn't working as well as it could. I just bit the bullet and made all the changes in parallel so all parts of the business were heading in the right direction at the same time.

'At the time I don't think I fully appreciated how big that exercise would be. It was 18 months before I managed to get all those elements under control and free myself to start building the business again.'

Paul says that while he took care to find out as much about Hillmark as possible before buying the business, 'the devil is in the detail'.

'I think my overall knowledge of the business would have been helped if I had access to all of the employees, rather than just the owner. I didn't have that access because right up until I bought the business my dealings were only through the business owner.

'Input from the employees would have helped me know what they knew about the business and what I may have had to change after taking ownership. By making sure everything was on the table that may have affected the purchase price I paid and it certainly would have helped with my broader knowledge of Hillmark before I walked through the door.

'It was a concern at the time because there seemed to be so much that needed my attention, but I'm not too worried about it now. Two years down the track the business is booming and in another two years our turnover will be double what it is now.'

Part of the challenge for Paul was to broaden and boost Hillmark's traditional 'behind the scenes' distribution. For instance, until Paul took control SteelKleen was mostly marketed via manufacturers of stainless steel kitchen appliances who included SteelKleen samples with each appliance sold. Consumers could then purchase subsequent containers of SteelKleen from the appliance retailer.

This form of tied distribution gave Hillmark an exceptional marketing advantage but Paul believed a large, untapped market existed in the nation's supermarket aisles.

Paul's new packaging and point-of-sale merchandising gave Hillmark a bold new image to encourage supermarket sales. He says the new marketing material has been 'critically acclaimed' by the many distributors and supermarkets that now carry Hillmark's growing range of products.

Hillmark's cleaners are approved and recommendeed by leading appliance manufacturers including Fisher & Paykel, Maytag Australia, IXL, Electrolux (Westinghouse, Chef, Simpson) and Kleenmaid/St George.

Cerapol now has the lion's share of the Australian ceramic cooktop cleaner market and Hillmark's stainless steel cleaning products have approximately 45 per cent of their market.

Paul has also adopted a more proactive approach to marketing Hillmark's traditional lines such as the cooktop element covers – a range that he says was 'dying on the vine'.

'Sales of element covers were declining by 20 to 30 per cent per annum. They are sunset products and won't be our stars into the future, but I did not accept that we should not put any marketing effort at all into them.'

Paul spent time visiting and talking with retailers and distributors about element covers, which at the time were sold in box sets made up of one large and three small covers. He found out that while this combination was fine for the older style of stoves, modern European cooktops had different burner configurations and required two large and two small element covers.

Armed with this knowledge, Paul quickly changed the packaging. Within six weeks he released a new selection called the 'European Collection', breathing new life into an old category.

He sent complimentary sets of the new collection to each of the stores that suggested the change and within a few weeks had received thousands of dollars in additional orders.

'I think the lesson is that just because a product isn't performing well you shouldn't give up on it. All your product lines don't have to be growing to give overall business growth. Slowing down or avoiding a decline in some products can assist you build the business.'

Lessons Learnt:

* Short-term pain can lead to long-term gain. Paul Haysman spent 18 months revamping Hillmark's products, packaging and marketing at significant expense, but the move worked. Sales are now rising sharply off the back of a more integrated marketing approach.
* Don't ignore 'sunset' products. Slowing the decline in sales of any product can help sustain the growth of the company overall.
* Listen to your customers. Paul created a new sales opportunity by talking with retailers and discovering a need to repackage stove element covers to suit European appliances.

Advice to Others:

* Spend time learning as much as possible about a company before buying it. Where possible, gain access to existing employees and other associates of the business so you can gauge what they know about it and where any problems may lie. Additional research before signing on the dotted line may avoid finding 'skeletons in the closet' later.

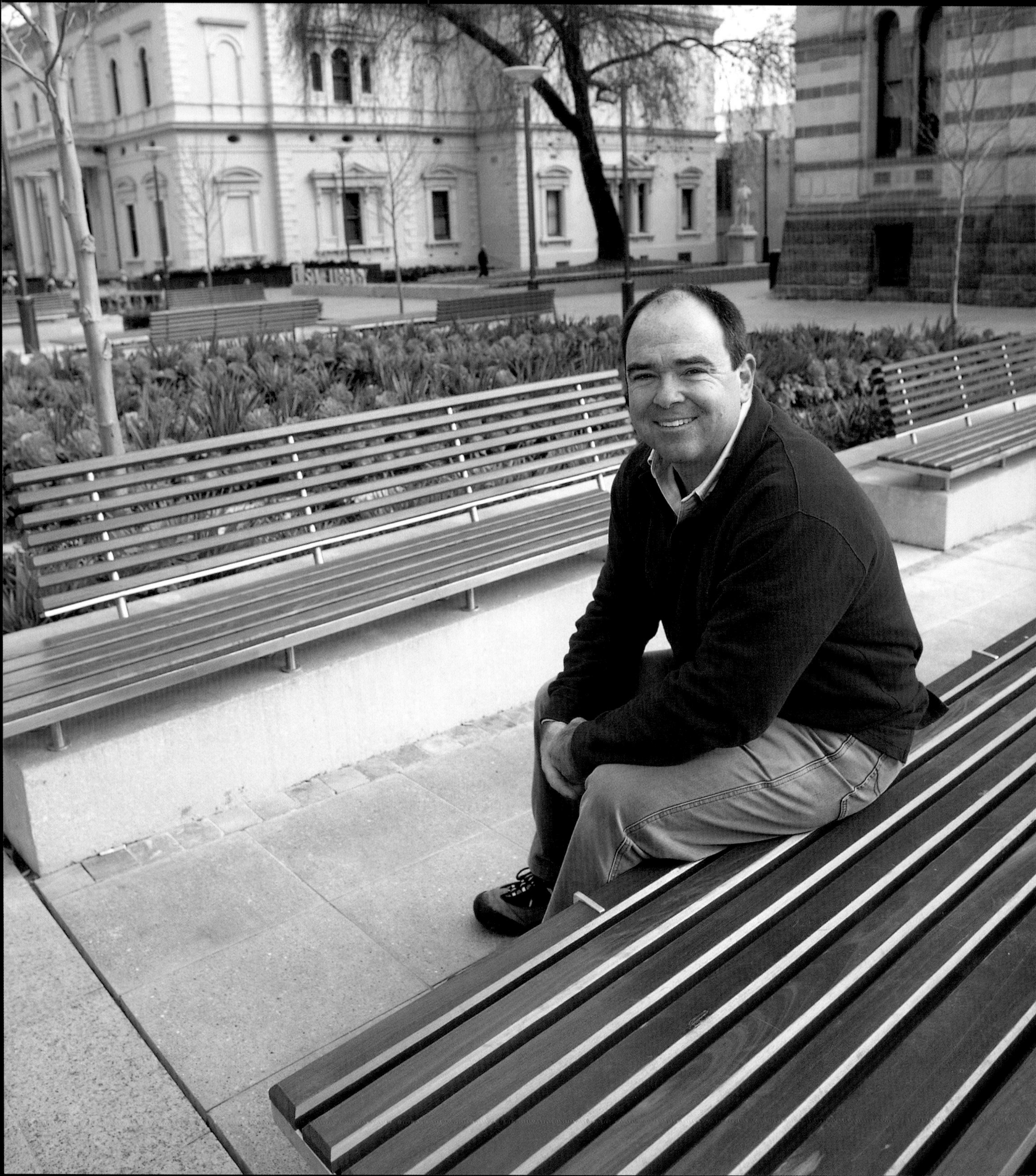

Cameron Johnston

Cameron Johnston has convinced customers to buy products that his business, Street & Park Furniture, hasn't even designed or manufactured yet.

Such is the company's ability to adapt and willingness to 'try anything'.

This attitude has enabled Street & Park Furniture to grow from a South Australian backyard operation into the leading furniture supplier for some of Australia's most significant urban developments.

The company designs and manufactures a broad range of products, including seats and benches, tables, bins, bollards, lighting and light poles, tree grills and tree guards, signage, drink fountains and bike racks.

These products are made from a variety of materials including iron, steel, timber, concrete and stone.

Major projects undertaken by Street & Park Furniture in South Australia include furnishing the 189 hectares of open space at Mawson Lakes, the City of Adelaide seat program and the redevelopment of the North Terrace precinct.

Interstate projects have included furnishing the 3000-lot Taylors Hill housing subdivision in Melbourne and installing street lighting for Broadbeach Mall on Queensland's Gold Coast.

'I'm a bit of a dreamer and so I'm lucky that I have a team around me that always helps me to deliver.

'It's a bit of an in-office joke these days where my colleagues will say to me, "What have you sold now, and how are we going to make it?"

'But it is our ability to adapt that has been the key to our success. We're prepared to try anything and it would have to be a fairly difficult project for us to say we don't think we can do it.

'We're yet to find something that's beyond us.'

Street & Park Furniture was founded in the mid 1980s by businessman Richard Haynes in his backyard. By the late 1990s, at the age of 60 and having run the business for 12 years, Richard was looking to wind down.

During a discussion one day with his neighbours, Cameron's parents, Richard jokingly suggested that perhaps Cameron could buy the business from him. A year later in 1998, seeking a new challenge and having plucked up the courage to leave the perceived safety of working for large corporations, Cameron signed on the dotted line and purchased the business.

Street & Park Furniture was a solid performer in terms of sales and profitability, but Cameron risked everything financially to buy the company.

The purchase was a change of pace from his decade-long career in marketing, but provided the opportunity to blend his desire to have his own business with a keen interest in the practical aspects of manufacturing.

Since receiving his degree in Business Marketing, Cameron had worked in senior marketing roles in both Adelaide and Sydney in everything from oil firms to packaging companies.

'Whenever I worked for manufacturers I always gained a great deal of satisfaction from walking through the factory, grabbing things and pulling them apart, and learning and talking to the people who actually made the items.

'I've always enjoyed the practical side of manufacturing and had an active interest in good design.

'This business provided the ideal opportunity not only to become a managing director and use my marketing skills, but also to spend time designing and creating the products themselves. A business that allowed me to combine all my interests was very appealing.

We're prepared to try any-thing and it would have to be a fairly difficult project for us to say we don't think we can do it. We're yet to find something that's beyond us.

'I wasn't looking for a way to make a million dollars, but I did want to make a meaningful contribution. I wanted something that got me out of bed in the morning and after more than 10 years in straight marketing roles I wasn't getting that enjoyment anymore.'

While Street & Park Furniture still supplies the standard product range that the company had when Cameron bought it, the number of products on offer has been considerably expanded through new additions, such as light poles, and a growing market in customisation for companies such as Telstra.

Street & Park Furniture's customers are primarily landscape architects, councils and developers who are impressed with the breadth of the company's product range as well as its focus on innovative design.

A growing emphasis by developers and councils on good urban design and the creation of more 'liveable' suburbs has been a boon for the company, tying in with Cameron's philosophy that better streets and civic spaces are a vital part of community well-being.

The company's motto is 'better cities begin at street level' and Cameron believes Street & Park Furniture has raised the bar in terms of street furniture standards.

Recognising that design considerations, rather than price, are the drivers in determining what company's products a landscape architect or council will use, Cameron's future priority is on producing a more contemporary range of furniture that reflects changing trends in urban design.

One element of this expanded range includes solar lights which Street & Park Furniture literally created 'from the ground up', following a request from a developer customer.

'Our solar lighting was developed from first principles – the only knowledge we took from the solar industry was the measurements of a standard solar panel.

'Everything else we developed ourselves, from the computer that runs the technology, to the design unit and curved solar panels, which we believe to be the first of their kind in the world.

'We were determined to curve the solar panels for aesthetic reasons. Generally, other solar lights on the market put performance ahead of design appeal, but we approached it from the opposite perspective.'

For Cameron and the team at Street & Park Furniture, the project was a lesson not only in the development of solar lighting, but also in the benefits of working collaboratively with others.

'Not having much knowledge of fibre-glassing, we contacted a surfboard manufacturer on the south coast. While we designed the panel and soldered the individual cells together, it was only with the assistance of this other manufacturer that we were able to combine the cells with the fibreglass.

'Similarly, we sought help from another company with the electronics component of the lights.

'It really highlighted to us that if you say to others, "look, this is new to me, I need some help", most businesses will give you a hand.

'It was a great thrill for me to see the way our suppliers really bought into the project. Don't be embarrassed to ask for help.'

The company expects the solar lights to be a major seller in coming years, with a considerable amount of enquiry already from throughout Australia.

While happy to be able to develop a specific product to meet a customer need, for the Street & Park Furniture team it was also the thrill of the challenge that was appealing in designing and manufacturing the solar lights.

One of the team members who played a major role in the development of the lights, Paul Gill, is a former farmer with no specific experience in solar lighting, electronics or working with fibreglass.

'But he was able to pick up the ball and run with it – he was integral to ensuring that we could deliver the product that the customer wanted. It shows that with the right people on board, you can take your ideas and turn them into reality.'

This 'can do' attitude has seen Street & Park Furniture expand its customer base from its original focus on South Australia to become a company that exports half of its products to the eastern seaboard.

The company's innovative website has been an important tool in allowing existing and potential customers around Australia to find out more about the company and its product range.

Cameron is now considering the best way to further develop the company's business interstate.

'One of my biggest passions is that there's no reason why any business in South Australia can't service the rest of the country.

'I'm amazed at how many people are surprised that an Adelaide-based company is selling products to the eastern seaboard. It has never entered into my mind that we wouldn't sell outside of South Australia.

'Location is no reason for not participating in a market. If we're sending a truck full of street furniture to the outskirts of Adelaide, it's just as easy to keep driving until it gets to Cairns.'

Cameron pays tribute to the ever-patient spouses of entrepreneurs. He says it would be almost impossible for businesspeople to take the risks required to grow a business without the encouragement and support of those who would also be impacted by a venture's potential failure.

'This is particularly the case with my wife, Rachel. The risks in this case were as much hers as mine. If it all went pear-shaped she too would have lost a house and a home. With two young children this certainly requires courage.'

Lessons Learnt:

* It's good to dream, but make sure you can deliver on your promises. Build a team of people who can work with you to help turn your dreams and ideas into reality.
* A reputation for being adaptable and prepared to try anything is a great way to build customer support and repeat business. It can also take your business on all sorts of interesting new tangents.
* South Australian companies can match it with their interstate counterparts. Rather than asking 'why' we should be selling our products interstate and overseas, we should be asking 'why not?'

Advice to Others:

* Don't be afraid to ask for help and don't underestimate the value of getting a different viewpoint from those outside your industry. No one expects you to know everything. Some of the best results for Street & Park Furniture's customers have come when the team 'thought outside the square' and benefited from the different perspective and skills of others.

Mark Kirtland

In 2000, Mark Kirtland's neck was broken when a chiropractic manipulation went wrong. His neurosurgeon told him he might never walk again. Three years later Mark competed in a gruelling Iron Man triathlon event that involved a 3.8km swim, a 180km bike ride and a 42km run.

The amazing turnaround illustrates the determination and discipline that Mark has used to build a stable of successful water industry companies over the past decade.

The incident also serves as a constant reminder to Mark that life is short and that balance between business and lifestyle is essential.

Mark owns or holds a major shareholding in six diverse water industry companies: Australian Industrial Pump Systems; Butlers Pumps and Irrigation; Caprari Pumps Australia; and Aquaflex Australia (all in Adelaide); Watercorp Irrigation (in Mount Gambier); and Lawries Pump Sales and Service (in Berri).

The evolution of the group is a credit to Mark's strategic and marketing skills – and to his core philosophy of business planning.

Mark spent 16 years working for pump manufacturer Finsbury and diversified manufacturer Clyde Apac before forming Australian Industrial Pump Systems with a former colleague to distribute Southern Cross industrial pumps.

It was a huge risk. Mark walked away from a secure and well-paid job to launch a business in an unfamiliar and competitive market. Within a year, AIPS was teetering on the brink as the fickle pump market and a tough trading environment threatened to send the fledgling business to the wall.

'We had to make some changes – and quickly. I went to Melbourne and saw that a couple of companies there were developing well in the fire pump market. When I got back to Adelaide we changed our whole focus to concentrate on building pump systems for the fire protection market.'

It was another big risk – but it saved the company.

'At the time the Australian fire pump market was dominated by one large manufacturer. Because they had the market to themselves they were perceived as charging too much and their service was relatively poor. We came in as the only South Australian manufacturer and picked up a big slice of the market almost immediately.

AUSTRALIAN INDUSTRIAL PUMP SYSTEMS

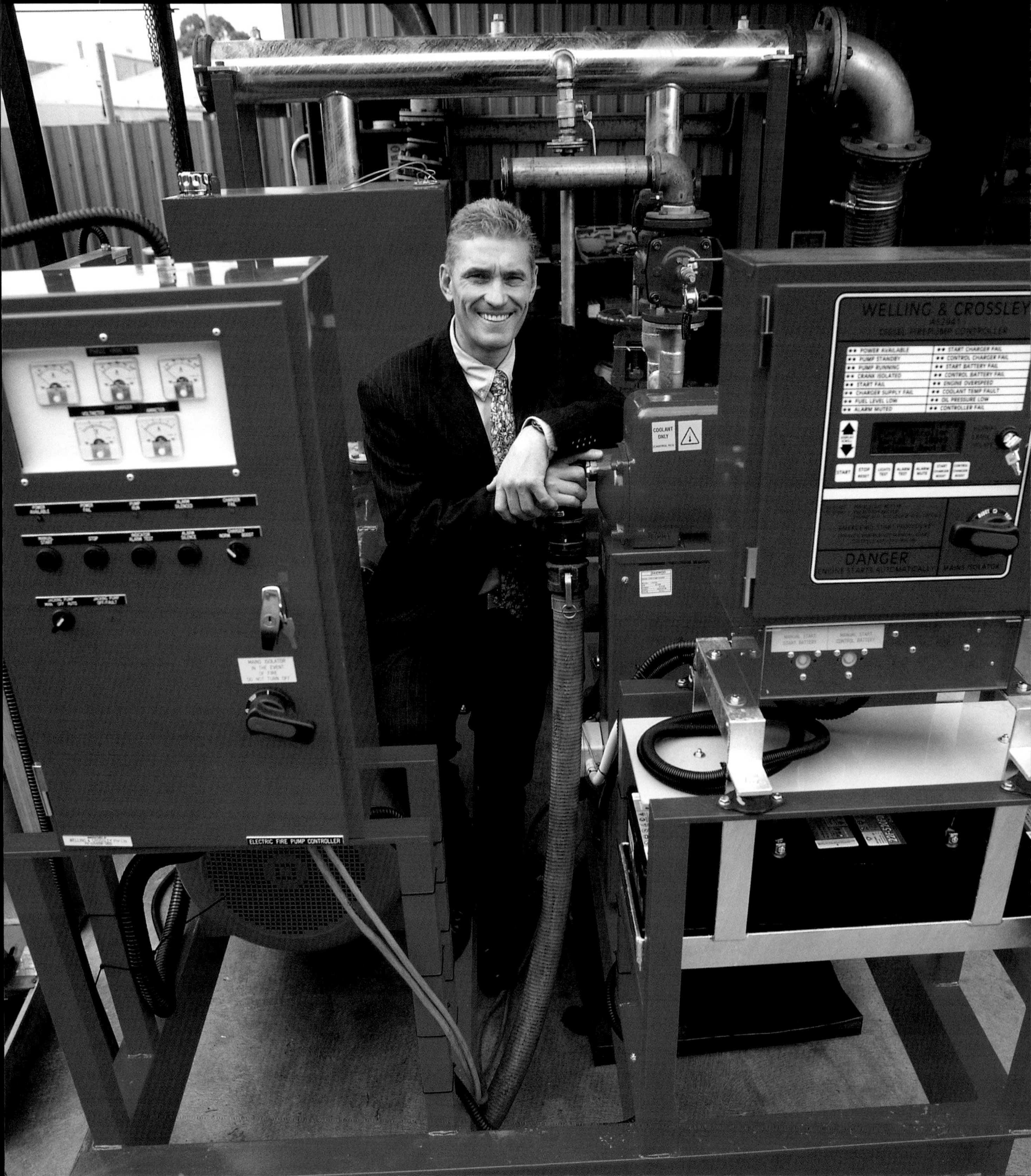

'We had an excellent knowledge of pumps and engineering, and we started to deliver competitively priced systems.'

In what had been virtually a monopoly market, Mark says customers were 'screaming for change'.

'The first thing I did was go to the market and said that if they wanted a small independent to survive in South Australia they were going to have to support me – and they did.'

Because of their near-monopoly position, Mark's opposition had become complacent about how they dealt with customers. For instance, Mark learnt that many of his competitor's quotes for work were hand-scrawled one-page notes that were then faxed to customers.

'I developed a very professional sales quote format that included photographs of pumps we had installed previously and a spreadsheet showing all the financial data. That way the client knew exactly what the quote included. There was no uncertainty.

'That won us a lot of work because even though we didn't have a big company behind us we were able to portray a high degree of technical competency in the quote that we gave. It added a new level of professionalism that had been missing from the market.'

Within two years, AIPS had 50 per cent of the South Australian fire pump market and Mark had secured the company's future. He subsequently bought out his business partner.

AIPS now dominates its market. It has about 90 per cent of South Australia's fire protection pump market and is enjoying strong growth in Victoria and Western Australia.

In 1997, Mark purchased the then Southern Cross irrigation business in Mount Gambier, now known as Watercorp Irrigation. Turnover was up 50 per cent in the first year under Mark's ownership and, following the appointment of a strong management team, Mark and his team have since transformed Watercorp into one of South Australia's most successful rural irrigation businesses. In 2003, Mark sold 50 per cent of this business to his much-respected manager, Daniel Grosse.

In 2000, Mark bought Butlers Pumps and Irrigation, which supplies irrigation systems, fountain pumps and other garden equipment throughout metropolitan Adelaide. Once again, Mark installed a new management team to rejuvenate the business. With a strong emphasis on business planning the business is now very profitable.

Then, in 2003, Mark established Aquaflex Australia (in partnership with irrigation industry stalwart Brian Lawrence) to nationally market and distribute a revolutionary soil moisture sensor for sports fields, golf courses and agricultural irrigation applications.

When Lawrie's Pump Sales and Service in South Australia's Riverland hit financial strife in 2003 Mark bought that business too, re-hiring the former owner and helping rebuild the business.

> The lesson is, do your homework. It's important not to get wrapped up in the emotions that go with establishing or buying a business. You can't just do it on gut feeling.

In 2004, Mark established Caprari Pumps Australia – once again with Brian Lawrence – to market and distribute Australia-wide the quality pumps made in Italy by the Caprari family company.

Mark now has a portfolio of complementary companies covering almost every aspect of water pumping and distribution. The group's combined turnover is about $7 million, but Mark says a target of $10 million is 'just around the corner'.

The group's outstanding success owes much to Mark's focus on in-depth research and strategic planning. He prepared a comprehensive business plan on each of the businesses before any investment was made, carefully researching the market to understand the opportunities.

'I have always prepared detailed business plans. It's one of my disciplines in corporate life. A business plan enables you to take the emotion out of decisions about a business.

'When I bought Watercorp, AIPS was still in its early days and we weren't as strong as we are today. But I did a detailed business plan on Watercorp and took it to three banks and they each said they'd lend me the money for it. I did the same again with the Butlers purchase.

'A business plan shouldn't only be a document you prepare to get money from a bank. You should be using it to prove to yourself that the business is a goer and that it's worthwhile borrowing the money because the business idea is sound.

'The lesson is, do your homework. It's important not to get wrapped up in the emotions that go with establishing or buying a business. You can't just do it on gut feeling.

'I once spent five months working on a business plan before deciding not to pursue the business because it didn't stack up. That's not wasted time. It stopped me from making a bad decision.'

Mark's business plans have been crucial to the creation of two of his companies. With both Caprari Pumps Australia and Aquaflex Australia he had to convince offshore parent companies that he could successfully distribute their products throughout Australia.

In fact, Mark's voluminous business plan on the creation of Caprari Pumps Australia was the linchpin to convincing the Caprari family in Italy why a comparatively small South Australian company should be given Australian distribution rights.

Until Mark came along, Caprari had no formal distribution arrangement in Australia, even though the brand was widely recognised as one of the best turbine pumps in the world.

Mark travelled to dozens of irrigation and pump specialist dealers around Australia, researching their pump requirements before preparing his comprehensive business plan. The research showed that dealers buying from Caprari's competitors were frustrated at the long wait – sometimes months – from the time a pump was ordered to its delivery date.

'Everyone was getting incredibly frustrated with existing pump suppliers and said that if we could hold stock in Australia to guarantee quicker delivery times we would get their business. That was a key element of the business plan.

'When I visited the Caprari family in Italy they sat me down in their boardroom for three days, asking detailed questions about every page of the business plan. Because I'd done the research I had answers to all their questions. If I hadn't done my homework they may not have chosen to partner with us.'

By the time Mark left the Caprari family's headquarters he had secured the Australian distribution rights.

Delegation is another factor in Mark Kirtland's success. His knack of being able to pick good people and then empower them to run the day-to-day operations frees him up to take more of a strategic overview of the group.

Also, 100 per cent ownership is not essential to Mark. He would rather have 50 per cent of a successful company run well by competent managers than own all of a business that requires his hands-on involvement every day.

That helps him achieve his other goal of finding balance in his life and ensures that he has plenty of time for his family and health interests.

'Up to the point where my neck was broken I was devoting too much time to business and my health was starting to be affected. I thought I had a balance but I realised that without your health you have nothing. I started making some changes.

'I certainly devote time to my businesses but I have honed my business planning, management and delegation skills even further to ensure a holistic approach.

'I work fewer hours but I have taken on more challenges and achieved more personally, so I can feel good about the balance I have found.'

Lessons Learnt:

- A business plan is not just a document for the bank. It enables you to analyse your options regarding a business – and it can stop you from making the wrong choices.
- Hire good people and empower them to manage. It will save you from being consumed by your business.
- Take a professional approach to the way your business deals with customers.

Advice to Others:

- Learn to step back from your business. Life is too short to be consumed entirely by work. Don't become a fanatic – balance all your interests.

Anthony Kittel

Anthony Kittel didn't know what a power converter was until he bought a company that manufactured them.

When the opportunity arose to purchase REDARC Electronics, Anthony – then General Manager at ROH Wheels Australia – had to ask a colleague what a power converter was.

'Even when he explained it to me, it still went over my head,' Anthony recalls. 'I quickly embarked on a steep learning curve.'

REDARC was founded in 1979 by Bob Mackie, an electronics engineer. While it had a solid – rather than a spectacular – track record, it did have a reputation for innovation, with Bob undertaking all the R&D work on the company's products. Bob's death in 1995 saw the business run under management and a slow but steady decline in REDARC's performance.

Despite his lack of knowledge about the product, Anthony bought the business with his father-in-law Denis Brion in 1997. At that time it had eight employees and an annual turnover of $800,000.

Anthony's background was in manufacturing and Denis had owned a plastics manufacturing business. The purchase of REDARC followed several years of discussion about the possibility of going into business together, and a lengthy and extensive search to find a business that met the criteria of both.

The pair weren't too bothered about the type of product being manufactured, but they did want a business that was profitable (even if only just), made a quality product, had a stable workforce and offered plenty of opportunity for improvement. After considering dozens of potential candidates, REDARC was a match.

REDARC specialises in the research, design, development and manufacture of a range of power conversion products for the trucking and automotive industry. This includes electronic voltage converters, inverters, power supplies, battery chargers, turbo timers, trailer braking products and associated automotive products.

Unlike passenger cars, trucks have different voltages depending on where they are manufactured. American trucks operate on a 12-volt system, while European and Japanese trucks are 24-volt. REDARC's products convert the voltage up or down as required, providing standardisation.

The company's products are used by major truck manufacturers including Mercedes Benz, Iveco, Mack, Volvo, DAF and Isuzu as well as auto electricians who fit REDARC's converters as an after-market product.

While REDARC has minimal direct exports to New Zealand, the US and the Middle East, the company's products are often used as original equipment on trucks manufactured in Australia which are then exported.

Having purchased the business, Anthony's first priority was to meet the company's customers in order to gain an understanding of the market and to shore up support for REDARC under the new ownership.

'In the few years before we took over there had been major problems with customer dissatisfaction with both the product and the service they were receiving. We had to let our customers know that we were aware of the issues and that we were keen to address these as a priority to ensure they stayed on board with us.

'We quickly adopted the fundamental rule that "the customer is king" and we highlighted that with both our customers and employees.

'Staffing was the next issue to be addressed and we decided to keep everyone on and give them the opportunity to prove themselves, which they all did. Every single one of those original staff members has stayed with us, even through the major operational and cultural changes that we have implemented.

'I've had external consultants tell me that there would be staff losses from some of these changes and that there could be up to a 20 per cent fall-out, but it's never happened.

'That's a result of how we've gone about introducing and implementing change. We've been proactive, educated staff about why we're making the changes and involved them in the process. We've never hidden anything.

'We've run REDARC like a family business and have always appreciated the people who we have here.'

REDARC's products were the next to be evaluated by the new owners. Complaints about product faults and a lack of reliability were straining customer relations.

Hand-in-hand with ironing out the product problems was the introduction of a range of 'customer friendly' philosophies to make the company more responsive to buyer feedback.

REDARC graduated from begrudgingly, and sometimes rarely, honouring warranty claims to a 'no questions asked' approach whereby a problem product is immediately replaced with a brand new one. Returned products are analysed to determine the source of the problem and if no fault can be found discussions are held with the customer and suggestions provided on how to eliminate other possible causes.

A free telephone technical assistance service has been established which runs 'red hot' with enquiries and reinforces REDARC's commitment to helping customers, while also proving an excellent avenue for market intelligence.

'Our customer service approach is best highlighted by what we do when something goes wrong, as it provides us with the best opportunity to delight the customer.

'We don't have customer problems; we have customer opportunities and try to turn a negative into a double positive. Not only is the problem fixed at that time but generally they're a loyal customer for many years afterwards because they know we do the right thing by them.

'We might lose money at the time but if that customer keeps coming back to buy further products, it guarantees the longevity of the relationship. That's vital in a company like ours which relies on repeat business and has a high referral rate.'

Repeat and new business have seen REDARC's sales grow by 30 per cent annually in recent years. Sales revenue is expected to reach $10 million in the next few years.

The company has been named in *Business Review Weekly* magazine's Fast 100, the Deloitte Technology Fast 50 and the Top 20 SA Technology Company lists on numerous occasions and REDARC's customers regularly award the company with 'top supplier' status.

As planned when the business was purchased, Anthony bought out Denis's half share of the company in 2002.

While a proactive approach to customer service, improved business systems and some minor product refinements put REDARC back on track in the first few years after its purchase, increased investment in R&D and new product innovation have been integral to the company's success in more recent times. Anthony says this is the key to continued growth in the future.

Hundreds of customer comments, queries and suggestions – coupled with the input of employees – have been considered and analysed and are being used in the design and development of new products.

You just need to focus on the fundamentals and ask yourself, 'how can we make this company better?'

'As a result of our approach to working so closely with our customers we've gathered a lot of information and ideas which are now filtering through as new product ideas.

'I can't emphasise enough how critical it has been for our senior people to be out in the field talking to customers and users of the product. You hear about their problems and that presents an opportunity for you to develop a solution for them. For us that's been the best driver for new product development.

'It has also seen us increasingly customising our products for particular customer needs, giving us the reputation as a "one-stop shop".

'We used to be quite casual about how we kept track of suggestions and feedback, but as we began to recognise the value of these ideas and how they could influence our future products and focus, we took a much more formal approach to documenting and recording this input.

'Even if it's not implemented immediately, it might be very relevant in a few months or years down the track.'

While Anthony has learnt a thing or two about power converters since purchasing REDARC, he has learnt even more about turning a struggling business into an entrepreneurial treasure.

'There are so many businesses that can be greatly improved just by looking at their policies and procedures, how they manage staff or market their products.

'You just need to focus on the fundamentals and ask yourself, "How can we make this company better?"'

Lessons Learnt:

* Entrepreneurship isn't only found in start-up businesses. The same skills and dedication can be applied to an existing business to take it to the next level.

* Excellent customer service is a great form of market intelligence. Initiatives such as technical assistance hotlines and customer visits provide an excellent opportunity to learn more about your own products and how they can be further developed to meet the needs of your customers.

* Avoid the 'slash and burn' approach to managing your workforce when you come into a new business. Explain to your employees what you want to achieve and give them time to prove themselves. Chances are they will be keen to be part of an invigorated company.

Advice to Others:

* You don't necessarily have to understand everything about your business – including its products. Vision, energy and sound business and industry basics will enable you to make a success of the business and identify new opportunities for growth. You can learn the 'nitty gritty' as go you.

Michael Kohn

When Michael Kohn started his air charter business, Air South, he founded it on the philosophies of third century Chinese military hero Kuan Gung.

To the Chinese, Kuan Gung represents loyalty and righteousness, considered to be the two most important virtues of mankind. According to legend, Kuan Gung fought many battles with courage and endurance – two traits that have been integral to Michael's initial business survival and later success.

Michael's father gave him a plaque of Kuan Gung when he started the business and it stills hangs in his office today, constantly reminding him of the importance of these attributes in his own business dealings.

'When I first entered the air charter business I was mocked by many of my competitors, who didn't believe that I would succeed in such a volatile industry. Many before me had failed trying to create a similar type of company.

'But I loved flying and I knew that if I remained committed and had the courage to create my own opportunities, then success would eventually come.'

Michael established Air South in 1993 as a 22-year-old with two young pilot friends.

Disillusioned and unemployed after completing their pilot training, the trio established Air South to help gain the flying hours needed to make them more employable.

With one telephone and a $200 contribution from each of them, Air South commenced its chartered scenic flight operation. Despite their persistence and commitment however, the enterprise was not financially viable and Michael's two colleagues subsequently abandoned the business to work for commercial airlines.

Michael wanted to persevere with the business but Air South's tight finances eventually forced him to seek work with another airline. Still, he persisted with his dream and continued to build Air South on a part-time basis.

The major difficulty faced by Air South in its first few years of operation was the uncertainty of aircraft availability for the company to provide its services. Due to the high capital costs involved aircraft are usually leased, but aircraft owners are reluctant to guarantee an aircraft to a charter company unless it has a proven record of use.

Despite this, Michael's absolute focus on service, with customers the first and foremost priority, saw the business slowly grow. As a result, Air South was guaranteed an aircraft within its first year of operation, a vital step in ensuring the viability of the company.

After several years of hard work juggling both full-time employment and trying to keep Air South running, an opportunity arose in 1997 for Michael to provide crew transport for mining company Heathgate Resources. Seizing the opportunity, Michael tendered for the contract – even though he did not have an appropriate aircraft to perform the task or the funds to lease the aircraft.

To help work out which air charter company they would choose, Heathgate Resources decided to use a selection of air charter companies once, with a decision to be made after an evaluation of the services provided by each of them.

'When it came to my turn, knowing that the crew members on their way back to Adelaide would be longing for a drink after two weeks in the desert, I loaded the aircraft with a carton of cold beer.

'While it was only a small act, it certainly made an impression with the company and was enough for us to be awarded our first long-term contract.

'This event further reinforced to me the difference that the small things could make to the business and how these things could differentiate Air South from our competitors.

'However, while I was elated at winning the job, I had to quickly find a suitable aircraft to service the contract. After a brief search I found a plane in Queensland and managed to convince the owner to fly the aircraft to South Australia and to defer the lease payments for a couple of months, giving me time to build up the revenue to make the payments.

'Since that first contract, our competitive advantage has continued to be our commitment to clients and the ability to provide exceptional service at a lower price. These two factors have been the difference between us and our competitors.'

That first major contract was the launching pad for Air South's long-term success.

Michael says Air South now has the largest air charter fleet in South Australia, with about 50 per cent of the total charter business in Adelaide.

The company's main customers are medium to large companies needing to transport cargo or personnel to regional and outback destinations.

I've never considered myself an entrepreneur. I just think of myself as someone who pays the bills doing something that I love.

One of Air South's 'bread and butter' contracts is transporting the *Advertiser* newspaper to regional areas. This contract was originally won with Ansett Cargo in 1998. Following the collapse of Ansett several years later, Air South again won the contract with Aus Air Express.

While Michael managed to salvage the contract, it also provided him with a sobering business lesson.

A few days before the collapse of Ansett, Michael received a $36,000 cheque from the company for transporting the *Advertiser* – a considerable sum of money for Air South at that time. However, a busy flying schedule meant Michael didn't get to the bank for several days.

On the day the cheque was banked, Ansett's accounts were frozen. Michael lost the money and joined a long list of Ansett creditors. Needless to say, Michael now makes it a priority to bank all cheques on the day they are received.

'My wife and I joke that one day we'll write a recipe book called "101 ways to cook potatoes", as that was basically the only food we could afford during those early years and following experiences like the Ansett collapse.

'Air South has allowed me to achieve my ultimate dream of making a living out of the two things I am the most passionate about – flying and running my own business.

'As many business owners have experienced, in the early days that dream came at the price of long hours and financial constraints. It was these obstacles though that were so valuable in my professional and personal development as the company progressed.'

When financial success did eventuate after many years of hard work, Air South was able to purchase its first aircraft in 2002. The only one of its kind in South Australia, the 11-seat Cessna Titan is substantially more cost-effective to run than similar sized planes and was purchased after extensive research by Michael.

It provides Air South with a real competitive advantage – the ability to provide the same level of service as competitors at a lower price while still achieving high margins. This has seen other charter companies either lose customers to Air South or make a financial loss on contracts that they do win.

The Cessna Titan is in addition to the six planes that the company leases and Michael hopes the company soon will be able to purchase its second plane.

The company still services Heathgate Resources, along with Dominion Mining and Henry Walker Eltin. Michael is now looking to further expand Air South's air charter services into the mining and resource sector, as well as develop corporate air charter services for large local companies.

The next major phase of Air South's future growth may well come from the very place where Michael's flying career started. In 2003 the flying school where Michael underwent his pilot training, ROSSAIR Flying Centre, went into external administration.

Recognising that this could add a new dimension to the company's operations, Michael purchased the flying school, which now specialises in providing pilots with instrument flying training.

The new Air South Flying School began operating early in 2004 with a particular focus on providing practical and real life scenarios, something Michael feels is missing at established flying schools. Michael's aim is to equip his students with the best knowledge as well as practical experience to gain employment.

The flying school has enabled Michael to come full circle, allowing him to provide others with the same skills that allow him to live his passion every day.

'While I enjoy flying, having my own business – and all that I've learnt from that along the way – has been the most fulfilling.

'I've never considered myself an entrepreneur. I just think of myself as someone who pays the bills doing something that I love.'

Lessons Learnt:

* Bank your cheques as soon as you receive them. You never know how financially secure your customers are, no matter how big they may be.
* Enjoy whatever you do. The day that you stop having fun at work is the day you should leave.
* Not only do you need to be open to opportunities, you also need to have the courage to seize them. It's no good recognising an opportunity but letting it pass you by.

Advice to Others:

* Don't overlook the small things in servicing your customers. They can be the difference between you and your competitors in a tight market. A carton of cold beer was the catalyst in Air South winning its first major contract.

Mark Langford

At GameTraders, everything old is new again.

Founder and Managing Director Mark Langford launched the company in 2000, creating a niche market for the sale of second-hand computer games, consoles and accessories.

By the close of the first day's trade at GameTraders' pilot store in the Adelaide suburb of Mitcham, the fledgling company had managed to make a modest profit.

GameTraders has since become one of South Australia's fastest growing franchise brands, employing more than 90 full-time and casual staff nationally with a turnover of more than $10 million per annum.

GameTraders' rapid growth came because it filled a gap in the marketplace, and was driven by an increasing demand for second-hand computer games.

In addition, GameTraders continues to provide a service that remains unmatched by any other company in Australia.

With a background in real estate and hotel broking, Mark initially cut his teeth in retailing with the establishment of a leisure store, Leisure Land, selling everything from computer games and kites to board games and jigsaw puzzles. It was at this time that the Pokemon craze took off and Mark's store did a lively trade in the buying and selling of second-hand Pokemon cards.

As the popularity of Pokemon waned, Mark could see the opportunity in developing a store with a similar concept, concentrating on second-hand computer games. He started buying second-hand games and quickly built up a stockpile.

'I knew from the outset when I went into retailing that I was going to franchise a concept.

'When I opened up GameTraders I made sure the store was professionally designed to have a franchise look from the beginning.'

That first day's profit was repeated day after day and the store's stock built up quickly with kids and their parents embracing the opportunity to make some cash or trade in unwanted computer games. Mark did virtually no advertising, with word-of-mouth at local schools proving the best form of promotion.

'Within three months I could tell that this was a concept that people loved and I knew I should franchise it as soon as possible before someone else copied the idea, leaving us to play catch up.

'I started working with a franchising consultant and it took nine months to do all the paperwork and put the operation manual together. We sold our first franchise – at Findon – just 11 months after the opening of Mitcham, which is very unusual. Normally a business takes four years to get the model right and then franchise.

'It was a simple model and is totally unique. I had been in business since I was 26 and had operated a real estate franchise previously, so franchising came quite naturally to me. I knew what I had to do.

'I found it easy to sell that first franchise and still do now. Selling is not about convincing a person to buy something, it's about getting people to put their trust in you as a person. When a potential franchisee meets me they make a judgement as to whether they think I'm a trustworthy person.'

Encouraged by the rapid financial growth enjoyed by these two stores, Mark Langford quickly expanded GameTraders' franchise network over the following 12 months with the opening of eight additional outlets in metropolitan and regional South Australia, before setting his sights interstate.

There are now more than 25 outlets in South Australia, Victoria, Queensland, West Australia and New South Wales.

Despite the fast growth of the group, Mark has been careful to ensure that GameTraders' expansion is controlled, resisting the temptation of doing too much too soon.

'If we had wanted, we could probably have twice the number of stores that we currently do, but I've been cautious about biting off too much.

Selling is not about convincing a person to buy something, it's about getting people to put their trust in you as a person.

'We waited quite a long time before opening our first store in Sydney, despite the attraction of entering into Australia's largest market. We had the stores here in Adelaide and initial ones in Melbourne, Perth and the Gold Coast with a business plan that was focused on establishing stores in Victoria, so I wanted to make sure we didn't overstretch ourselves.

'The move into Sydney was only made after I felt comfortable that our existing stores were bedded down and the model we had was right.'

Another key to GameTraders' successful growth has been the recruitment of internal expertise as well as the use of professional external consultants, with Mark recognising that he couldn't be an expert at everything – and didn't have the time to be.

Staff with marketing and merchandising/retailing experience were appointed and the advice of an external business adviser and public relations consultancy was utilised to help take GameTraders to the next level.

While this put pressure on the cashflow of the group, professional support was seen as the only way of 'becoming big'.

'Appointing staff and using consultants results in a massive increase in your overheads and I probably did it before I really had the cashflow to fund it, but my reasoning was if you've got a tiger by the tail and you lose control of it then it's going to come back and bite you.

'If you can't handle the growth you've got unhappy franchisees who aren't getting the support they need, so I felt I needed to put that infrastructure in place sooner rather than later.

'I think many entrepreneurs do make errors in not calling in qualified expertise soon enough. The business model always needs to be improved.'

While the initial focus of GameTraders was solely on trading second-hand computer game products, its business activities have since been expanded to encompass the sale of new games, a broader range of accessories and rentals in both new and second-hand games.

The company caters to the full range of computer game formats developed since the 1970s. These include the current Xbox, Gamecube and PS2 systems through to original formats such as Atari and Sega Megadrive.

Despite the success of the original GameTraders model (which has won a national Franchisor of the Year Award and state Franchisee of the Year Awards), it is constantly evolving to reflect the dynamic nature and pricing of the computer games industry.

With early game formats, new games were expensive to produce, pricing them out of the reach of many families. GameTraders' second-hand games were considerably cheaper, in some cases up to 90 per cent below the new retail price, providing a real price differentiation.

More recent formats have games that are easier and cheaper to manufacture, flooding the market and forcing GameTraders to drop its prices on its second-hand offerings.

'The market changes so quickly that a game that was retailing new at $100 a month ago could drop to $49 today. Second-hand obviously always has to be cheaper than new, so if there's a price drop we have to reduce our price as well.'

Extensive market research showed that customers also wanted GameTraders to stock new games, a move that was eventually made despite Mark's concern about the financial pressures associated with holding new stock that might not sell as trends changed.

The initiative has paid off however with a healthy increase in sales across the group.

The introduction of rentals on new games as well as second-hand has also proved a successful move, as has stocking a unique range of games accessories and launching a website that allows customers to search online for a particular title at any GameTraders store.

Off the back of these changes Mark aims to continue building the group in the coming years, with the ultimate goal of 200 to 300 stores Australia-wide, recognising that achieving this will require all his skills.

'When you're running a business it takes a long time to understand who you really are. I think I'm fortunate in that while I see myself as an entrepreneur and I love being creative and coming up with ideas, I'm also a businessman.

'I know what I have to do to run a business and make the nuts and bolts of it all work. That's so important for long-term success.'

Lessons Learnt:

* Begin with the end in mind and have a vision of how you want the business to look. From the first day of GameTraders Mark knew he wanted to make the concept a national franchise. Having that vision enabled him to put the measures in place to achieve that reality.
* Jump in the deep end – don't be afraid. While it's important to research, think and plan, at the end of the day you have to take action, even if it means facing your fears of failure or financial ruin. This can be confronting but it's very empowering.
* Don't try to do everything yourself. You can't be an expert at everything so get professional assistance and qualified staff to fill in the skills gaps.

Advice to Others:

* Don't twiddle your thumbs. Do it right but do it quickly. If GameTraders had not capitalised on its initial success by moving into franchising within a few months of starting up, the company risked being gazumped by an agile competitor.

Ron Langman

Ron Langman is best described as a 'serial entrepreneur'.

Since leaving school early to chase a career in photography, he has launched so many innovative ventures that he has emerged as something of an entrepreneurial icon in South Australia.

In fact, the business for which he is probably best known, the national Home Ideas Centre chain, initially came about in the late 1970s because no one else would touch it – but Ron saw its potential.

The Home Ideas Centre group is now the world's largest network of building and home improvement exhibitions. The concept is deceptively simple. Basically, suppliers of building products – from bricks to security doors, tiles to pergolas and, yes, even the kitchen sink – pay for space to display their wares all under one roof.

It means a home-owner can view hundreds of building products at one spot rather than waste days driving around to check products at individual company locations.

Ron Langman's route to the Home Ideas Centre concept was circuitous and typically entrepreneurial.

I'm definitely not a gambler. I'm a risk taker in situations where I can have a major influence on the outcome.

As a young man he headed to London to pursue a career in fashion photography. Unpredictable weather in the United Kingdom meant most fashion shoots were indoors using basic – and quite boring – backdrops. Ron began travelling and photographing anything that could be used as a backdrop – from the Eiffel Tower to ancient Greek temples – and selling the transparencies to studios around Europe that had installed front projection systems.

On returning to Australia, Ron launched a specialist food photography studio, pioneering many photographic innovations now considered standard.

Meanwhile, Ron's innovative spirit continued to bubble. Inspired by an odd product he had seen in Europe, he manufactured the first bean chairs in Australia, although a later competitor gazumped him by securing national distribution for a smaller version now known as the 'bean bag'.

Another of his concepts involved attaching rollerskate trucks to the bottom of thin slats of timber – an early version of what would later become known as skateboards.

In the mid 1970s, Ron co-founded Consumer Databank, a buyer advisory service.

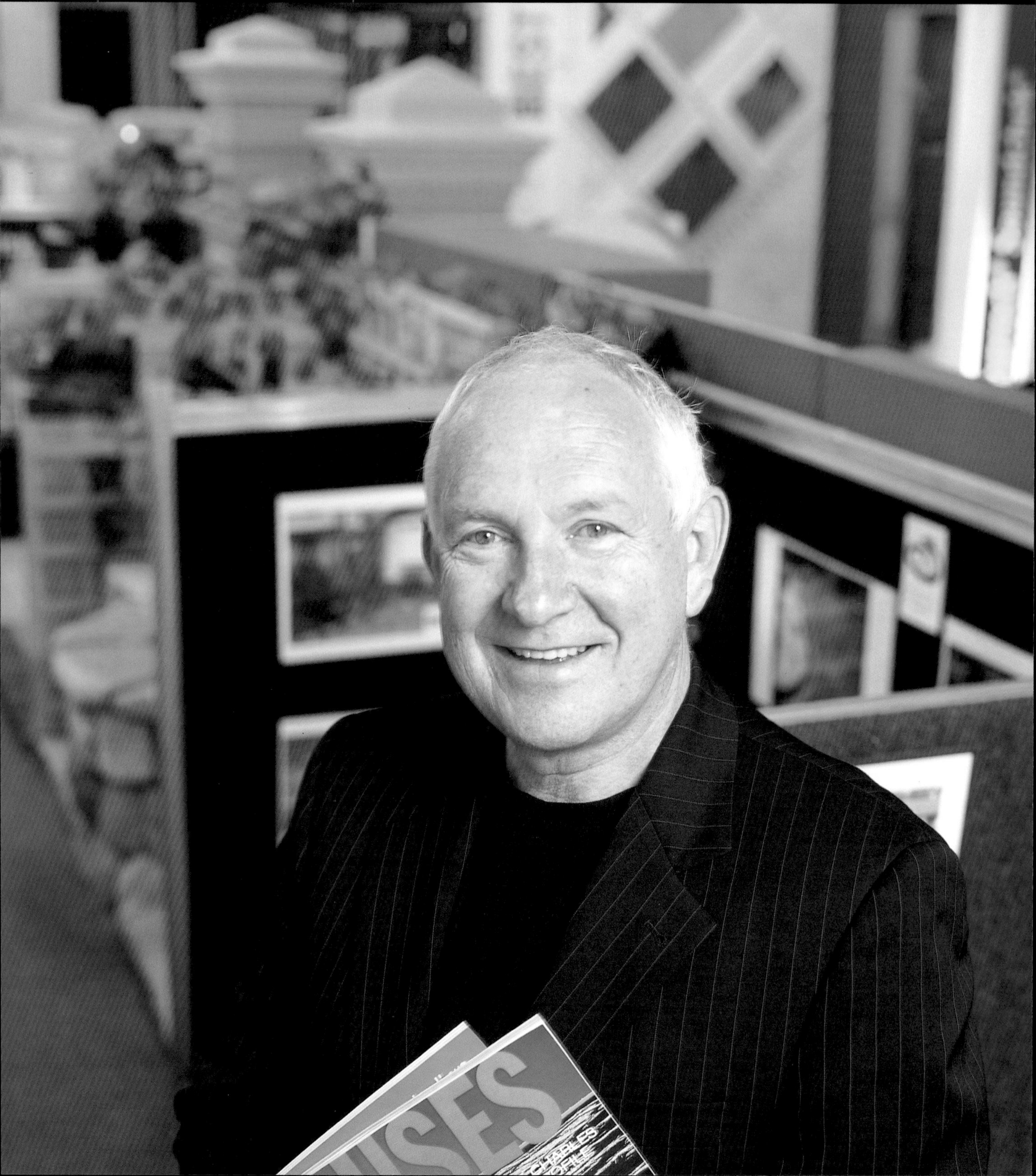

Then, in 1978, another opportunity emerged. At the time the Master Builders Association and several other exhibitors ran a small home building exhibit in Adelaide, but it wasn't financially viable and was facing closure. Ron was on the exhibitor's committee.

'I did some back-of-an-envelope sums and saw that it would be a good business. So I called a meeting of all the companies that exhibited in that centre and convinced them it would work with one subtle difference – we would run it not just primarily as a service to the community but as a service to them, the people who were exhibiting at the time and who were paying the bills.

'We turned it from a community resource into a marketing tool.'

Ron bought an old car dealership site on the corner of Anzac Highway and South Road – a huge showroom on one of Adelaide's busiest intersections.

The Home Ideas Centre (then known as the Building and Home Improvement Exhibition) quickly became a 'cash cow'. The companies displaying their goods paid for space in the Centre, which within a few months was drawing huge visitor numbers. The more space they wanted, the more they paid.

Keen to maximise the benefits to exhibitors, Ron systemised the viewing process and fine-tuned the walk-through design. Visitors to the Centre were shepherded along on a snaking journey past almost all the exhibits. Each exhibit was numbered, with visitors able to mark numbers on small cards and collect product information at the end of the visit – a great research and sales tool for the exhibitor companies.

Within a few years Ron expanded into Melbourne and joint ventured with another exhibitor in Brisbane. He has now created a chain of Home Ideas Centres in most states and has strategic ties as far afield as South Africa.

In the late 1990s, using the Home Ideas Centre as his model, Ron launched Selector.Com, providing an on-line building product resource for architects and specifiers. Selector.Com is profitable and growing well – one of the few money-making survivors of the 'dot.com' crash.

Ron has mentored many young South Australian entrepreneurs. He partnered with one young businessman in the development of a unique chain lock, the Python Lock, which was subsequently licensed to Masterlock, the world's largest lock company.

Ron's marketing nous and knowledge of licensing and intellectual property (he is on the Federal Government's Intellectual Property Advisory Council), enabled him to identify a gap in the lock company's international product mix which made his Python Lock a 'must have' for the international group. As a result, he was able to secure a lucrative deal that provided the duo with an annual six-figure income from the lock for another 15 years.

While it would be easy to paint Ron Langman as an energetic man driven by a need to innovate, he has a simpler explanation.

'All through my life these things have occurred as an opportunity to fill intellectual vacuums. I need another project, but I don't need any more money. I have never been driven by money.

'Whenever I've felt that my brain wasn't being used enough I've taken on something – including flying a helicopter or learning to play the saxophone. It's just something to fill the gap.

'I guess one of the reasons I have done well at things is that I try to keep roughly 25 per cent of my time and intellectual capacity free to open up new opportunities. The moment my day-to-day activities occupy more than 75 per cent of my time and intellectual capacity, I'll delegate and shift the work on to someone else.

'To be honest, I've almost never worked long hours or terribly hard. I strongly believe it's better to have four people doing the jobs at 80 per cent as well as I can do them than trying to do four times as much work myself. I think delegation is a key to success.

'Of course, you have to understand that delegation has its costs. The people to whom you delegate may make mistakes and they may cost you financially or in goodwill terms. But in the long term you can't move forward if you try to do everything yourself. If you get a team around you the outcome will always be much greater than anything you can ever achieve on your own.

'As long as people are not delegating then almost all of their intellectual capacity and probably a great deal of their time is committed to the day-to-day activities of their business. This means they are unable to step back and take a strategic view.'

Ron advocates taking calculated risks – but not stupid ones.

'I think some businesspeople are like gamblers. They actually get a buzz from betting the whole farm on a particular business deal. I may put some of the farm on the line but I always look carefully at how much I can lose and how much I can make.

'I look at what the downside is and if I get to the point that I've lost what I was prepared to lose, I will then throw it in and walk away from it even if I am only five steps away from success. I'm definitely not a gambler. I'm a risk-taker in situations where I can have a major influence on the outcome.'

In his youth, Ron twice badly damaged his right hip and was bedridden for almost two years, short-circuiting his formal schooling. He says much of what he learned of the world was from adults and American comics.

'I know many people who are much better qualified academically than I am, but not having gone all the way through an empirically-based education process has produced positive results for me.

'It is inherent in academic education that there is a "correct" answer. Life's not like that. So not having embraced that system where there has to be a correct answer to things, I have been able to grab any answer and be prepared to run with it, and abandon it if it proves wrong.

'Also, I take what's sometimes described as a lighthouse or beacon approach to things. It's faster and more efficient to get from one place to another if you can see where you're going and you're drawn to it.

'I have an ability to see what something's going to look like when it's finished and work back from that position. That avoids the zig-zagging and hitting all sorts of obstacles that comes from just starting out heading in a certain direction. I think people can learn that talent.'

Lessons Learnt:

* Take calculated risks – but never stupid ones. Bet on yourself in a situation where you can influence the outcome. Anything else is gambling.
* You don't have to work ridiculous hours to be successful. If you work at 75 per cent of your intellectual capacity that leaves 25 per cent for inspiration and to pursue new ventures.
* Take a 'lighthouse' approach to business and ideas. If you can see the end point and work your way back from there, it will be easier to reach your goal.

Advice to Others:

* Delegate, delegate, delegate – or you'll never be able to step back and take a strategic overview of your business. Accept that a team of people with only 80 per cent of your capabilities in some areas – and who may make mistakes – will still be able to achieve much more than you trying to do it all yourself.

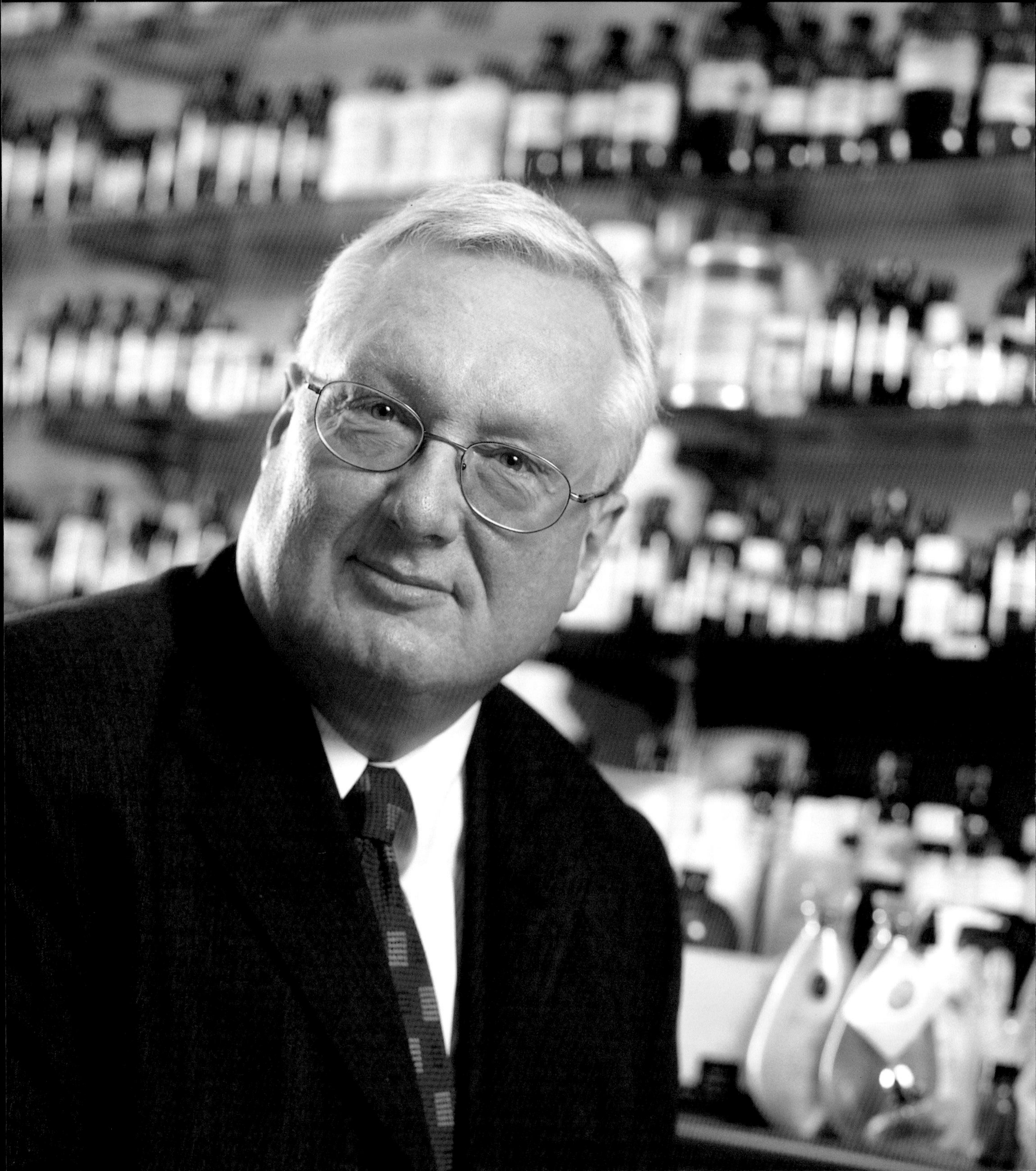

Roland Lever

From a company that originally operated in the spare room of the family home, J.H. Lever & Co has grown to become one of South Australia's genuinely 'sweet' business success stories.

As the State's leading fragrance and flavour manufacturer, the Richmond-based company credits much of its success to an ability to embrace change and remain relevant to evolving consumer needs.

In fact, the company's Managing Director, Roland Lever, believes companies should not be afraid to steer a 180-degree change in business direction if it means better meeting customer requirements and facilitating long-term business success.

As a result, J.H. Lever & Co is proving to both local and overseas fragrance companies that an Australian manufacturer can – quite literally – 'mix it with the best of them'.

J.H. Lever & Co specialises in the production of fragrance concentrates, some equal in quality to the world's best-known designer perfumes. Its fragrance bases are used in a wide range of products including shampoos, sunscreens, candles and air fresheners, while its flavourings and essences are ingredients in foods such as chocolates, yoghurts and sweets.

The company today services about 200 clients, including most of Australia's leading food, cosmetic, aerosol and toiletry manufacturers. J.H. Lever & Co's customers include such names as Avon, Blackmores, Cussons, Delta Laboratories, Faulding Pharmaceuticals, H.J. Heinz and Co, Red Earth, the Sara Lee Group – incorporating Nutri-Metics – Schwarzkopf, Wella and Yoplait.

Roland's father, John Lever, founded J.H. Lever & Co in 1957, with fragrance importing and distribution as the sole focus of the business.

Previously having worked for an aroma chemicals company in the Netherlands, John brought with him to Australia a major distribution account for Mane, one of the world's top 10 fragrance houses in France. Some years later, he secured representation for Swiss company Cosmetochem, a world leader in natural plant extracts and cosmetic ingredients.

Both of these relationships continue to thrive today.

After working in the business part-time for more than six years, Roland and his wife Jolande bought the family company (then based in Colonel Light Gardens) in 1986.

In the mid 1990s continuing growth led to consolidation of operations at larger premises in Richmond where, in 1995, Roland made a business decision that would cement the company's long-term future.

At the time, Mane was reducing its marketing support to Australia to focus on growing markets, leaving unserviced many of the small and medium-size customers on which J.H. Lever & Co relied for 85 per cent of its annual turnover.

It soon became apparent that importing and distributing these types of products would no longer be viable as the company's primary focus.

Instead of reducing J.H. Lever & Co's involvement in the industry, Roland initiated the significant step of opening an in-house manufacturing arm, Australian Aromatics.

'Instead of "hiding" behind Mane and feeding off its success, we were courageous enough to take a risk – and responsibility for our future – and start manufacturing the same quality products previously imported from our French partners.

'We effectively shifted the focus of our relationship with Mane in a way that guaranteed our future survival. The manufacturing arm now gives us a strong edge over our competitors by enabling us to answer product design requests within lead times that are faster than our competitors, and closely tuned to local market conditions.

'Projects beyond our capacity are referred to Mane, which is effective for them.'

A decade later, Australian Aromatics products account for more than 75 per cent of J.H. Lever & Co's annual turnover.

In hindsight, Roland describes the expansion decision as one made 'somewhat naively' – but it was a decision he was not afraid to make.

My experience is that too many businesses today are more interested in fulfilling their own needs, rather than those of their customers.

'Sometimes companies need to be willing to embrace significant change in order to remain relevant to their customers' needs and, in turn, generate business growth.

'Consequently, these companies are more likely to achieve long-term success than those that are resistant to change.'

J.H. Lever & Co's production currently exceeds 3000 kilograms of concentrated fragrances and flavours per month.

Selling a large proportion of its products to companies in New South Wales and Victoria, J.H. Lever & Co has retained its home base in Adelaide because of the South Australian capital's lower operating costs, and efficient and reliable freight services.

'Adelaide has access to the most streamlined and economical freight transport systems in this country, which means our deliveries are virtually guaranteed to reach our customers – both national and international – on time.

'Rather than customers being forced to endure lengthy waits for goods, as they have had to do with other suppliers in the past, in most cases we can guarantee delivery within 48 hours. This ability has proven to be a winning "edge" for the company.'

Roland credits a quality product, the pride staff take in their work and a constant focus on working with winning customers, all on a strong financial management foundation, as additional keys to J.H. Lever & Co's success.

'The importance of good financial management often is forgotten by people just starting out in business. Brilliant ideas alone just don't work.

'For any company to stay profitable and generate growth, business owners must view their product, customer service and financial management processes as an essential three-tiered business strategy.

'Compromise in any one of these areas is selling short a business's chance of success.'

J.H. Lever & Co's ability to reposition itself as a manufacturer rather than being solely an importer and distributor of fragrances has given the company a strategic edge over its competitors.

Because of the decreasing availability of international product supplies and services, J.H. Lever & Co has been able to secure a niche in the Australian marketplace by providing local food, cosmetic, aerosol and toiletry manufacturers with an alternative base from which to source their fragrance concentrates, flavours and essences.

Australian manufacturers have been quick to realise the many advantages of J.H. Lever & Co's 'rapid response' capabilities, which are driven by its ability to produce custom-made products to exact specifications while setting the pace with the shortest possible lead times.

Roland recognised the financial and time demands often faced by his contract manufacturer clients as they work to meet their own customers' requirements. As a result, J.H. Lever & Co has extended its focus to assist contract manufacturers achieve their productivity and performance goals.

By strategically marketing its strengths – product quality, availability and responsiveness – J.H. Lever & Co has been able to provide contract manufacturers with a wide range of services to help them fulfil the productivity demands placed on them by their large multinational customers.

Through targeting the special needs of contract manufacturers, the company's financial performance has remained stable throughout its transition from fragrance importer and distributor to product stockist and manufacturer.

Roland realises that each customer has very different requirements. As a result, products and services are tailored to suit individual customer needs.

'We engage an external consultant to conduct an annual customer survey, which I believe is a vital tool in monitoring the business's performance.

'Comments generated by these surveys enable us to catch changing customer needs, to which we can then respond accordingly.

'Customers are surveyed on our responsiveness to product orders, our use of innovation in helping achieve business goals, and our technical expertise and price competitiveness.

'The results of these surveys enable us to improve our understanding of customer needs, helping us focus resources more heavily on delivering services and products that are the most needed.'

Feedback from recent surveys identified that some customers wished to work more closely with J.H. Lever & Co on the development of new fragrance product concepts. As a result, the company is now becoming more actively involved in its discussions with clients in order to educate them on current market trends and help them develop more successful products.

J.H. Lever & Co is examining a range of options aimed at generating further market growth in the next decade, including additional diversification of its product range and the construction of a new purpose-built manufacturing facility with room to grow.

Roland says that ultimately the company's future lies in 'continuing to make sure our customers are winners'.

'That's what everybody here is continually working towards. My experience is that too many businesses today are more interested in fulfilling their own needs, rather than those of their customers.

'We know that our future relies on our long-term customer relationships. If we can assist a customer to successfully position their product in the marketplace, we are the ultimate beneficiaries because we receive the customer's loyalty in return.'

Lessons Learnt:

* Brilliant ideas alone don't work. Sound financial management needs to underpin good ideas if a business is to be successful.
* Nurture long-term customer relationships. Help your customer become the best at what they do, and you will win that customer's loyalty.
* Deliver a better and faster service than your competitor. It has the potential to win you new customers.

Advice to Others:

* Sometimes a complete change of direction is essential to set a company on the path to greatness. These decisions can be scary, but don't be afraid to make grand leaps if you want to reap significant rewards.

Les Mann

Les Mann has two key business mantras. The first is: 'Be prepared – then act quickly.' The second is: 'Don't assume anything.'

With these business parables stamped into his personal Business Bible, Les has carved a reputation as a shrewd entrepreneur with a keen eye for a great investment and a 'take no prisoners' approach.

As he says: 'Don't stuff around. Just do it. Do your research, put everything in place to make it work and then clinch it quickly.

'I do a lot of number crunching, but once I've done the numbers I make quick decisions. If it's the right investment there's no point mucking around or someone else will beat you to it.'

Perhaps Les's best-known investment was his 10-year ownership of South Western Manufacturing, a boutique timber furniture manufacturer that became famous for its ubiquitous 'Sou Wester' director's chairs and card tables.

Since selling South Western in 1999, Les has made numerous strategic investments, including many that he has sourced and syndicated to involve friends and associates.

In 2000 he took a substantial shareholding in Brauer Natural Medicine, which he has subsequently helped build into one of Australia's leading natural health companies.

He is also an investor in agricultural IT company Kee Technologies and has holdings in numerous Adelaide commercial properties including Zurich House in Kent Town.

Les's skill lies in being able to carefully analyse each investment and hone in on those that offer multiple benefits for the investor. By looking past the obvious, Les often identifies multi-dimensional opportunities that give him a double-whammy of benefits as an investor.

South Western Manufacturing is a classic example. On the face of it, Les appeared to be simply buying a furniture business. The existing owners were motivated sellers who had recently lost a major customer. Also, they had not aggressively marketed the products so there was plenty of upside for the business.

Just as attractive to Les however was South Western's location on a prime parcel of land in suburban Unley, and he saw a chance to make money on a future rezoning.

'I saw that South Western could benefit from a growth in lifestyle products like the director's chair, which could be made into a fashion item. Also, it was sitting on a great piece of land. I believed that we were heading into another land boom so I did the calculations, negotiated hard and we did the deal.'

Over the next few years, Les almost doubled South Western's turnover to $7 million and built the peak seasonal workforce to about 130 people. The range of director's chairs and card tables was expanded, with new colours and fabrics making the products much more attractive to householders.

'I started heavily promoting the brand and building strong relationships with stores like Kmart and Big W.

'We lost Freedom Furniture though. I made the blunder of telling them we were providing them with almost $1 million worth of product. I don't think they really knew how much we were supplying to them, so they decided to manufacture offshore and we lost that account.

'From that point on, I made it a rule never to tell anybody how much business they had with us unless they mentioned it first.'

Ultimately, South Western won an impressive 70 per cent of the Australian market for director's chairs and card tables, and export was shaping up as the company's only option for growth.

Les joined a business acquaintance on a trip to Japan and secured strong orders on his first visit. By exhibiting at the major European outdoor furniture fair in Germany, Les also developed business in the United Kingdom, Germany, Spain and Greece, eventually boosting exports to about 20 per cent of South Western's turnover.

Les had always pledged to retire from day-to-day business by the age of 50. He negotiated the sale of the South Western business and left the company at 49.

He held the land however and sold it separately to take advantage of South Australia's land price boom. It was a two-pronged exit strategy that provided Les with funding to pursue his dream of becoming an independent investor.

'Effectively, South Western paid for the property. It sounds strange but in many ways I built the company because I needed it to survive and thrive so I had a tenant for the buildings until the rezoning. The company was driven hard and provided the cash to pay off the mortgage on the property, so I emerged with two sound investments from the original business transaction.'

The next investment to come under Les Mann's microscope was Brauer Natural Medicine. Les made what was then a relatively high-risk investment in a little-known South Australian company struggling to compete nationally.

Marketing and product development were boosted and Brauer products are now listed in about 4200 pharmacies and health food outlets Australia-wide.

'Sometimes you have to invest in something that won't have a great return for a while. Brauer has now turned around and it's growing at 25 per cent a year in a growing sector. It's now making a great return on investment.'

Les could buy into Brauer because he was positioned to fund the opportunity when it was presented. It's the same with his other investments. Generally he already has his finances and partners in place – even if he doesn't know what the next investment will be yet.

'One of the reasons a group of us were able to buy Zurich House was the fact that although we weren't the highest bidder we offered a very simple cash settlement with no ties. The higher bidder had lots of strings attached. We had flexibility because we had the finance in place, so we got the property.'

Les's focus on preparation gives him plenty of leverage for his investments – and he makes no apologies for negotiating hard to secure the best deal.

Don't stuff around. Just do it. Do your research, put everything in place to make it work and then clinch it quickly.

'It's nice when someone approaches you with a deal and says: "Here's our deal and our terms" and you can say: "Here are our terms and conditions, so forget about yours. That's the deal. You either want it or you don't."

'It gives you a position of strength to work from. It's also about knowing your opposition. You have to know who you're dealing with and how they work.'

Les is happy to be described as an 'Adelaide investor'. One of his golden rules – at least these days – is not to make long-distance investments.

'For instance, if you are based in Adelaide and the investment is somewhere else, my recommendation is don't do it. You need to be right on the spot. You want to be able to get into a car and go and talk to the people you are involved with.'

It's a lesson Les learnt the hard way a few years ago when he spearheaded a syndicated investment in an eastern states toy company.

'It was a disaster. I assumed that if you made good toys kids would buy them. Unfortunately it's about the most competitive business you could be in. You have to come up with 100 new ideas a year and get six to market. Then hopefully every two or three years you will have one huge success which carries you through to break-even. Scary stuff.'

Soon after Les' initial investment the toy company lost the license to produce one of its leading products, leaving it with reduced revenues.

'I had put a substantial amount of money in and also syndicated with other people. One of them was my brother-in-law who subsequently became my ex-brother-in-law. Every board meeting was an absolute disaster. There were stand-up fights. We couldn't agree. The company was in crisis.

'It was very stressful – especially when you've got substantial amounts of money tied up in a company and you think you've lost it.'

Eventually the toy company had its next 'hit' product and Les cashed out.

Les believes communication and understanding underpin good business – from the shop floor level all the way through to Board involvement.

'One of the lessons that I've learnt in dealing with people is to never assume that they know exactly what you mean and can therefore put it into practice. You need to spend some time explaining what your values are so they can see where you are coming from.

'Whenever I've had conflicts with employees, it's often been based on my assumption that they know what I am talking about.

'At one stage at South Western we were giving instructions on the assumption that everyone could read and write, but it turned out that some of our employees were illiterate. So we invested in numeracy and literacy programs to help them through that. You just can't assume anything.'

Lessons Learnt:

* Plan ahead. It gives you control. Line up your finances and business partners so you are ready for the next deal that comes along.
* Don't assume anything. Make sure you explain exactly what you want so your employees, business partners or fellow investors understand what you expect from them.
* Wherever possible find more than one reason to make a particular investment. Look at it from different angles to find out what else you can 'squeeze' from the investment.

Advice to Others:

* Do your groundwork but then act quickly to make the most of worthwhile investment opportunities.

Tiffany Manuell and David Buck

When Tiffany Manuell and David Buck started their Happy House business at the age of 26, they felt they had the benefit of youth on their side. If the venture didn't work, they figured they still had enough time to start again.

Eleven years on, more than $45 million a year in retail sales, distribution to more than 40 countries and a gift and homewares product line numbering 1500 and growing, and the married couple have never had to worry about that 'what if . . .' scenario.

Instead, they are now managing the challenges associated with rolling out a chain of franchised stores throughout Australia and protecting the integrity of their designs from cheap, unauthorised copies – a flipside to achieving enormous overseas success with their products.

Happy House started from Tiffany's love of illustration and design. While she studied fashion design she was never a 'fashion junkie'. On returning to Adelaide after several years in Melbourne, she decided not to continue working in the fashion industry, instead choosing to make a 'very meagre' living making and selling cards, supplemented by waitressing.

Orders with three or four stores quickly followed, which saw both Tiffany and David juggling their day jobs with working well into the night hand-making gift cards.

'Each of the cards was fully hand-painted, hand-cut, hand-threaded and stamped. It was very hands on and very laborious,' said Tiffany.

'But it was such a brilliant learning curve because it really did make me appreciate just how much I loved doing that kind of work.

'It was also great for market research because I learnt what designs people really loved. It was very inspirational and I totally enjoyed the process.'

The business started growing to the point where it became a full-time focus for Tiffany. Once it then became too much for one person, the decision was made that David would leave his business banking role and join Tiffany in taking the business to the next level. They sold an investment property to help expand the business.

'A lot of people look back at that move and say "you really took a risk", but for us, we were just so excited at the prospect and wanted to give it a go. We both felt that if we didn't do this, then we'd never know,' said David.

'We were 26 and our attitude was "let's give it a crack and if it fails it fails, we'll just start again". We were prepared to back ourselves and it was an almost natural progression for both of us to evolve into our own business.'

'I actually look back at that time now and realise that it was all about gut instinct,' said Tiffany. 'We really did just what we felt was right and still do.

'We've had people say to us, "you guys don't really seem to do anything by the book, you don't seem to follow any rules", but we had no idea, it was a totally new experience for us. We didn't know there were any rules.'

The move quickly paid off with orders pouring in from throughout Australia. In those early days the company did all the design as well as the manufacturing, distribution and wholesaling, selling to gift stores and newsagencies.

By 1999 Happy House started licensing to manufacturers and distributors, allowing Tiffany and David to focus on design.

Happy House products now include everything from clothing, watches, fashion accessories and bags, to bed linen, gift items, plush toys and stationery.

In Australia, the biggest fans of the company's products are girls aged nine to 14. However, in Asia (including the company's biggest single export market of Korea) customers are generally 18 to 24-year-old women.

Thousands of stores stock Happy House products, with 35 concept stores in Korea alone.

The company's mission statement is 'Make it fun!' and all products have to visually represent a happy and fun approach.

'It's so integral for us as a company and as designers to be true to that,' Tiffany said. 'Thankfully our artwork has been really well accepted here and across the world, but we have to be careful of not falling into the trap of designing products that are too culturally specific, although we are conscious of the different markets in the different countries.'

While Happy House does very well in the Middle East, a country like Dubai that buys a large amount of product won't consider one of the company's best selling icons because consumers prefer not to purchase anything with a pig on it. Frogs do exceptionally well in some countries but not in others, while the Little Princess character tends to sell well in most countries.

In Australia, the company has strong sales with its general icon products – butterflies, flowers and hearts – whereas in Asian countries they are far more interested in characters.

According to David, Happy House's core demographic simply 'fell' out of the products the company designed.

'That's an interesting part of our evolution. It wasn't as if we said, "Here's a gap in the market, let's concentrate on this market segment."

'The products were so well received that it was just a snowball effect that we then had to keep up with. The market needed and expected freshness and innovation. The perception is that you can't sell the same product for more than six months – so we had to keep evolving.

'We were lucky that most things that we did were well received in the marketplace.'

One of the downsides to such success has been the unlicensed copying of the company's products, particularly in Asia, with cheap copies of new Happy House products often being sold within days of the official product hitting the shelves.

According to Tiffany, this copying has both positive and negative aspects for the company. While flattered by the fact that such copying means the company's products are enormously popular and have considerable appeal, it is a problem for Happy House that is becoming increasingly frustrating.

'There are some brilliant counterfeit companies around the world who base their whole business on feeding off successful designers.

'We try to see it in a positive light and not be affected by it so much. It will always be there, it's just something that we will always have to deal with for as long as we are unique.

'The key to it is continuing to be innovative and fresh and new, because then the people who are feeding off your ideas will always be one step behind. That's the only way we can continue to support our licensees and distributors – come up with a new product all the time, because the item that's being copied is exactly that, a copy.'

We were 26 and our attitude was 'let's give it a crack and if it fails it fails, we'll just start again'. We were prepared to back ourselves.

Both are conscious of not letting the negatives of this issue take up too much of their energy or focus, and they are reluctant to become entangled with ongoing legal action.

'Basically from a commercial point of view it's really just making a decision on whether the issue is worth pursuing,' David said. 'We really just have to make an economic judgement. If it is upsetting our market perception and eroding any potential sales we could be making in that market, then we'll go for it legally. But sometimes you have to know which legal battles to leave.'

Instead, the company's current focus is on the rollout of a series of Happy House stores throughout Australia. The ultimate aim is to have up to three or four stores in each capital city. Some will be company owned, with the majority being franchises.

Having achieved so much success in recent years, the move into retail is helping both Tiffany and David to capture that excitement and energy associated with the early days of the business.

'Having our own stores allows us to have our product in the marketplace the way we want it presented, representing our values and philosophies around the brand. It's not just about the product on the shelf – it's the experience that goes with it,' David said.

'Seeing a Happy House store is a very visual representation of everything that we have achieved over the past 10 years or so, encapsulated in a 100-square metre retail outlet.

'For us, it's about "making it fun", enjoying the journey and enjoying the people who we are on that journey with.'

Lessons Learnt:

* Test the waters with initial small-scale production runs to see how your product is received. Use this as a market research exercise to fine-tune your product before going to larger-scale production.
* Be selective about where you focus your energies. If there are aspects of your business outside of your control, do what you can to manage them, but don't let them take your eye off 'the main game'.
* Be mindful of your target markets, but don't allow them to completely dictate or change your business.

Advice to Others:

* Commercially-driven decisions are a necessary part of any business, but unless you enjoy what you do and who you do it with, corporate success at all costs is just pointless.

Malcolm May

Make friends, get involved and learn from others are at the core of Malcolm May's home-spun business credo.

In fact, those simple philosophies have helped him build the company he co-founded, Balco, into a multi-million dollar agribusiness.

Balco was launched by Malcolm and three friends – Geoff Spence, Murray Mickel and Murray Smith – in 1990, to develop exports of hay to South-East Asia. The venture has proven a spectacular success. Today, Balco sells almost half the hay exported from South Australia and 18 per cent of the national hay export market.

Balco is based in the mid-north South Australian town of Balaklava. In fact, the company came about because of the need to re-invigorate the business heart of Balaklava, which in the late 1980s was slowly dying as a regional service centre.

At the time, Malcolm May was on the local development board formed to lure businesses to Balaklava – but none came.

As a result, he and his three partners started Balco with a $200,000 bank facility and dreams that a hay-driven recovery would pull their town out of the doldrums.

Turnover is now about $30 million. The company has about 90 staff and an annual throughput of about 130,000 large square bales.

Balco also produces about two million 46kg hay blocks that are wrapped in plastic and exported to countries including Japan, Taiwan and Korea.

Among its diverse uses, Balco hay is consumed by beef and dairy cattle in Japan and racehorses in the Middle East.

'Hay is a unique product that lets us do all the value-adding at our end where it is grown. There is nothing that needs to be done to our hay when it reaches its final destination. The customer just breaks open the bale and feeds it to their animals.'

Japanese cattle producers once sourced all their hay from the US, but Balco's ability to tailor its product to niche markets – even to the extent of sorting by hay colour – has enabled the company to win a significant market share.

Balco has helped drive the growth of the Australian hay industry, charting its own future along the way.

It's one of the reasons Malcolm advocates 'getting involved'. Balco has had representation on numerous organisations and committees driving the development of the sector, ranging from the Australian Fodder Industry Association (AFIA) and industry export group AExCo through to the Australian Quarantine and Inspection Service (AQIS). As a result, Balco has helped steer decisions and initiatives on quality assurance, certification, research, production, distribution and marketing.

As a leader you have to do things differently. And you have to accept that a few failures may be part of that.

'Since the early days we have been fairly active in creating the industry and steering the development of product and quality control. It was critical to the development of the industry so we took the lead. We really encourage everyone here to be on as many relevant committees as possible. We're helping to design our own industry.'

At Balco, there is a heavy emphasis on vertical integration. Every link in the supply chain is seen as equally important to the quality of product that reaches the end user.

'We have up to 200 farmers growing hay for us. We are in regular contact with them, through newsletters and personal contact. We have farmer meetings in September before the season starts, bringing them up to speed on everything about the market and what's required. We run a very open company.

'To a large extent our ongoing success is about the trusting relationship we have built up with everyone from our farmers to our staff and our customers. We treat them like we want to be treated ourselves, and really look after them.'

Local involvement has been another linchpin to Balco's fortunes. From its first day of business it has had the strong support of the Balaklava community and the company's loyalty to that community is set in stone. It is ironic – and symbolic of Balco's role as a mainstay of the town – that the company's headquarters these days is an old bank building in the centre of Balaklava.

'The support of the community here has been mind-boggling at times. I can honestly say that if we had set up in Adelaide in the first place we would not be here today.

'We have had our tough times. In the early 1990s there were three hay processors in South Australia and that went to 13. Things weren't good at the time. Even so, we had local businesspeople giving us credit and there was strong support from everyone. If not for that support, we would have gone under. They just said: "We need you here."

'The local newsagent at the time said we could book up anything we liked at his shop and pay when we could – and if the whole thing didn't work we didn't have to pay him back at all. That sort of support is phenomenal.

'We see it as part of our corporate responsibility to repay that generosity and support the town.'

The economic fortunes of Balco and the region are intertwined. Staff are hired locally whenever possible. Goods and equipment are generally bought from Balaklava merchants even when it may be cheaper to buy in bulk from Adelaide.

Factory hay processors who exceed certain production requirements often receive vouchers from Balco for $50 or $100 to be spent at the local butcher or supermarket. Balco also pumps money into local charities and sporting organisations, further entrenching it as the lifeblood of the Balaklava community.

Malcolm May is a reluctant 'local hero'. As Managing Director and key strategist he is the public face of Balco but he says the company's growth has been a team effort.

'If there hadn't been four of us in the business originally, it wouldn't be as strong as it is today. Everyone had different skills and thresholds of pain, and that meant we were all there to support each other at different stages of the journey. We learnt as we went.'

Balco has used its strength to diversify. Increasing demand for commodities prompted the formation of a division that now supplies a comprehensive range of grains and mixed fodder.

Malcolm is also quick to admit that – as with most companies – mistakes were made. An abortive attempt a few years ago to sell branded vitamin water into the UK cost $600,000 but it taught the team some lessons about when to pull out of a project. Balco has since applied that knowledge by exiting another venture in Queensland before more funds were required.

'You have to draw a line in the sand. In the early years we were doing things by the seat of our pants. Eventually, instead of working on gut feel you have to go to the next level and get professional help. These days we will do a feasibility study and research it to death.

'At the same time you need to explore change, whether people in the company like it or not. Many people don't like change and are scared to change. They stick with what they know because the unknown can be frightening.

'As a leader you have to do things differently. And you have to accept that a few failures may be part of that.'

Balco now has independent board members with valuable specialist skills. The company has recently changed its structure to fine-tune its operations and introduce more staff shareholders. Succession planning is on the agenda.

At the same time, a cautious approach to capital raising means the original four investors still own more than 70 per cent of the company.

Balco continues to evolve. It recently struck a joint venture arrangement with transport logistics giant Patrick Corporation to operate South Australia's first inland rail terminal linked to Balco's plant at Bowmans, just outside Balaklava.

Business is already booming. Malcolm May expects that up to 20,000 containers will eventually go through this hub each year, providing Balco with yet another lucrative income stream.

His next challenge is turning the 3000 tonnes of waste hay 'fines' (left over from the baling process) into pellets for the livestock industry.

Malcolm says the ideas and support of others have been paramount in Balco's ability to find and reach new markets. For him, personal development has been as important as watching the company grow.

'You learn from everyone around you but you have to learn not to keep everything to yourself. You have to talk and work together. Others have different perspectives and skills and can help make the thing work. I have found that other people can lift me up. I learn from everyone I meet.'

Lessons Learnt:

* Know what your company stands for – and make sure everyone else does too. If your organisation is about family and community, and you genuinely care about those around you, they will be there to help you through the tough times.
* Get involved. Wherever possible, seek a position on committees or authorities that can help steer the development of your industry. Your company can benefit if you are helping shape the sector, set the boundaries and write the rules.
* Learn from those around you. Success is a team achievement.
* Don't be scared to 'tell it like it is'. Balco's open policy with the Balaklava community and its farmer suppliers helped it through the financially tight early years.

Advice to Others:

* You don't have to be a 'bastard' to build a great business. Don't tread on people. Nurture a family environment with your staff, suppliers and customers. Work closely with them and take them with you on the journey.

Martin Radford

Under Martin Radford's direction, his company Complete Fire has become one of South Australia's best-known and fastest-growing fire services companies.

He credits this largely to its emphasis on building trust with customers as their businesses are fire-proofed.

It sounds simple enough. Doesn't every customer want to know they can trust their supplier? Yes, says Martin, but in his business people's lives or livelihoods can depend on the reliability of their fire protection.

'My whole team knows that when they finish a project they have to make sure that it's 100 per cent right. I expect my employees to be proud of their work.

'We saw on television recently a shopping centre fire where some unprotected shops were completely destroyed, but a fire door we had been involved with operated perfectly and protected the rest of the building.

'That's the very tangible result of a job well done.'

Complete Fire – based in the western Adelaide suburb of Marleston – specialises in installing and servicing fire extinguishers, fire sprinkler systems, fire detection and special hazards systems. The company has more than 40 employees and contracts with some of South Australia's leading companies.

The focus on customer confidence has certainly paid off. Complete Fire's turnover is now about $8 million and Martin's sights are firmly set on $10 million within the next couple of years.

A large proportion of work comes from Complete Fire's construction arm but Martin is continuing to build business in the portable fire extinguisher market and the firm's service division.

'Success in this business is based on trust. Too many businesses have been burned – if you'll pardon the expression – by unprincipled suppliers charging for services that have not been provided.'

Importantly, Martin says Complete Fire works hard on not being 'invisible'.

'Most of our clients have some form of technical background so they understand what we are doing. We could simply and quietly come in and do our work or check the equipment, and the end result – technically – is the same.

'But if the client doesn't see the fire guy for three weeks, how do they know he was there and that the paperwork hasn't been fudged? It happens in our industry. It's our job to make sure they know we have been there doing our job.

'We can give them the confidence not only that they are getting what they've paid for, but that the system will work if it's required.

'That's how we have separated ourselves from our competitors. With us, we make sure we are a visible presence and that the clients know we are on the job.

'Also, we only sell the clients what they need and that builds trust and loyalty.'

Complete Fire has come a long way since it was founded in 1991, when turnover in the first year was just $28,000. Courageously, Martin established a business in a well-established and highly competitive sector, then fought hard for market share, so he knows all about perseverance.

I used to stew over the bad decisions but not any more. Now I get over any disappointment, learn from it and move on.

'The first years establishing the business were extremely hard. I didn't pull a wage for the first two years and if it wasn't for my wife having a good job we would not have been able to do it.

'It was an intense time and you live it 24/7, but I was convinced that I was building a successful business. It all comes down to holding your nerve when times are tough. Panic and you will lose the lot.'

The unpredictability of the construction industry has certainly provided a few shocks and some good learning experiences for Martin and his team.

'There have been times when cash was tight. I've had my fair share of jobs go bad in a big way. A project that's worth $400,000 can actually lose $100,000 if things don't go right, and that's happened to me before.

'I used to stew over the bad decisions but not any more. Now I get over any disappointment, learn from it and move on.

'Keeping fresh and not becoming bogged down in the day-to-day routine adds years to your business life expectancy.'

Another factor is Martin's ability to re-invent the company every few years, changing its structure and pursuing new ideas and markets. In a specialist company this is not always easy – but Martin believes in creating his own opportunities rather than waiting for the market to find him.

For example, in the wake of the 2001 anthrax alerts in the US, Complete Fire built a decontamination spray unit for one of Adelaide's major hospitals. It was non-core activity, but it demonstrated the company's flexibility and opened up new markets.

'Some of our competitors wouldn't have been able to do that. With us it didn't have to go through 15 levels of approval and 12 months of self-examination about whether it was right for us. We just did it.

'In this business, you have to be adaptable.'

Martin is continually putting his role in the company under the microscope. Many company owners who started as hands-on technicians struggle with their gradual shift to become a strategist and direction setter.

By regularly picking up the tools and pitching in with his team at the coal-face of major jobs, Martin has proven that it pays not to lose touch.

'When you start out you have a small but very good team around you and that's part of why you are so successful.

'Then, as most companies grow, they hire new people who don't understand what it was like in the early days and often they don't have the same respect for the company or the CEO that the original team may have had.

'They don't know that the CEO worked 80 hours a week and went out in the middle of the night if there was an issue with a client that needed to be solved. Those who join the company 10 years later just see the CEO driving a nice car and sitting in his office calling the shots. I guess it's only natural, but sometimes they think: "Well, what does this guy know and why should I respect him?"

'One of the ways I have gained some respect with these newer team members is that I've gone back to the tools and worked with these guys on-site, and it helps give them a totally different view of me. They think: "Hey, this guy's not an idiot. He really does know what he's doing."

'It's good for the people who work for you to see that you can actually do what you say that they should do – that you actually walk the talk. I think more CEOs should get down off their pedestal sometimes and do that.'

Martin says it's just one more benefit of being a medium-sized company in the fire industry rather than a multinational – and he says he is glad that 'the buck stops with me'.

'That's the number one difference between my company and the larger companies. If a client is not happy they can get on the phone and ring me 24 hours a day, seven days a week and say: "Martin, I'm not happy." Then I can decide how to deal with that.

'The clients like that. I can go to the site if there is an issue. If they are right, I'll back them 100 per cent and they know they won't be charged or the job will be done again.

'With my competitors it can be very difficult to find the person who makes the decisions. There is no ownership with them. That's the real difference.'

Perseverance is another Martin Radford catch-cry.

'I don't know of any successful company that gave up when the going got tough. They just keep going. They dig in and it can help create a better company. If you can deal with it when the chips are down it gives you a great feeling.

'As I solve one problem and turn it into a success, turn a negative into a positive, somehow I actually get a renewed confidence that is very rewarding. The more you can roll with the punches, the more you learn to deal with difficulties. Then the next time something goes wrong you have more in reserve to deal with it.'

Finding the work-life balance is never easy, especially in the seven-day-a-week construction environment. A few years ago, Martin was the first in the office and the last to leave.

'I have since learnt that time away from the office to recharge or look at the business from outside these four walls is extremely productive.'

Lessons Learnt:

* Whatever business you think you are in, you are also in the business of building confidence. Talk regularly with your clients. Don't be shy about showing them you are doing the great job they expect of you.
* Don't be afraid to pick up the tools and work shoulder-to-shoulder with your team. Sometimes it helps give them a new appreciation of your expertise.
* Delegate – even if just to get you out of the office. Recharging the batteries is important to maintain your energy at work.

Advice to Others:

* When the going gets tough – keep going. Successful people and companies don't give up.

David Raffen

David Raffen is fast emerging as 'Mr IT' in South Australia.

His various companies – including Dr PC, Microarts and the Southern IT Group – are involved at virtually every level of the information technology sector, from installation and maintenance of personal computers for the home user through to the design and management of electronic information systems for corporate and government entities.

Dr PC is one of South Australia's fastest growing IT businesses.

The company's black and gold vans with their distinctive medical crosses are instantly recogniseable as they race to the next computer 'emergency'. They are not only the technicians' mobile workshops; they are also bold and bright moving billboards, fulfilling an important marketing role.

The name certainly leaves no doubt about what Dr PC does – and for David Raffen that is part of the joy of owning the company. It is a brand that speaks loudly for itself.

David Raffen didn't start Dr PC but he was shrewd enough to recognise the potential value in the brand when the company came up for sale in 2003.

Until then the company's development was relatively low key, but David has drawn on more than 25 years' experience in the IT sector to accelerate Dr PC's expansion. He expects to sell more than 300 Dr PC licenses and franchises nationally within the next few years, changing the face of home computer service.

The power of the Dr PC brand hit home to David soon after he bought it. He was already considering licensing or franchising the brand but at that stage had not advertised to gauge interest from potential licensees or franchisees.

Cutting price to win work is a dead-end street. It doesn't win you loyalty.

'Our first licensee actually approached us direct and asked if he could become involved. That's how strong the brand was. He wanted to be involved before he even knew we were thinking of licensing it out.'

While many of Dr PC's competitors scramble for market share by slashing product prices, David Raffen's focus is on providing clients with reliability, predictability and accountability.

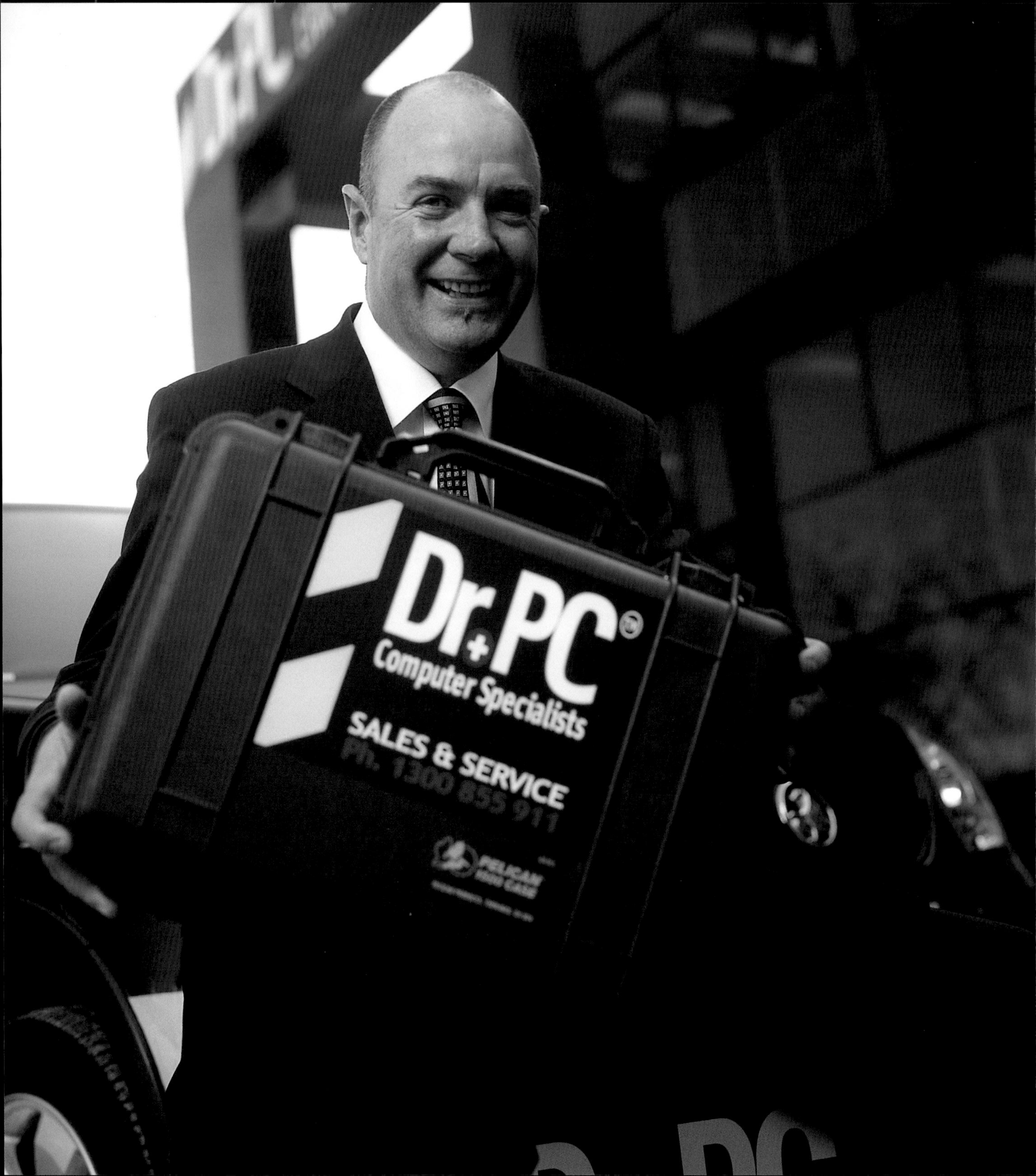
Dr.PC
Computer Specialists
SALES & SERVICE
Ph. 1300 855 911

It sounds like a cliché: give great service, do the right thing by the customer and your business will be a success. But David says the home computer repair industry has been characterised – and unfortunately badly tarnished – by appalling service levels.

'In the past the market was dominated by a lot of cowboys operating out of their home laundry. The home computer user didn't know where to turn. Computer repair shops would start up and sell them a computer, but then they'd be gone a few weeks later and there was no one providing back-up service for the equipment they installed.'

Dr PC gives consumers the comfort of a well-branded focal point and a long-term supplier – one they know will be around in a few weeks, months or years and who is already familiar with their computer set-up.

Moving away from the 'bargain basement' approach to winning business was a risky move in such a competitive market, but it is paying off for David Raffen.

'Cutting price to win work is a dead-end street. It doesn't win you loyalty. When it comes to buying computers, many people are happy to purchase their equipment over the internet to snap it up at the best price.

'The real problem for them comes with the installation. They buy the cheapest computer but when the equipment and programs arrive the user often has little idea how to piece it all together and set it up.

'Everyone thinks they can just load up the software. Home computer use was supposed to be "plug and play" but for most householders it's more like "plug and pray".

'Much of our business is going out and helping people who already have a computer but who have decided to purchase and install a new CD burner or printer. They find that the software they have installed has stopped another application from working on their machine or something else goes wrong.

'The last thing people want to do is unplug all the wires and try to do it themselves because they won't remember what went where. Even if they do unplug it, in the past they had to haul it out to the car and drive it somewhere to get it fixed – and even then they didn't know where to take it.

'Dr PC goes direct to the customer. We turn up with all the necessary parts, diagnose the problem and solve it on the spot. It takes the stress out of dealing with the computer, which is the biggest issue for some people.

'People are happy to pay for good service and convenience. We are not always the cheapest but we offer a service where we go direct to the customer and we even have a 24-hour emergency service if they want to pay that little bit extra.'

All Dr PC licensees must complete the Microsoft Certified Systems Engineers (MSCSE) and Cisco Certified Network Associate (CCNA) qualifications, which are recognised worldwide.

The company also operates its own training school to ensure its operators are appropriately qualified in the technical aspects of the job. Importantly, technicians are also taught how to explain to customers exactly what will be required to fix their computer problems, in terms that the user will understand – just as a doctor would speak with a patient before an operation.

'Users need to hear what's wrong with their computer in everyday language, not geek-speak. They need to know what they are paying for and be part of the decision-making process.

'These days, in a competitive industry like ours, we have to be accepted by the consumer as a trusted organisation that provides value for money, honest feedback and services the customer the best way we can. It's about the consumer knowing what you are doing, and the service provider doing the right thing.'

For David Raffen, this is the core of Dr PC's success in the South Australian marketplace – and the backbone of his strategy to license and franchise the brand Australia-wide.

'People are happy to pay well for quick and efficient service from people they can trust. That trust is paramount.

'Having your computer fixed is a bit like taking your car to a motor repairer. If the mechanic tells you something is wrong under the bonnet, unless you know something about cars you are never going to know whether it's true or not, so you need to be dealing with someone you can trust.

'In our case, that person is a trained technician who can find and fix a computer problem, but also someone who's going to explain it carefully and who's only going to sell the customer what they need to be sold.'

While Dr PC has the home user market covered, one of David's other companies, Microarts, services the corporate sector, designing networks and infrastructure, providing the hardware and undertaking installation and ongoing support.

David Raffen has played an integral role in shaping the development of the IT sector through his involvement with the Australian Information Industry Association and Information Telecommunications Council.

David also founded the Southern IT Group – an innovative consortium of more than 20 South Australian IT companies with a combined turnover of more than $100 million – to pitch against large multinational IT companies for work that the individual member companies may not have won on their own.

The creation of the Southern IT Group gave a new dimension to the local IT sector, significantly boosting the fortunes of local companies. Microarts is a member company, so David is helping steer his own destiny while broadening the opportunities for local IT companies.

'A few years ago local companies were often losing out to much bigger international companies who tended to win large IT contracts in South Australia.

'The Southern IT Group pools resources and creates a critical mass. As a result, we are able to get together to tackle the same types of opportunities as the larger international companies. It has also enabled us to gain the attention of government, because we are now a major industry force in our own right.'

David Raffen says his aim is to 'comprehensively service the IT community, from mums and dads to the largest corporate businesses in Australia, by providing professional, value-for-money service'.

The continuing success of his stable of companies demonstrates that this straightforward business formula appears to be just what the doctor ordered.

Lessons Learnt:

* You don't have to create a great brand from scratch. Sometimes you can buy a brand with potential and build it from there. Keep your eyes open and be ready to pounce if an opportunity arises to buy the right brand.
* Don't bamboozle the consumer with technical terms – no matter what your industry. Don't assume they understand what you do for them and what they are paying for. Explain it simply so they can understand and value your service.
* Be a leader. If you join an association or organisation make sure you strive to take an active leadership role. That way you can add value, your voice can be heard and you can help shape your industry. Don't just sit there!

Advice to Others:

* It is possible to create an extremely successful business as a 'white knight' – a problem solver who rides in to save the day. If you can fix it well, fix it fast and take the stress out of the transaction, you will win customers.

Mike Rankin

There was a time in the late 1970s when Mike Rankin's dream of business success was being able to write all his cheques at one time without having to estimate whether there was enough money in the bank to cover them.

'It was a steep learning curve in the early days, with all the pressures of financial management. I had to ensure there was enough money in the bank and stagger my cheques. At the same time I would be fielding calls from impatient creditors demanding that they be paid.'

Things have changed. Mike Rankin's company Holco is now one of South Australia's largest meat suppliers, with customers including supermarkets, butchers and the food manufacturing and hospitality industries.

With more than 200 staff and turnover in the tens of millions, Holco is a vertically integrated company that takes its product 'from paddock to plate', providing its hundreds of clients with a full range of vacuum sealed, frozen, pre-minced and semi-processed meat products.

Beef steaks from Holco are eaten in some of South Australia's finest restaurants, while the company's boneless beef is used in meat pies sold nation-wide and its portion-controlled meats are served in hospitals, hotels, nursing homes, hamburger outlets and mining camps. If you are eating a meat meal anywhere in Adelaide, there is a good chance it has come from Holco.

The origins of Holco stretch back to 1975 when Mike, a few months before he completed his butcher's apprenticeship, bought a butcher shop for $2200. Two years later he sold it for six times the purchase price, then bought two more stores.

The entrepreneurial seed was sown. Mike subsequently incorporated his umbrella company Meatpak Australia in 1980 with $10,000 of working capital, and began supplying minced products to independent supermarkets.

'I had a strong desire to grow a business. I was pretty bored at being stuck in a butcher shop and wanted to get cracking on something bigger. It was just a case of seeing a niche and having a go at it.'

As a commodity business, the meat trade traditionally had been price-driven. Mike believed vertical integration could provide a better product and service offering, differentiating him from his competitors.

Between 1980 and 1990 Mike worked to broaden the business by focusing on the wholesale market and supplying butcher shops and supermarkets with a general range of beef products.

Eventually the flourishing wholesale business required larger premises and in 1987 Mike purchased a disused export boning room in the outer Adelaide suburb of Peterhead.

Then, in 1995, Mike purchased Holco Meat from national company Metro Meat, a move that doubled the size of his business and opened up exciting avenues for potential growth.

Mike Rankin's meat empire is now made up of four clearly defined business units that neatly dovetail into each other:

- Holco Fine Meat Suppliers Wholesale Division – supplying butchers, supermarkets and trading meat Australia-wide
- Holco Fine Meat Suppliers Catering Division – supplying hotels, restaurants and the hospitality sector
- Springfield Butchers – a group of 13 retail outlets located in major regional shopping centres
- Paringa Farm – involved in lamb farming and livestock trading.

From the early days Mike has focused on flexibility and service to win and keep customers. The catering, restaurant and hotel trade did most of its ordering in the late evening, so Holco launched a night shift to prepare orders for next-day delivery.

Holco also introduced a staffed telephone service through to 11 pm each night and now receives a high proportion of its orders after 8 pm.

'You have to meet the needs of your market. We found that our key market, the food service sector, was working through to about 11 pm at night. We thought, well, we're not matching our market very well – what can we change?

'We also felt the industry needed a human interface. That's especially the case if someone in a major hotel or restaurant rings to say "my fridge broke down and I need to feed 400 people". All of a sudden we were able to offer solutions, adjusting volumes and delivery times, and generally helping them sort out any problems they may have. It worked well.'

Another key to Holco's success has been Mike's adherence to a 'small business' philosophy and what he calls the 'all-for-one and one-for-all' attitude he has fostered.

'Becoming too "corporate" too soon can be a danger. If you start thinking and acting like a big business too soon it can weigh you down with costs and overburden you with hierarchical structures. We have kept the business quite flat in structure. To the extent possible, it is run very much like a small business.

'At the same time we have pulled in the best parts of corporate thinking – such as high-level financial information – and applied it to the business.'

This down-to-earth attitude sees Mike don his white coat to work alongside his employees on the processing floor from 5 am every day.

'I can't imagine it any other way. I value our people and the personal interaction we enjoy. The staff also appreciate the time the management group spends on the floor. We are seen leading by example and doing the hard work, not just sitting back reaping the rewards. Everyone contributes.'

Mike says part of Holco's success has been his ability to take major but measured risks at times when it would have been much easier to stand back and be more cautious. This has gone hand-in-hand with the ability to envisage exactly where the business is heading and recognise that bold moves are required to achieve the goal.

'You almost need tunnel vision, I think, the same as with high achieving sports people. Sometimes you have to take risks that frighten the hell out of you – and you have to punch above your weight all the time.'

An example was Mike's decision to purchase the Peterhead property even though his investigations had shown that the local council would not grant a continuance of its use as a boning facility. At the time he signed to buy the property it seemed he would never get the permits he needed to operate from the new location.

'I took that risk on the basis that we had to keep growing and there were no other suitable properties available anywhere in Adelaide.'

Mike launched court proceedings against the council's decision and finally received a favourable judgement enabling him to operate from the premises. The litigation took its toll in time and precious capital, but the pay-off was a low-cost, well-located and entirely suitable property that immediately boosted the balance sheet, giving Mike greater borrowing capacity for further growth.

'There is a risk-reward ratio that underpins everything you do to a degree. You must have the capability to take the risk, so you need to have a good relationship with your lending institution so they will stand beside you while you make your move. Then you've got to have the fortitude to take the risk.

'Just look at some of the great entrepreneurs of the world. Richard Branson [Virgin] lays it on the line once a year – and he probably puts half his organisation at risk doing that.

'Once you have got some momentum going I have found that certain things fall into line and with Holco I have been able to incrementally step up the nature of growth. The hardest part is building that initial momentum but once you have it running you can start to think strategically instead of concentrating just on what's happening today or tomorrow. You can take a more long-term approach to running your business.

Sometimes you have to take risks that frighten the hell out of you – and you have to punch above your weight all the time.

'In hindsight, if I had the time again, I would take bigger risks earlier on in my career which would have increased the size of our current day operations. Hindsight is an amazing advantage though. At the time I felt I was taking enough risk.'

The early mornings and long days don't bother Mike. He says it comes with the territory and he thrives on hard work – in fact, he says it's the only way to create a successful enterprise.

'I enjoy the business and have always been a worker. There's no easy way. Success involves a lot of hard work and tough hours.

'The term "overnight success" is a bad cliché. Anything that looks like an overnight success usually involves someone working for 20 years in the industry beforehand.

'I don't know anybody who has become successful without hard work. Don't expect quick results. A successful business has often been driven over a long period of time and the owners have copped the setbacks and the knocks. When you are lying on the ground and bloodied from another kick in the guts you have to get up and go at it again.'

Lessons Learnt:

* Take measured risks to build your business more quickly. Use the momentum in the business as a springboard to take quantum leaps.
* Don't lose your 'small business' mentality no matter how big your company becomes. It is often the core to a successful culture.
* In a price-driven commodity business, differentiate or die. If you are not doing something better than your competitors, the choice for your customers will be based on price alone.

Advice to Others:

* Seek out successful people and network early in your business career so you can learn from others. 'There are amazing benefits available from being able to learn from people who have the experience of success and leverage off their knowledge.'

Terri
Scheer

In the lead-up to being named 2004 South Australian Small Business of the Year, Terri Scheer was fighting tooth and nail for the survival of her business, Terri Scheer Insurance Brokers.

It was a feeling of deja vu for the founder of Australia's only specialist landlord insurance provider, having faced massive obstacles nine years earlier to keep her business alive in its first few days.

This latest threat was in the form of Federal Government legislation, the Financial Services Reform (FSR) Act.

Under the legislation, Terri Scheer Insurance Brokers could no longer sell its landlord insurance in the same way it always had through its one and only distribution channel – real estate property managers – without these managers having to go through the onerous task of becoming licensed.

'As a result, we knew that most real estate agents would not have continued selling our insurance products – it was a catastrophe,' Terri said.

'We suddenly found ourselves having to deal direct with 90,000 landlords, rather than through a few thousand property managers.

'Having made the deliberate decision in the early days of the business to target property managers, rather than the landlords direct, we had to basically turn our whole business upside down to find a way to still utilise property managers to get our product to the market, but within the legislative requirements.

'In the initial stages we estimated it was going to cost us almost $2.8 million in lost business and costs associated with changing our business model to deal direct with landlords and property managers.

'As we investigated different scenarios and options, that estimate came down to $1.7 million over 12 months.'

A sharp negative spike in the growth trend of the company was reversed, after months of hard work by Terri, her team and lawyers, when the company developed and implemented a workable business model dubbed 'Scheer Simplicity'.

Ironically, when the FSR Act was first introduced, Terri Scheer was a 'trailblazer', with her company the first in Australia to be granted a licence under the new legislative regime.

'I strongly supported the idea of cleaning up the financial services industry, removing the cowboys and providing greater consumer protection,' Terri said.

'Little did I know this same legislation would nearly kill my business.'

While fighting for business survival, Terri Scheer Insurance Brokers was a category winner in the Telstra Small Business Awards and then took out the coveted title of South Australian Small Business of the Year.

A couple of months later the business was featured in the 2004 BRW Fast 100 Companies listing for its compound growth rate of 39 per cent per year over the previous three years.

Since its establishment in 1995, the company's turnover has rapidly grown, reaching $18.4 million in 2003/2004, up from $8 million two years previously.

This is despite the fact that the company wasn't expected to survive its first month in business.

Terri's involvement in the insurance industry began in 1977 when, at the age of 17, she secured a claims role. After training in all areas of commercial and corporate insurance broking during the 1980s, in the early 1990s she designed Australia's first insurance policy devoted to landlord protection while working for a large South Australian insurance brokerage.

Prior to this, owners of professionally managed rental properties had no access to insurance that would protect them from loss of rental income, or from tenants causing malicious damage to their property.

'While landlords had access to building insurance and contents insurance, the major problems they faced were tenants damaging their property, or vacating the property without paying rent,' Terri said.

'There really was nothing in the market to protect the landlord's income – or that of their agents – from tenants doing the wrong thing.

'However, even to this day many landlords are oblivious to these risks. They assume that once the agency has been put in charge of their property they no longer have any problems to worry about, and simply don't expect their tenants to do the wrong thing.'

Identifying the needs of this growing niche market, and following the success of the insurance product she had designed, Terri formed Terri Scheer Insurance Brokers as an independent brokerage in 1995.

However, Terri was quickly introduced to the cut-throat nature of the corporate world, with her previous employer placing increasing legal and financial pressure on her to close the doors of the new company.

On her third day in business, Terri's insurance underwriter withdrew its support. On day 10, her account executive returned to her previous employer. And on day 21, she and her partner separated – all this in addition to raising a young child.

After experiencing 'the hardest time of her life', and with a great deal of perseverance and determination, Terri overcame these obstacles to establish what is the world's only specialist insurance brokerage of its kind.

Today, Terri Scheer Insurance Brokers has offices in Victoria, New South Wales, Queensland and Western Australia, with operations in the Northern Territory, Tasmania and Canberra, while its headquarters remain in Adelaide. An office was opened in New Zealand early in 2004.

With research by the company showing that up to one in six investment properties in some suburbs will suffer damage by tenants or loss of rent, the success of Terri Scheer Insurance Brokers has been based on its ability to consistently service these specific insurance needs.

If you become too focused on a financial target you tend to mentally limit yourself to that. Instead, I say, 'Let's do the best we can, allow the company to go where it wants to go and give it a life of its own'.

This has been achieved not only by catering to landlords, but by offering a sound support system for the agents who manage their properties.

'While we now also deal direct with landlords, professionally managed rental property agencies are still the key focus for our business,' Terri says.

'While the landlord owns the property and is thereby very involved in the insurance process, it is the real estate agent who needs the support. They're trying to keep both the landlord and the tenants happy, and meanwhile they are trying to run their own profitable business.

'Terri Scheer Insurance Brokers' philosophy is to provide excellent service and support to property managers, so if they run into trouble they know they can ring us for help.

'In fact, not only can we help them with insurance, we also have a team of property management staff who can provide assistance and advice to agents on a variety of residential rental property management issues.

'This focus on rental agencies in turn adds value to the service they provide to their clients.'

Three of the country's largest real estate groups – Ray White National, L.J. Hooker and First National, and in South Australia, Raine and Horne – have selected Terri Scheer as their preferred financial services provider, in addition to several thousand individual property managers.

The company recognises that insurance is just one aspect of a property manager's responsibilities to their landlords, so the focus of Terri Scheer's customer service strategy is to make this process as simple as possible.

The company also plays a key education role in the property management industry, with Terri a highly sought speaker at conferences and training seminars on the issue of risk management, as well as a strong sponsor and supporter of the industry.

While the company's competitors spend much of their time playing 'product catch up', improving their policies to remove any differentiation, Terri Scheer remains a product leader. Other insurance providers often use Terri Scheer's policies as a template, and when the company makes improvements to its products, competitors generally follow suit.

Terri believes a contributing factor to the rapid growth of her company is that, unlike most businesses, she does not set concrete annual financial budgets to achieve.

'If you become too focused on a financial target you tend to mentally limit yourself to that. In addition, I don't think the best way to motivate staff is to give them a dollar figure to achieve.

'Instead, I say, "Let's do the best we can, allow the company to go where it wants to go and give it a life of its own". If you love something set it free!

'I find that to be a much healthier attitude – and it has resulted in the company naturally over-achieving.'

However, Terri would like to see the company reach turnover of $40 million in the next few years, with 75 per cent of market share of each state of Australia.

By continuing to provide superior customer service and support, Terri's objective is to 'raise the bar' so high that it will be impossible for competitors to enter the market. Few would be brave enough to even try in the face of such formidable determination.

Lessons Learnt:

* Product specialisation can provide a real competitive edge, creating an unprecedented level of know-how in the market and allowing you to identify and develop new products.
* Make it easy for your clients to do business with you and help them to look good in their own clients' eyes.
* Find out how you can help your employees to achieve their goals and dreams. Take them on the journey with you and you'll all benefit.

Advice to Others:

* Don't let setbacks deter you from achieving your vision. Inspiration can come from many sources and some of the most traumatic and stressful times in Terri's life have motivated her to want to achieve even greater success.

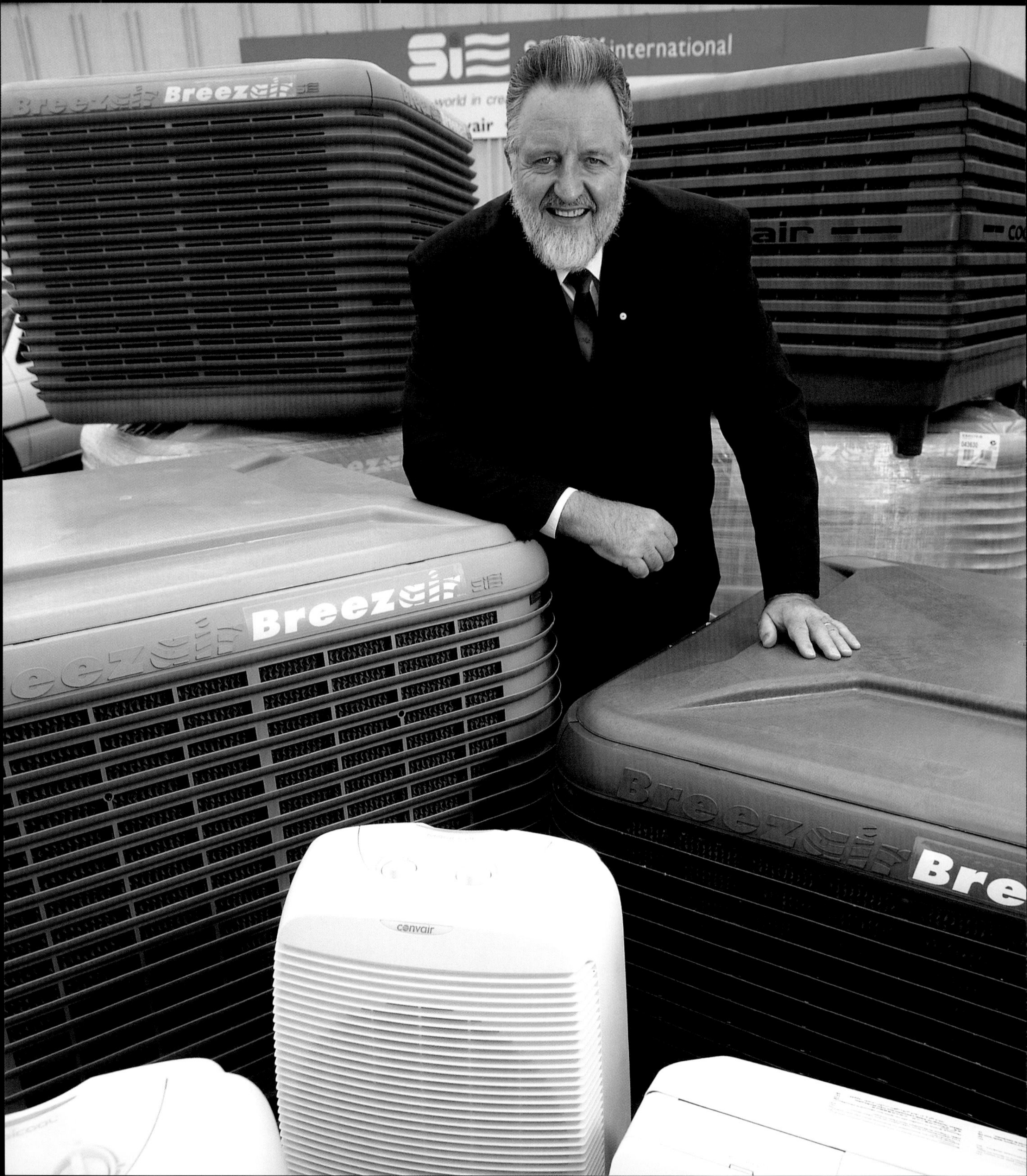
Breezair
Breezair
convair

Frank Seeley

Frank Seeley became an entrepreneur at the age of 10 when his mother wouldn't give him the money to buy a yo-yo. Frank spent the next few days door-knocking and offering to do odd jobs for the neighbours to raise the money.

His career moved to the next level when he was 16 and learning to play the piano accordion. Frank was a tinkerer who wanted to learn how the complicated instrument worked, so he took one to pieces.

The shrewd young businessman saw an opportunity in purchasing old and dilapidated piano accordions, doing them up and selling them for a profit.

The early experience paid off. More than 30 years later, Frank Seeley is Chairman of Seeley International, Australia's market leading designer and manufacturer of portable and ducted climate control systems for the home, commercial and industrial markets.

With a turnover of more than $90 million, Seeley International's award-winning air conditioning and heating products are sold in more than 60 countries under the renowned Breezair, Braemar, Coolair and Convair brands.

After starting his career as a primary school teacher, Frank moved on to become a successful commission agent selling portable evaporative air coolers with his brother Cedric.

When Cedric died suddenly, Frank found himself caring for two families at the age of 28 – and in desperate need of a steady and predictable income. A short time later however his cooler supplier withdrew from their business arrangement, and Frank was left with no income source.

By this time, Frank had realised that the biggest drawback to the acceptance of evaporative coolers was the life-limiting corrosion of their metal parts. He believed he could eliminate the problem by building a cooler entirely from plastic – a move that would also significantly expand the market potential.

In 1972, working from his garage at home, Frank prototyped an all-plastic cooler and set up a very basic production line, outsourcing all the components. As sales grew, increased cashflow enabled Frank to boost production and component manufacture was brought in-house.

In 1978, Frank designed a totally new portable evaporative cooler. Again, it was constructed entirely of plastic with no metal parts. With some inspired lateral thinking, Frank also insisted that the design have no separate fasteners to hold it together, a concept that was a decade ahead of the rest of the world and made possible by the design flexibility of plastics.

In one move, Frank had reduced the number of components required from 386 to 56 with dramatic savings both in the cost of parts and their assembly. Frank's initial design strategy is now commonplace in the climate control industry.

In 1979, Frank's motor supplier had established a monopoly in Australia and became intransigent on price. Frank responded by building his own motor facility and within a year he was producing over 100,000 motors annually.

The same year, Seeley International began exporting – almost by accident. One of Frank's managers had visited Iraq to try to win sales of the company's innovative coolers. Unfortunately, he was unsuccessful but decided to leave a sample cooler with an Iraqi government department rather than ship it back to Australia.

'The Iraqi Government department tried out the sample model and were so impressed that we received a fax from Iraq with an order for 20,000 of the portable air conditioners.

'Before we could finish production they faxed us again ordering another 20,000 units. They ordered 100,000 the summer after.'

Seeley International now exports globally and has 60 per cent of the portable evaporative air cooler market in the US. The company has sales offices in the US, UK, Spain and France.

In 1983, in an Australian first, Frank applied the principle of all-plastic construction to the roof-top evaporative air conditioner. This meant overcoming significant technical problems to convert all components to plastic, resulting in numerous solutions that Seeley International was able to patent.

These patents enabled Frank to exclude his competitors from the market and retain Seeley International's significant cost advantages. They also underpinned a portfolio of designs that still lead the world.

Seeley International's success in leading-edge design owes much to Frank's commitment to re-invest up to 7 per cent of turnover into research and development.

'Our R&D started with the use of plastics, which facilitated multiple-function parts. That was a first. The elimination of metal components in so many areas was groundbreaking technology.

'All our new ideas are thoroughly researched to overcome problems and provide additional benefits for customers. They are also rigorously patented throughout the world. This approach has enabled us to fully protect and exploit new technologies and designs.'

Seeley was the first company to introduce a rounded and low-profile rooftop cooler that was more aesthetically appealing.

Recently, Frank's team developed what he believes is the world's quietest air-conditioning motor. The only sound that can be heard is the sound of air being gently circulated throughout the system.

Frank says 'creative innovation is the last great unfair advantage that we have'. With that in mind, he formed Seeley International's 'Innovaction Group' to drive continuous improvement of manufacturing processes and enhance the quality and features of existing products.

'An entrepreneur these days is everything that the entrepreneurs of the 1980s were not. An entrepreneur takes a basic commodity and transforms it into something extraordinary, which is totally reliable, offers more consumer benefits, costs less and is capable of delighting all who use it.

You have to treat employees with respect – and be willing to move on quickly when an employee makes a mistake.

'It's also important to note that honesty and entrepreneurship should go together.'

Frank is also a sworn enemy of 'the hard sell'.

'I learnt about selling from my late brother Cedric, who coached me not to sell, but to learn how to help people buy. People don't want to be sold – they want to make a decision about buying a product based on how good that product is and its benefits.'

Staff motivation and management have been vital in building the Seeley International business. Hand-in-hand with that has been Frank's desire to achieve a non-political work environment.

'I have had previous business experiences where internal politics impact on staff morale, motivation and performance. We have specifically acted to instil a culture of fairness and open communication at Seeley International.

'I show a real interest in my employees' personal issues and I try to be a humble leader. I don't have to be the one getting all the congratulations. It's not important who gets the accolades as long as we get the results required.'

Frank is also an adherent to the philosophy of 'servant leadership'.

'It's all about acknowledging that your employees have different skills to you but that as a leader and entrepreneur you can serve them to assist them to do their job better.

'You have to treat employees with respect – and be willing to move on quickly when an employee makes a mistake. Communication with all employees is the basis for building commitment to the overall business objectives and strategies.'

This holistic philosophy extends beyond the workplace. Frank and his family have been involved with helping disadvantaged children for the past 20 years. In that time Frank has hosted more than 25,000 disadvantaged children in his home.

At Seeley International, Frank has established an experienced board including a number of external directors with diverse backgrounds and experiences.

'I am a strong believer in not being surrounded by "yes men". The external directors are anything but "yes men", as are all my people in key roles.

'In order for the company to grow, we need to be continually challenged and benefit from sharing ideas and skills between the directors, as well as between senior and junior executives.'

Seeley International's future growth will continue to be driven by development of new technologies and products. The company's most recent development of the Icon Series range of evaporative coolers, containing the Hushpower motor, is already breaking new ground in energy efficiency, quietness and running costs.

It is also paving the way for the next growth phase, which will allow Seeley International to enhance its position in Australia and provide a platform for taking the company's technology to the world.

One of Frank's personal goals is to positively contribute to the business until he is 100.

'I want to maintain my involvement in the company for as long as I am capable of contributing in a meaningful way.'

So where would Frank Seeley be if he had not become an entrepreneur and pursued his dream of building a better air cooler?

'I would now be a dissatisfied, disgruntled and unsuccessful ex-school teacher.'

Lessons Learnt:

* You can build a thriving business by changing an industry. Frank Seeley created a highly successful company by making the world's first all-plastic cooler and changing the shape of his industry forever.
* Work towards creating a non-political work environment. Internal politics impact negatively on staff morale, motivation and performance.
* Embrace the concept of continuous improvement. Being the best is not good enough, as others will always catch up. Keep improving your processes, products and services to stay ahead of the pack.

Advice to Others:

* Don't surround yourself with 'yes men'. An entrepreneurial company needs to be constantly challenged – and that can't happen if everyone around you simply agrees with the boss.

Drew Sellick

Drew Sellick likes to joke that if someone has ever given a urine sample or blown into a breathalyser they are familiar with his product.

Plastic medical specimen jars and disposable breathalyser mouthpieces are just two of more than 700 products made by Drew's company Techno-Plas – a business that has made its name as a manufacturing innovator in Australia.

His commitment to improving manufacturing practices has taken him from sweeping floors to running a trailblazing business based on a highly computerised and technical 'lights out' 24-hour, seven-day-a-week operation.

Drew found himself working in a junior role in a plastics factory at the age of 18. It was his first job out of high school, and by the time he was 22 he was running that business. After helping to build the company over several years, in 1980 he moved to establish his own plastics business.

Within six years the company was operating 18 injection-moulding machines and servicing a list of large clientele. When one of his key customers listed on the Australian Stock Exchange they also offered to buy Drew's business as a way of guaranteeing product supply.

Drew sold his company for a multi-million-dollar sum and found himself in the comfortable position of being able to retire at the age of 37.

Eighteen months into retirement, boredom had set in. Looking for a new opportunity, Drew established Techno-Plas in 1988 in the middle of a recession.

While he was cashed up from the sale of his previous business, there were enormous costs associated with establishing the plastics business and purchasing the required machinery at a time when interest rates were at 19 per cent.

There are a number of times in your life when a door will open, but many people aren't prepared to walk through it.

'Manufacturing is financially hard work – you need to have plant, equipment, dies and products to show before you can go out and start selling. You have to put your money where your mouth is.

'From the outset we focused on winning work on price and quality; we wanted to be the lowest cost manufacturer. We knew the importance of offering product consistency, but we also had to price ourselves slightly under the rest of the market.

'The key to achieving all of that was technology. We invested heavily in equipment that we adapted. Most baseline machines are pretty much the same; it's the difference in the mould design and how you handle the product that is critical. And that's where we've been innovative.'

The sophistication of the high-tech equipment used by Techno-Plas, including robotics and complex computer systems, allows the company to manufacture around the clock and to spread its fixed overheads over seven days a week, rather than five.

Such a high level of automation originally saw the business virtually eliminate the need for after-hours factory floor staff, with employees leaving at the end of the day and the systems still operating overnight during 'lights out' and on weekends.

In recent years however, manufacturing employee numbers have been boosted to provide absolute control over the process as a result of changes in customer requirements and supply chain management, and in order to simplify the company's operations.

'That's been one of the biggest lessons for us; the dangers of over-complicating the business. While the technology has many benefits it was starting to get too complicated and difficult to manage.

'It got to the point where the factory operations, pallet stacking and dispatch were almost entirely robotic, which is fine if nothing goes wrong. But no one was there to fine-tune things if there was a problem with the automated systems.

'We learnt that it was important to automate to maintain a competitive advantage, but not to over-complicate things. We have now found a good balance of automation and on-site staffing to ensure things run smoothly.'

While Techno-Plas's original focus was primarily on medical and laboratory consumables – such as specimen jars, test tubes and Petri dishes – this has been expanded to include products for the food, wine, pharmaceutical and cosmetics industries.

The purchase of a Melbourne facility in recent years, renamed Techno-PET, is now seeing the company manufacture PET bottles and containers for a range of customers, particularly in the food and beverage industries. This provides new opportunities for the company, further reinforcing its competitive advantages.

A driver behind purchasing the Melbourne plant was a desire to be closer to the eastern states markets, particularly those customers who are diversifying and have an increasing focus on exports. Drew sees the Melbourne location becoming much more important to the company's operations because of supply chain management and the freight cost advantages.

About 10 per cent of Techno-Plas's annual turnover of $10 million is in exports, but a much higher percentage is used by Australian-based customers in their own products which are subsequently exported.

In recent years much of Drew's focus has been on implementing the right infrastructure, systems and people, so the company is strongly positioned to operate in what he believes will be an increasingly challenging environment.

Integral to this has been developing a strong executive management team – with decisions now made by a committee of the company's leading managers – and seeking outside support and guidance through Drew's involvement in the international peer networking group TEC (The Executive Connection).

'Our commitment to operating 24/7 is a huge bonus in Australia where manufacturers traditionally haven't looked beyond a five-day week. It's very quickly coming to the point where local companies are going to have to address this or face being in all sorts of trouble.

'Manufacturers in our neighbouring Asian countries are thinking and working 24/7, so any company that's competing either in Australia or overseas is going to come under huge pressure because they're under-utilising their resources.

'I see manufacturing having to change, very much like retail has – the doors are always open. And if they don't, there are countries not too far from Australia that will capitalise on that. We're seeing more changes now than we have in the past 20 years and those that aren't ready for it are going to get hurt.

'Timing is everything. We started operating this way early on and have had the time to build up the business and our capabilities.'

Techno-Plas's proven track record and performance has seen it attract some of Australia's largest companies as customers – including medical, health and pathology groups that operate globally – while its competitors are left to play catch-up. Having 'name' companies on its customer list has provided Techno-Plas with a critical marketing advantage, and its capacity and economies of scale are difficult for potential customers to ignore when seeking suppliers.

A large product range and diverse customer base has helped spread risk in the business. No one debtor accounts for more than 8 per cent of Techno-Plas' turnover – and even that customer's business is spread over eight different products.

Drew has an 'open book' approach with clients and has increasingly focused on pooling resources with other companies, including competitors, in order to win business.

'Like many companies, 10 years ago we were very protective of telling anyone anything about the business. Over time we have found that having a much more open approach with our customers has proved extremely beneficial as they learn more about how we can assist them, and that we are a successful, thriving company that is here for the long haul.

'Equally, partnering with other companies to share experiences and build business has provided good results for us. This is particularly relevant for companies in industries like ours that are capital intensive. It can be very worthwhile sharing equipment and resources in an environment where each piece of machinery can cost hundreds of thousands of dollars.

'Understanding more about other businesses also helps us to benchmark – financials, production, people and systems. Know your competitor's price and quality standards. It's all about an absolute customer focus. If you're not measuring you're only pretending.'

Drew believes Techno-Plas' future success will come from capitalising on the opportunities arising from the hard work of the past and the 'can do' attitude on which the company prides itself.

'We tell our customers, "give us the work, and we'll get it done". We see ourselves as problem solvers and that means we take on projects that other people would say no to. We've really instilled that in our people.

'Positive management and guidance equals a positive company. Like I say to my people, "even if the roof falls down, we'll just come back the next day and repair it".

'There are a number of times in your life when a door will open, but many people aren't prepared to walk through it. Some of the things we have achieved I put down to timing, but I do believe our journey of success has largely been as a result of taking the opportunities that have been presented to us.

'To me, that's the entrepreneurial spirit – the willingness to take a calculated risk.'

Lessons Learnt:

* Spread your risk. Specifically target growth areas, but also ensure that you are not reliant on a single large customer.
* Don't be reluctant to pool resources with other companies. Be open to partnering with others to lower costs, maximise opportunities, share experiences and grow business.
* Position yourself early on in your business to capitalise on future opportunities. Running a sophisticated 24/7 operation from the outset has allowed Techno-Plas to compete internationally while its competitors play catch-up.

Advice to Others:

* Maintain a competitive advantage – but don't over-complicate things in the process. It's possible to be too clever and to over-use technology. 'Keep it simple' is Drew Sellick's mantra these days.

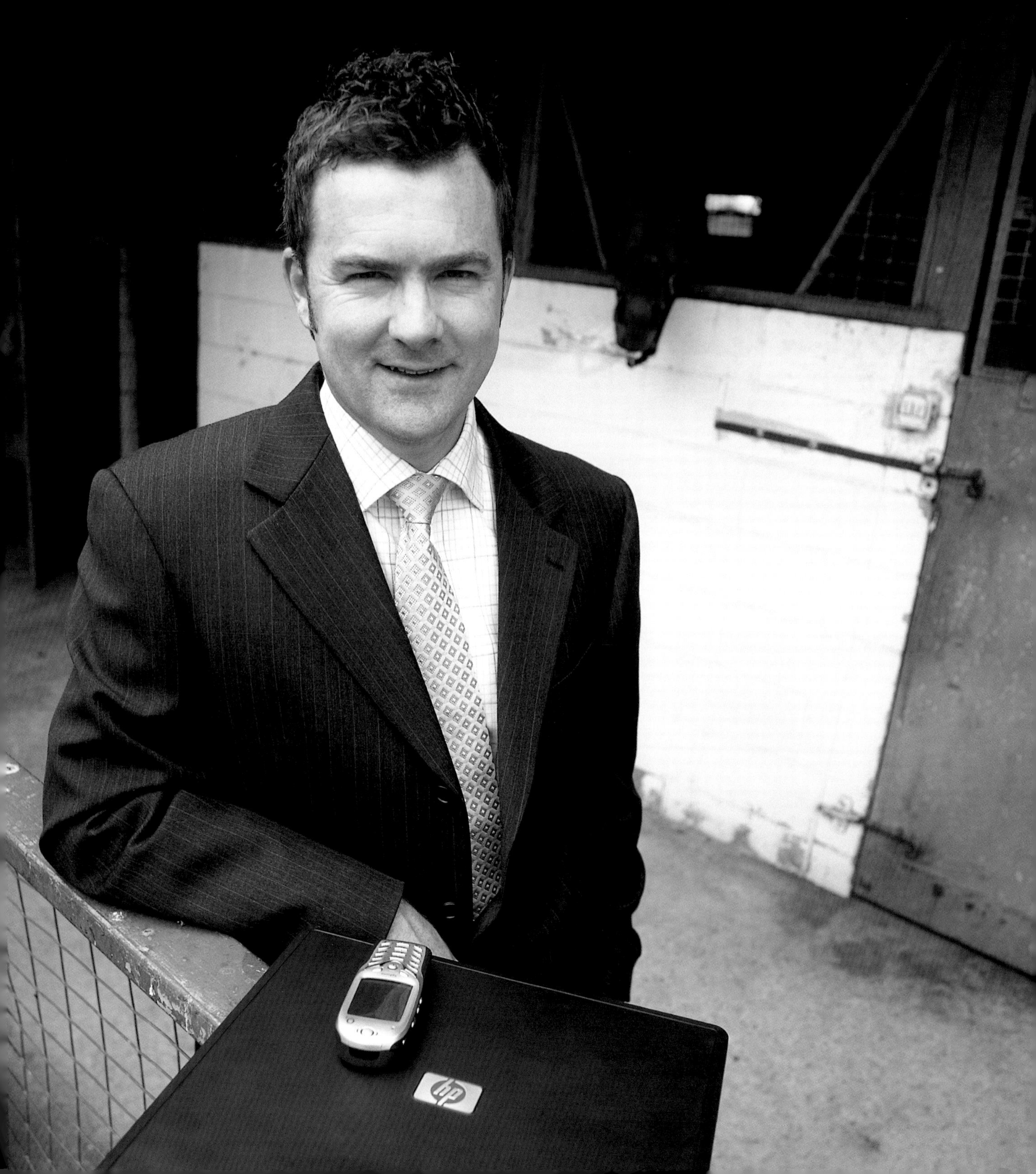

Darren Shaw

Darren Shaw reckons the best thing he ever did in business was to change his company's name.

Having established his IT business as Shaw Solutions eight years earlier with his father John, Darren changed the name to Promadis in 2003 in line with the company's branded range of software products.

As well as achieving consistency between product and company names, the main driver behind the decision was Darren's belief that the company was large and well established enough not to have to 'hide' behind the Shaw name.

'At that stage of the business we were increasingly moving into selling our own programs under the Promadis badge, rather than being a "body shop" and selling other company's products. We wanted to address that inconsistency and we thought calling the company Promadis made it a lot simpler to tell our story.

'Being called Shaw Solutions also implied that there was a heavy reliance on anyone with the surname Shaw to keep the company humming along, and that's just so far from the truth. I didn't want customers thinking that because I have the surname Shaw that I was the only person they could speak to, or that I was any more important to the company than any other member of our team.

'It was the best move we ever made. It's funny how things started to really fall into place for us following the change.'

Promadis is now one of the few Australian IT companies that can truly claim to offer a total, one-stop information technology service. This approach was developed after listening to numerous businesses that were tired of having to deal with multiple IT suppliers.

As a single-source supplier, Promadis can be more cost-effective. Just as important though is the firm's ability to build a closer relationship with the client, who can simply contact Darren's team about virtually any IT issue.

In fact, this one-stop approach has led to the company marketing itself as a business solutions provider, rather than an IT company. Darren believes too many IT companies focus on technical issues rather than ways to improve their clients' bottom line.

'We want to be talking to the board members, not just the IT department, about how we can help a company improve its overall performance. We get our thrills from seeing our clients' businesses improve.'

Despite the broad range of services it provides, the heart of Promadis' business is still software – the focus of the company's early days. The range of Promadis software programs is the company's flagship.

While Darren is a very talented computer programmer, he has never undertaken any formal training. Working as an errand boy at a computer company in the late 1980s, Darren started reading manuals and decided to 'give it a go'. Thus began his career in programming. Over the next few years he worked for large IT companies in Adelaide and Sydney before establishing his own company with his father in 1995.

One of Darren's most successful software programs has been Promadis Raven, which manages births, deaths and marriages records. Originally developed for the Births, Deaths & Marriages Registration Office in South Australia, the program is now also used by the Northern Territory and Australian Capital Territory Governments.

After investigating what other similar software programs were available internationally, Darren discovered that the Raven program was in fact world-class, leading to the decision to consider sales opportunities overseas.

Off the back of the move into overseas markets, Promadis' annual turnover is nearing $4 million and Darren believes international sales are integral to the company's future success.

Promadis' client base is diverse and reflects the company's broad product range. Client industries include but are not limited to local government, property management, medical, manufacturing, and rural produce processing and distribution.

Shareholder or not, you should always fulfil your role properly. Do what your company relies on you to do — or get out of the way and let somebody else do it.

The company has recently developed a forensic science package now used by Forensic Science in South Australia and Tasmania, while a major poultry group slaughtering 750,000 chickens a week uses Promadis Distribution.

Promadis Financials is used by a wide range of companies to run their core financials such as accounts payable/receivable and payroll, while several diagnostic, medical and hospital groups have purchased Promadis Medical.

'Our clients are not run-of-the-mill companies that can go and buy any old system and put it in their business. We only work with clients that value IT, and who understand the value that computer and software systems can add to their business.

'With Promadis you obviously get software, but you also get us – the people. We'll want to be involved closely in strategic discussions and decisions because that's how we add value. We can't do that if we're kept at arms' length in a more traditional supplier arrangement. Our clients need to see that their investment with us each year will improve their bottom line.

'As a company, we are now judging ourselves on the world stage. Our international push with our registry and our forensic programs will define us through the next 10 to 15 years. That's where we excel and it presents a massive opportunity.'

With this opportunity comes considerable risk, but Darren sees that as the hallmark of entrepreneurship as Promadis builds and dominates niche markets.

'Our dream has always been to own a market. For us, that means when a forensics or registry office in an obscure region somewhere around the world needs a new system, they think of Promadis. We don't expect to be a household name, but we do want to own the market.

'That has been our motivation in going overseas. We know we have world-class products and people, and that there are markets out there that we can own. That has given us the confidence to take on that risk and not see it as the gamble that others might view it as.'

This same confidence has enabled Promadis to boldly bid for and win projects without always knowing how to execute them at the time.

'People say "how are you going to do that?" and often we don't know; but we do have the confidence that we will develop a plan that works. That's not being blasé or bidding for work that we can't do – it's about avoiding analysis paralysis.

'We need to be nimble in business, especially when you're our size in a small city like Adelaide. You can't hit the world market and be staid and plan every step in great detail – you have to be confident you'll be able to do it when the time comes. That's how we've always been.'

Promadis doesn't operate under quotas, targets or hours billed. Instead, the company's staff are expected to carry out their daily work under five key company values – be brilliant; make it happen; crave integrity; grow relationships; and enjoy.

Underpinning these values is Darren's call-to-action philosophy: 'If nothing changes, nothing changes'.

All members of staff, whether a receptionist or the managing director, are expected to use the five values to measure the success of their daily tasks and their contribution to the company.

Darren developed the values while founding Promadis, driven by a desire to understand what 'makes' a company.

'I spent two days agonising over the question – what is a company? A company is not an individual, or the shareholders, or the board. People come and go; products change – it's not these things.

'I worked out that a company is defined by a set of values, and a business should stay true to these values no matter what changes may take place.'

On the topic of shareholders, Darren believes that owners who are also employed in a business must prove their value by fulfilling their day-to-day roles – otherwise they are anchors dragging the company down.

'Too many businesses are nowhere near as good as they should be because they have people who think that just because they are shareholders they have a right to hold all the most senior positions and not pull their weight.

'Shareholder or not, you should always fulfil your role properly. If you have to sweep the floors, sweep them. If you have to make decisions, make them. Do what your company relies on you to do – or get out of the way and let somebody else do it.

'You need to keep your role within the company and your roles as a shareholder or board member very separate. You also need to understand where your strengths lie and not be so proud that you can't own up to your weaknesses and appoint people who can do it better than you can.

'That's been another benefit out of our name change – the staff can see that no single person is more important than anyone else here and that everyone is valued equally. You don't need to have the surname Shaw to be a vital contributor to this company.'

Lessons Learnt:

* What's in a name? Plenty. Be cautious about naming the company after yourself as this can give the impression that the business is all about you.
* Benchmark yourself against the rest of the world; you may be surprised at the results.
* Being a shareholder doesn't relieve you of your responsibility for doing your job. Get on with it and carry out your roles within the business to the best of your ability.

Advice to Others:

* Own your market, or better still, create your market. Focus on niche sectors to make them your own.

Greg Siegele

Greg Siegele gave up a promising career as a lawyer and lived on bread and water for three years while trying to get his company, Ratbag, off the ground.

Ratbag has since become one of the world's leading computer and console games developers, but when the company was founded in 1994 it seemed the odds were against Greg and his business partner Richard Harrison.

Ratbag entered the games industry at a time of fierce competition. More than 2000 games products were being released each year worldwide and only about 100 of those broke even. The statistics were frightening.

Ratbag also faced the tyranny of distance. Game development is a high-risk endeavour and in the 1990s most publishers refused to invest in projects in Australia because the distance made monitoring extremely difficult.

As a start-up company, Ratbag also had significant capital requirements. It takes 15 to 30 people up to 24 months to develop a game, and the budgets for just one project can be up to $5 million. Established game developers could develop superior products more cheaply from their existing technology base.

Greg's company did have one thing in its favour, however, and that was timing. Up to the early 1990s, games for Sony, Playstation and Nintendo 64 used two-dimensional graphics. From 1994 – just as Ratbag was being launched – the industry moved to three-dimensional graphics, which meant everyone in the industry had to start from scratch developing 3D technology.

'The new technology cycle created the opportunity for us to enter the industry. Over the next three years we developed a 3D PC graphics engine that was the fastest in the industry, to the extent that it is still used today to benchmark new 3D graphics hardware all over the world.'

Greg's goal was to sell the rights to Ratbag's first game in advance and get the publisher to fund the $2 million cost of development. This was a considerable investment for a publisher to make in a project for a start-up with no track record.

In the end it took Greg nearly four years to attract Ratbag's first publishing deal.

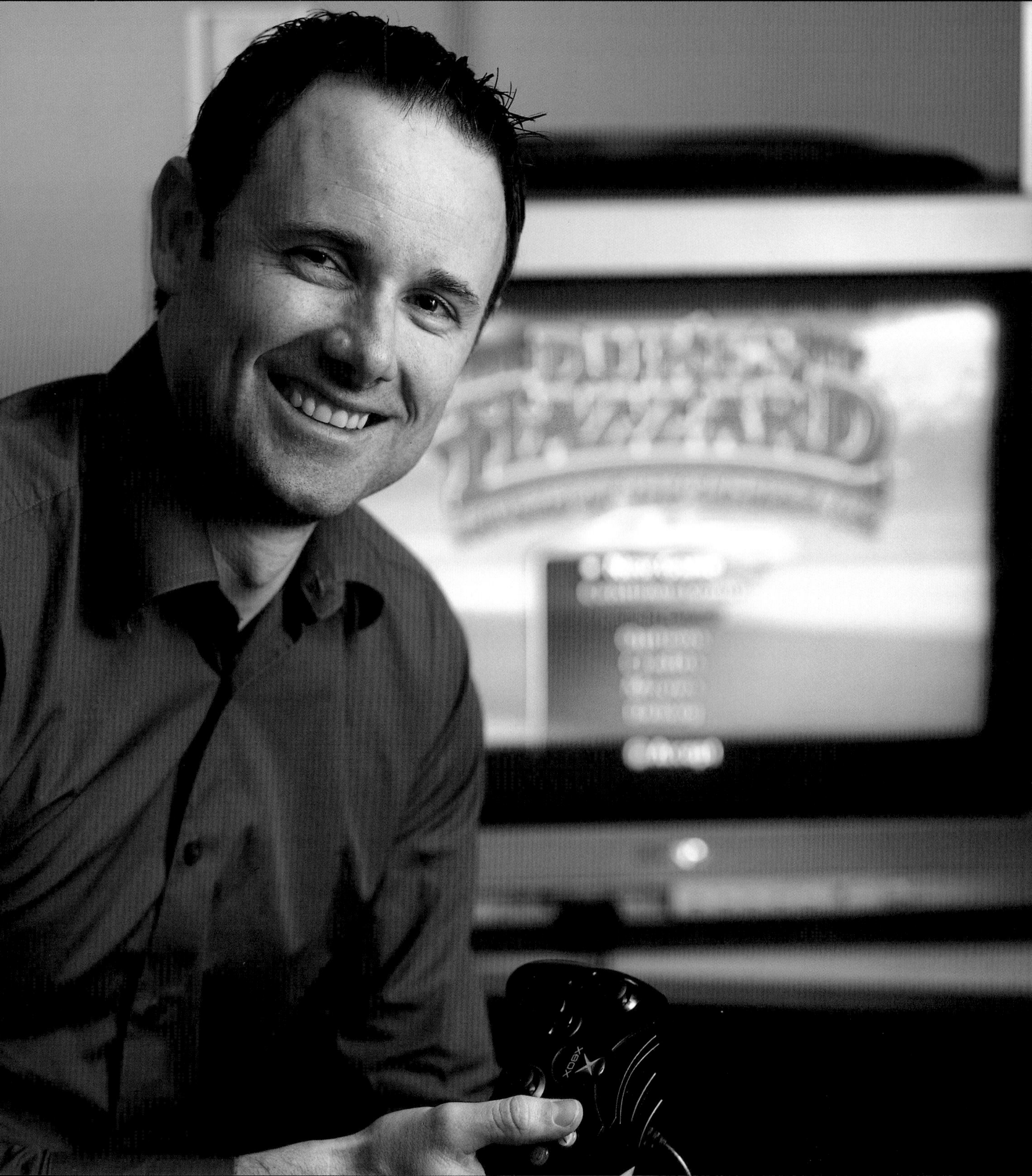

'Looking back on it now it was four years of failure – constant rejection. However, at the time we didn't see it that way. We had confidence we would succeed and we simply didn't give up.

'With each rejection we improved our technology, our content and our approach until finally the publishers could not refuse what they saw – a brilliant prototype of our first game, Powerslide, that would make them buckets of money.

'After they had all knocked us back for years, we eventually had an auction between eight of the world's top nine publishers.'

Powerslide was an instant success, pre-selling 180,000 units and being awarded PC Racing Game of the Year. Then, just as Greg and his team were getting ready to collect the royalty cheques, the games publisher went broke.

'They couldn't fulfil the orders so we never saw any royalties. Worse still, they pulled out of the second project we were developing for them without paying a cent for the six months of development we put into it.

'We were facing extinction just 12 months after we thought we had it made.'

Greg's team immediately scrambled together a design for a game they could build quickly and cheaply using their existing technology base.

'To stay alive, we cut our operating costs to nearly zero. We agreed on a deal with our 15 staff where they would work the next five months on $200 gross per week and in return receive a larger slice of the profits on this project.

We ploughed every cent we had into this game and I went out into the market and sold my butt off. Two months before we were due to run out of money we secured a publishing deal.

'We ploughed every cent we had into this game and I went out into the market and sold my butt off. Two months before we were due to run out of money we secured a publishing deal.'

That game, Dirt Track Racing, went on to become one of the best-selling PC racing games in history and established Ratbag as a serious game developer.

Ratbag has now released a total of five games, selling two million copies in more than 30 countries.

All up, Ratbag employs more than 65 development staff. Greg says Ratbag's enduring success is due largely to the loyalty and enthusiasm of its employees. As a result, he has focused strongly on creating the best possible work environment.

'One of the most impressive things about the people who work at Ratbag is their loyalty to the company and to each other. I suppose that comes from the company's loyalty to them. We employ really good people. They have a lot of respect for each other and they care for each other and we also want them to be the best at what they are doing.

'When you bring a bunch of people like that together and they all get caught up in the excitement of where they are going together, that creates a very strong team.

'We maintain a relaxed and creative atmosphere in the office. The focus is on each team and each individual's results. Staff can wear anything they like to work, and arrive and leave as they want. Teams and individuals have an enormous amount of autonomy, which I believe is essential in a creative business.

'We also play a lot. We have massive multi-player games sessions at work on Tuesday nights. Then there's paintball and go-kart racing, rock climbing and all manner of activities each month on a Friday afternoon.

'The passion that our people have for their work and Ratbag is such that you will always find people in the office after midnight. Many of them would rather be at work than do anything else.'

Unlike many of his competitors, Greg recognises that Ratbag has two types of customers – publishers to whom Ratbag sells the games, and consumers who buy the games.

Most developers focus solely on making games, but Ratbag has its own Marketing and Public Relations Department to maximise sales and promote the Ratbag brand.

Ratbag simultaneously releases its games globally in five languages. This boosts sales opportunities while also reducing piracy by providing direct support to markets in Europe.

Ratbag's other innovative marketing initiatives include:

* Polling customers on-line for feedback on Ratbag's products, then incorporating the results into future games.
* Involvement at a grass roots level so the company understands the intricacies of a particular motor sport. As a result, Ratbag is renowned for creating the most authentic and in-depth motor sport simulations.
* Merchandise. A variety of Ratbag paraphernalia is available for fans – and Ratbag has quite a following in the US. When the company's presence is announced at a racetrack, fans queue up for autographs.
* A consumer website with 10,000 members.
* Ratbag is also the first company to exploit virtual advertising in games, receiving $100,000 to $200,000 in advertising revenues per game.

Recruitment has been one of Ratbag's challenges. Greg says finding experienced game developers in Adelaide has been difficult, so the company brings people in from interstate and, more often, overseas.

'We employ one international for every two locals. We have people at Ratbag who come from England, Scotland, Slovakia, New York, Canada – all over the place.

'That's had a strong effect on the employees we have from Adelaide. When we first started the company everybody was young. Like a lot of people they thought they should be living somewhere else, in a bigger city or overseas.

'But when the internationals started joining us and started telling our locals just how great Adelaide was, people started seeing it from a different perspective. Now everybody who works in our office is very proud to be based in Adelaide and they don't think about going elsewhere.'

Mentors are important for Greg. He says his ability to learn from other people has been critical for Ratbag.

'I actually never worked in a business before. I went through university, practised law for a couple of years and then started Ratbag, so I didn't really know anything about running a business.

'I have had to learn on the job and the best way to do that is from other people who have done it before and who know what they are doing. My appetite for learning from other people has been voracious.

'As Ratbag grows and develops through new stages, I am finding new people who have been through that experience and try to learn from them.'

Lessons Learnt:

* Growth can be difficult. Ratbag nearly went broke going from a small business to a medium-sized company. The implementation of management systems and controls helped put the company back on track.
* Morale and energy is vital in a creative company. Foster open discussions with your team so they know where the company is heading and can be involved and informed throughout the journey.
* Don't be afraid to ask for help. Collaboration with other companies has been important for Ratbag's success. You'd be surprised how helpful most people can be if you just ask.

Advice to Others:

* Find people who have done it before and learn from them – even if it means calls overseas to others in your industry. You'd be surprised how willing people are to share information.

Philip Speakman

It's hard to imagine any individual has had as much influence over South Australia's employment market as Philip Speakman.

In 1986, Philip founded the company that would become South Australia's largest specialist human resource and general management consultancy, Philip Speakman & Associates.

During Philip's involvement the company was directly responsible for the employment or contracting of more than 55,000 people. That's about 13 per cent of the job market in South Australia.

That figure doesn't include the several thousand employees Philip's firm trained to improve their skill base, creating management and efficiency benefits amounting to millions of dollars for local companies.

At one stage the firm contracted more than 2500 people each day to businesses state-wide.

'When you think that you have had that sort of effect on so many lives, so many households and so many families, it's a very humbling experience. It's only being able to stand back at the end of my time with the firm and look back on it that I can start seeing it in some perspective.'

Until the early 1980s all-encompassing recruitment firms were almost non-existent. Most South Australian companies conducted their recruitment and training in-house.

With the outsourcing revolution of the late 1980s and early 1990s, Philip's firm – renamed Speakman Stillwell & Associates after he joined forces with Adelaide psychologist Daryl Stillwell – grew through careful expansion into key areas ranging from executive recruitment and training through to psychological appraisal and career guidance, call centre recruitment and labour hire recruitment.

The firm became a human resource powerhouse, pioneering the industry's development in South Australia.

'The sector went from a cottage industry into a corporate industry – largely driven by our firm,' says Philip, who grew the firm 'from scratch' to the point where it had $100 million turnover and more than 150 employees.

Then, in true entrepreneurial fashion, he created his own exit strategy and sold the business – with impeccable timing – to international recruitment giant Select Appointments (Holdings) Plc.

'Part of our strategy was to take a great business model, hone it locally and take it global. We were very successful in doing that. The Select Group has now incorporated many of our business practices into its activities throughout the world, making the entire group stronger as a result.

'We also wanted to create an exit from the business.'

Philip always knew that his eventual goal would be to sell out of the company.

'I've been to Harvard Business School twice and they drill into you that a business is nothing more than a vehicle to maximise your wealth creation and your spiritual fulfilment. There comes a point that you have to exit the business to lock in the benefits that you have achieved.

'Your relationship with your business should not be a cradle-to-grave relationship. It should be a cradle-to-opportunity relationship.

It's never been about the money. You have to love what you do. Some people never get to that point. It makes you wonder how they drag themselves out of bed in the morning.

'That's why you see entrepreneurs like the Packers and Murdochs constantly selling businesses and buying into new ones.

'I would sound a warning to all business owners that nothing lasts forever. There is a saying that all businesses are born to die. You have to pick the top of the bell-shaped curve and get out while the business is booming.'

By the late 1990s Philip could see that the Adelaide recruitment market was becoming over-supplied, with numerous firms providing similar services. Ironically, many of Philip's eventual competitors came from his own ranks, leaving to compete against their old employer.

'We ended up spawning most of the industry in Adelaide and they were starting to cannibalise us. I could see that the same thing had happened in the legal profession and real estate, which are much older service industries than recruitment but which still mirrored us in many ways.

'All this competition came at a time when South Australia was losing major corporations. That meant our market was in danger of shrinking. I use the example of too many seagulls and not enough chips on the beach.

'It meant that all these human resource firms were competing and they were surviving but their margins were going down and the work was getting harder and sparser.'

By 1998 Philip could see that the time was right to orchestrate an exit. But how? Despite Speakman Stillwell's size in Adelaide it had no eastern states operations and as a result was not even on the radar of any potential purchaser.

'I worked out that it would probably require 18 months to two years to sort out an exit strategy.

'First, I had to identify potential purchasers, so I thought "let's think big". I jumped on the internet to work out the 10 biggest recruitment companies by their billings.

'Second, I put together a prospectus on how good the company was and I mailed it to all those companies with a map showing our access to Asia and emphasising that if we could do this in little old Adelaide, imagine what we could do when linked with Sydney, Melbourne and the rest of the world.

'Third, there was a very large recruitment personnel convention in Orlando, Florida, and about 80 per cent of the industry was going. I bit the bullet and contacted the 10 companies and said I would be in Florida for the convention and if you're interested I'd be happy to meet with you.'

Philip remembers it as one of the strangest experiences of his life. By day, he would meet individually with CEOs of the world's largest recruitment firms before or after the convention events. Then, during the evening cocktail events they would all totally ignore him, so none of their competitors knew they were in discussion.

'It was very odd. During the day we were best mates and at night they walked straight past me and wouldn't even acknowledge that I existed. Welcome to the international world of big business!'

These initial discussions sparked negotiations with two major groups, with Select Appointments ultimately offering the best terms and purchasing Speakman Stillwell.

Philip sold down part of his shareholding and was asked to continue with the new company while Daryl used the opportunity to exit altogether. The company's name was changed to Speakman & Associates.

'Really, the timing was perfect. The recruitment industry was still in a boom time and the international players were all cashed up with buckets of money to purchase companies like ours. The Australian dollar at the time was quite low, making us even more attractive.'

Philip stayed on as Chief Executive of the Adelaide operations for a little over five years, building up the company's operations even further and thereby maximising his final earn-out payment.

In August 2001, Select Appointments and Speakman & Associates announced the merger of their Australian and New Zealand operations, forming Select Australasia.

In 2002, Philip played a pivotal role in the Select Group's acquisition of executive recruitment firm Tanner Menzies, thereby completing his major goal of forming a truly national operation in executive recruitment.

With these tasks completed, in mid-2003 Philip finally decided that the time was right to sell his remaining equity in Speakman & Associates.

'We had achieved the maximum growth we could in Adelaide so the challenge had largely gone for me. Also, the industry had changed. I had been a pioneer in the industry during this tremendous period of growth, and I didn't really want to be pioneering its slide down the other side.'

Philip Speakman's advice to any business owner is typically blunt: 'Don't believe your own press.'

'Your success is only for a short period of time because we are now in global markets where things are growing so quickly that what's a good business today could be in mothballs in three or four years.

'Keep looking at your business and ways you grow it and add value. Don't stay the same. If you feel that you have reached the stage that you can't change or improve, then get out as quickly as you can.

'It's hard because when people start a business they are totally in love with it and it becomes their baby. They are reluctant to let it go.

'But a lot of people hang on for too long and then they reach the point where they have got a business that they can't sell. Remember that song by Kenny Rogers, "The Gambler" – you've gotta know when to hold them and when to fold them. That's what it's all about.'

Philip's impeccable timing has given him the choice of early retirement and not ever having to work again – but he still misses the cut and thrust of running his own business.

'It's never been about the money. Somewhere along the line you have to enjoy what you do. More than that, you have to love what you do. Some people never get to that point. It makes you wonder how they drag themselves out of bed in the morning.'

Lessons Learnt:

* Don't assume that a potential purchaser for your business knows you exist. Do something to get on their radar and convince them you are a business they need to buy.
* If you get to the point that you can't improve, change or add value to your business, that's a good signal that it's time to sell out and try another challenge.

Advice to Others:

* Have an exit strategy for your business – and make sure you sell it before the market turns against you.

Ulli and Helmut Spranz

'Build it and they will come' is not just a line from the movie *Field of Dreams* – for Ulli and Helmut Spranz it is a valid business philosophy that they have used to create one of Australia's largest bio-dynamic dairy products companies.

In fact, Ulli says she has had little choice but to take a 'softly, softly' approach to marketing the company and its products.

That's because until Ulli and Helmut began their company, B.-d. Farm Paris Creek, biodynamic farming and biodynamic food products were little known or understood in Australia.

The couple migrated to Australia from Germany in 1988 to fulfil their lifelong dream of establishing a farm that used no chemical fertilisers, insecticides, herbicides or fungicides on the property and nothing artificial to boost cattle growth or milk production. Such farms were commonplace in Germany, but almost unheard of in Australia at the time.

Ulli and Helmut spent a year travelling Australia before chancing upon 66 hectares of land at Paris Creek, about an hour's drive south of Adelaide.

'We had seen a movie called *Paris, Texas* and it was about somebody following his dream of having a little piece of land somewhere. It was a touching movie so when we saw the sign that said "Paris Creek" we felt drawn to turn off the road and have a look.

'A few weeks later we had settled on the contract to buy this property. It was a quick decision but well thought through because everything just sounded and felt right. The soil was good. There was plenty of good water available through bores. Good schools for our children were reasonably close. Adelaide was not far away, which was important logistically for our future plans. It was hilly, which reminded us of our home in Germany, and the sea was nearby, which was an extra bonus.

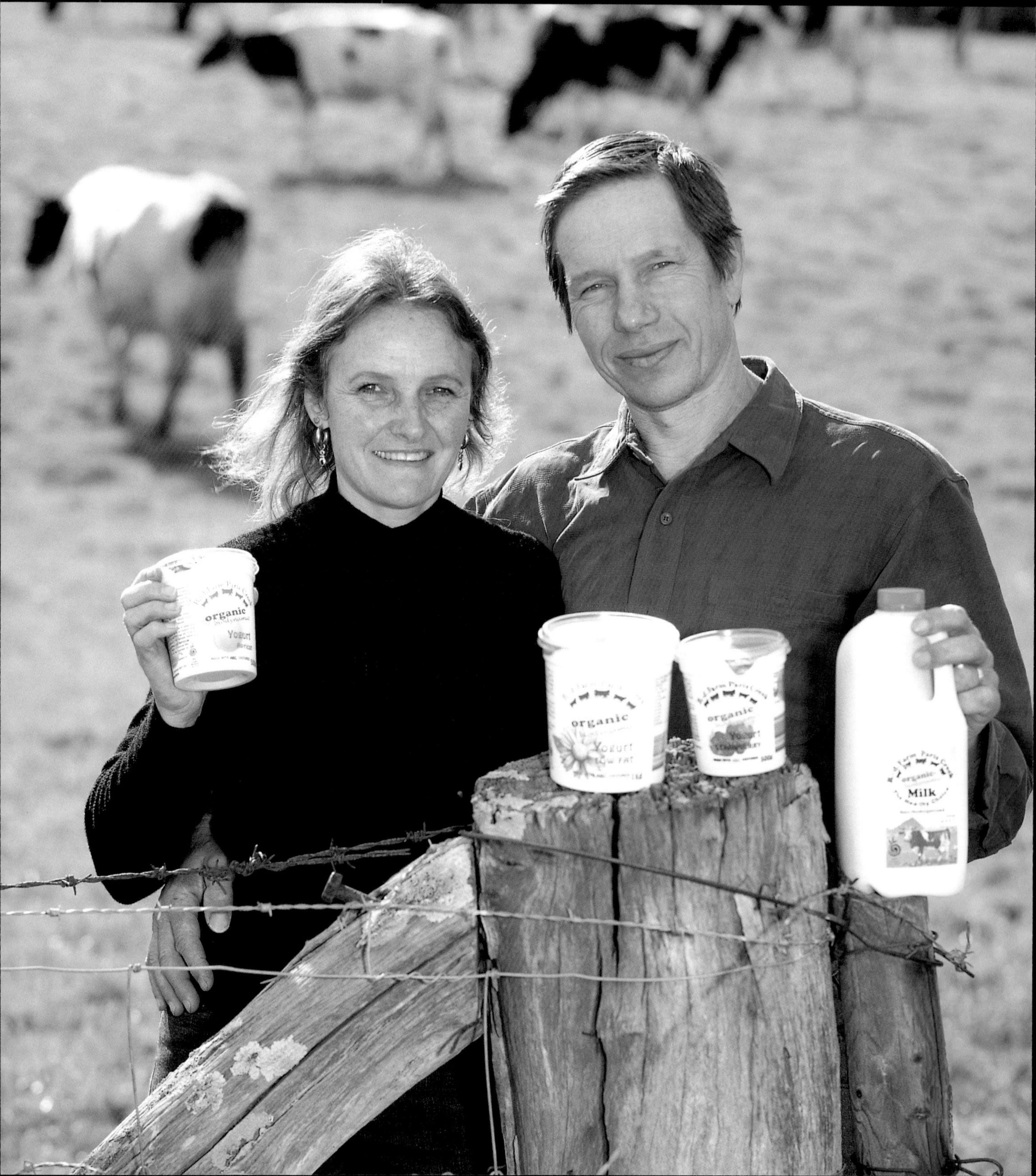
organic
Yogurt
organic
Yogurt
LOW FAT
organic
Yogurt
Milk

'Most of all we were fascinated by Adelaide, a very active city without being stressfully busy, and we could see a potential for future development there because of the variety of different cultures living in Adelaide and the Hills.'

Ulli and Helmut were in luck. The previous owners of the land had not used chemicals and the conversion to biodynamic farming was relatively easy, apart from the weed infestation which they had to deal with.

Biodynamic farming also avoids preventative drenching, antibiotics, hormones or genetically modified feed for the cattle. The health of the herd is maintained by close observation, well-balanced feeding techniques, herbal and mineral-based supplements, and – if needed – homeopathic remedies.

Soon Ulli and Helmut were providing their friends and neighbours with biodynamic fresh milk and demand grew rapidly. Before long they were also selling their milk and cream to top restaurants around Adelaide.

Then, to use the skim milk left over after the cream was removed, Ulli and Helmut began producing quark, a nutritious dairy product common in middle Europe. By now the company had well and truly outgrown the confines of the first little production area and they formed a company which they called B.-d. Farm Paris Creek after the location and the farm.

Ulli used her skills as a graphic designer to create a range of eye-catching packaging and a new Australian dairy category was born.

In 1994, Ulli and Helmut launched their yogurt range. It was an immediate success and sales spread quickly to all Australian mainland states.

As more supermarkets moved to stock the products it became obvious that a new processing plant was required and a state-of-the-art facility was built in 2001.

If the basic idea is good then people will see that and your idea will be successful.

Ulli admits that marketing throughout much of the company's growth has been by osmosis – but this has been a planned approach. Rather than embark on expensive advertising campaigns, B.-d. Farm Paris Creek has let the products sell themselves through their unique flavours and health benefits.

Along the way, Ulli has helped change the eating habits of thousands of Australians, but she has let them make the decision to shift to her products based on word-of-mouth referral.

It has been the same with neighbouring farmers, many of whom have now chosen to become biodynamically certified and supply B.-d. Farm Paris Creek with their milk and cream.

'We believe that education is best done by setting a good example, and so we did not try to convince people. If we had gone around and told farmers "this is what you should do", they would not have paid attention because biodynamic practices could sound a bit odd.

'One part of biodynamic farming involves burying cow manure in cow horns, which later is unearthed and the fertile content is used to improve the soil. If we had told people that in the early days they would have said we were crazy, but seeing how much our soil had improved and how well we were doing made the whole difference.

'Gradually farmers came to us to ask what we were doing because they could see that biodynamic farming was working here, that the cows were extremely healthy and the grass was greener – and they wanted to know why. We were happy to support them to achieve the same results.

'It's very similar with the marketing of the product. Initially people who tasted our product said: "This milk tastes so sweet and good, can we buy it from you", so we were delivering it to parents at the school. Five bottles became 10, and then 20, and then the shops approached us to stock the products and then the restaurants wanted the products. That's how it evolved. It looks like it accidentally happened, but in fact it was very well planned.'

B.-d. Farm Paris Creek now uses about 30,000 litres of milk each week. Its extremely popular milk, yogurt and quark ranges are available in health food shops nationally, in Coles and Woolworths in various states, in all Foodland stores in South Australia, and are also exported.

Ulli's purist production philosophy may be a marketing advantage but she admits it can make things difficult in a large-scale manufacturing and supply environment.

'Selling products through the large supermarket chains means a commitment to continuously high-quality standards, as well as ensuring that any quantity which is ordered can be delivered. That means that if the consumer trend goes towards raspberry flavour we need to increase our raspberry order – but there is a good chance that there may not be enough certified organic or biodynamic raspberries available in Australia.

'How would it be if we would say "sorry the growers have had a bad year". We can't. In this case we source our fruit from reliable suppliers overseas and we are lucky to have built a good relation-ship with suppliers who are willing to fill holes.'

Ulli smiles when asked about the name B-.d. Farm Paris Creek. She knows it's a mouthful and admits that many people cannot remember the wording in order.

'It actually means biodynamic farm at Paris Creek and when we came here, and thought of a name for this place, it sounded logical. At this time our English was not good enough for us to be able to pick the difficulty.'

Interestingly, though, it has become a marketing advantage. Ulli says the name is so distinctive that it has become a strong brand in its own right. It's 'that name that no one can remember properly', so it stands out – and as a result there are no plans to change it.

Ulli likens the gradual growth of B.-d. Farm Paris Creek and the popularity of its products to the overall philosophy of biodynamics.

'You nurture and stimulate the micro-organism in the soil, so that all the nutrients the plants need are readily available. If the basic idea is good then people will see that and your idea will be successful.

'I think our products stand out because they are different. People understand why they are different and that's OK for them. For instance, our yogurt is thinner than other commercial yogurts and I suppose that may not be to everyone's liking. But I think people know that it's a clean product without thickeners and other unnecessary ingredients and consumers trust us for our honesty in production. We keep that trust by never compromising the product.

'For instance, we use certified real vanilla bean and all our ingredients are certified organic or biodynamic. Other producers ask us: "Why do you do it that way?" They see us spend $500 on a kilogram of vanilla beans to flavour our yogurt and say that they can get the same flavour from vanilla essence that costs them $50.

'We believe that if you want to produce a healthy and real product and you are backing up that promise 100 per cent then you will find a way to spend that $500 for pure vanilla or for any other certified ingredient rather than take the $50 solution. It's as simple as that.'

Lessons Learnt:

* Make sure you are in a business that you love.
* Promoting your product does not always have to involve huge marketing budgets. If the products are good, word-of-mouth advertising is the best kind of promotion – and it doesn't cost much.
* Don't compromise your standards on the basis of cost – otherwise you risk losing the trust of your customer.

Advice to Others:

* Don't lose sight of what you want to achieve. Just go straight for it. If you think and feel that it's right and you can see that there's a future for what you are doing then don't divert from that path.

Peter Teakle

Peter Teakle is from the 'build a better mousetrap' school of entrepreneurship.

Back in the mid-1980s when his specialist wine label company Collotype Labels was trying to break into the broader Australian market, Peter needed a point of difference to differentiate him from 1400 other printing firms jostling for contracts with the country's largest winemakers.

At the time a big problem for wine companies was the scuffing of bottle labels during transport. After bouncing around in their cartons for days or sometimes weeks, the bottles were often badly scarred when they reached the retail outlet – a marketer's nightmare and a huge visual deterrent to the wine-drinking customer.

So Peter Teakle set about finding a solution.

'I sat in the back of a truck for a whole night watching bottles in their cartons, to see how they got scuffed. I worked out that one bottle of wine turned a full circle about every 60 kilometres on the back of a truck. I just sat there and watched these bottles turn while I was huddling under this truckie's tarpaulin. That's how I worked out why the labels were scuffing up in the carton.

'Then we set to work and came up with a label varnish that was pretty much bulletproof. This varnish was so good that it meant the wine company could take the cardboard separators out of the wine carton.

'That was an immediate cost saving of 50 cents – which was more than the cost of the new labels. I was able to go to the wine companies and say: "This is the price for the labels – but by the way, you can save more than that by taking away the separators in the carton."

'We were the first company in the world to do that. It gave us national dominance in labels for the wine and spirit industry.'

Collotype was founded in 1903 as a small print shop in suburban Adelaide. Today, with 350 staff globally and a $97 million turnover, Collotype is the world's most awarded label printer and the leading printer of premium wet glue and self-adhesive labels, with a specialist wine industry focus.

In its early days Collotype printed mainly fine art, ranging from tourism brochures and one-off promotional leaflets through to nostalgic prints of cricketing icon Sir Donald Bradman. It was quality work but only involved small print runs, so business was patchy.

In the 1930s, after Peter's grandfather Gilbert had purchased Collotype from its founder, the South Australian-based Angove winemaking family commissioned the company to print labels for its famous St Agnes Brandy. Now the print runs were in the hundreds of thousands, and orders were regular. This gave Collotype a new and more lucrative focus.

More than 70 years later, Collotype is still printing St Agnes Brandy labels for the Angove family – its longest contract and a lasting testimonial to the group's customer relations.

By the time Peter Teakle purchased the business in 1986, Collotype had clinched major label printing deals with most key South Australian wine companies and some interstate signature brands such as Houghton's in Western Australia.

But the eastern states market – then home to some of the largest Australian wine groups – was proving a tough nut to crack. After all, why should they divert business to a South Australian label printer when there were already hundreds of printing firms virtually on their doorstep?

The breakthrough was Peter's 'bulletproof' varnish, which spearheaded a major expansion of Collotype's activity nationally and subsequently internationally.

'Since then our research and development team has been dominant in responding to customer requests but also to coming up with our own innovations – ideas that add significant value to our customers and make us an indispensable part of their marketing mix.'

Innovations include Collotype's 'Wine Find' label which lets wine drinkers tear off part of the back label and pop it in their pocket, reminding them of a wine they liked when they next visit their bottle shop. Another initiative is the introduction of a label infused with DNA from the vine to provide proof-of-content for high-quality wines.

Collotype's approach is to 'go the extra mile' for its wine company clients by helping them to build their businesses, not just Collotype's.

'Instead of just dumping the labels in the foyer and walking away, we want to make sure they run well in the bottling line. I've often said that my father was involved in the printing industry, but I am in the wine industry.

'We have showed superiority because we have a passion for our product and we know the wine and spirit industry. We know bottling lines and that can benefit our customer.'

Collotype goes to extraordinary lengths to prove its product – even to the extent of hiring university students in major cities around the world to take digital photographs of wine bottles on supermarket and bottle shop shelves. Collotype can then demonstrate to customers the durability of its labels – and often how badly another company's labels have fared in shipping.

'We accept consequential loss with our product. If our product doesn't perform down the bottling line or its gets scuffed on the way to Chicago, we accept that. That's about putting your money where your mouth is.'

Peter is renowned among his customers for always having 'something up his sleeve' to help them improve their own business efficiencies. In one instance, Collotype worked out how some customers could each save about $300,000 a year on bottling line downtime. Other initiatives such as ice bucket performance, where the label can withstand four hours in an ice bucket, continue to reinforce Collotype's reputation for being one step ahead.

'No problem can withstand the constant assault of thought.'

These days, however, the window of competitive advantage is becoming much smaller – and Collotype must remain ever more nimble to remain ahead of its rivals.

'We use technology as a competitive advantage. But because technology is speeding up that advantage may be short-lived, so all the time you have to have your team checking the marketplace to find the next major advantage.

'In my grandfather's and father's time, because they developed embossing and hot foil stamping, these were competitive advantages that lasted for 10 years. Now we're looking at maybe 10 months before someone is able to copy your initiative.'

So, while technology may be one of the keys to Collotype's success, Peter says people are the real driving force behind the company.

'People are your competitive advantage. We get the right people and we train them in life skills. What we're looking for is a character and an attitude at Collotype. We get involved with kids in Year 12, before they leave school – and it's not an apprenticeship in printing, it's an apprenticeship in lifestyle.

'We have a lot of second generation employees here, so it's certainly a family business but not just by ownership.'

Collotype runs a ground-breaking employee program called Collo-Care – and its logo is a handshake.

'It's an all-encompassing cultural thing. To be able to really service a customer you've got to have people with the right character and attitude. The Collo-Care program encompasses that. We are so much more interested in character and integrity.

'It took me a long time to learn that you hire people on their credentials and you generally sack them on their character. So we turned our job interview program around and now we base it on character. It's about ethics and integrity – doing the right thing.'

There is no greater thrill than helping people make things happen. When you can take a young person and build their character and give them some life skills, haven't you really achieved something?

A few years ago Peter sold 49 per cent of the business to management and he now takes a more strategic overview of the company while enjoying the fruits of his years in business. He enjoys driving paddle steamers on the River Murray and spending time on his Akuna Station property near Waikerie, where he has developed his own vineyard and wetlands.

His over-riding interest is in making a positive difference to those involved in the Collotype 'family'.

'There is no greater thrill than helping people make things happen. When you can take a young person and build their character and give them some life skills, haven't you really achieved something? To me, that's creating wealth – and it's got nothing to do with anybody's bank balance.

'I remember fishing with my dad. He caught a salmon and handed it over to me and handed me the fishing line. I caught one and went to hand the fishing line back. He said: "No, I've caught one. I get more fun out of watching you catch it." I reckon I operate that way in my business and life.'

Peter believes that entrepreneurship is a state of mind.

'You have to have confidence and faith in yourself and your ideas – and success rarely eventuates without some risk-taking along the way.'

Now Collotype is targeting the US market, with expectations the group will double in size within eight years.

Not bad for a company whose fortunes were founded on Peter Teakle's one cold night in the back of a delivery truck.

Lessons Learnt:

* If you're not on the edge, you're taking up too much room. Take risks as you build your business.
* Patience and determination. One cold night in the back of a truck turned Collotype's fortunes around, but Peter Teakle could just as easily have stayed home in front of the fire.
* Create a positive corporate culture. To service customers well you have to have staff with the right character and attitude.

Advice to Others:

* Integrity is everything. Do the right thing by your people and your clients.

Anthony Toop

Innovation, innovation, innovation – rather than the old maxim of location, location, location – has been the key to Anthony Toop's real estate success.

In fact, it was a desire to do things significantly differently that prompted Anthony to establish Toop & Toop with wife Sylvia in 1985.

Believing there was a better way to run a real estate agency after 10 years working in the industry throughout metropolitan Adelaide, Anthony and Sylvia sold an investment property and used the $20,000 proceeds to start the business.

It was a big risk at the time, but Anthony believed he could offer the market a better service.

From the outset, Anthony's goal was not only to create a great individual business, but to become a global leader in real estate best practice, influencing the industry as a whole.

'It was instinctive to me that this was the right thing to be doing. I wanted to go down in history as changing the way the industry operates.

'To me, business success is a moving target. It's doing things that have not been done before. It's about being the best, but not necessarily the biggest, and trying out new ideas.

'I have always been passionate about real estate, as well as what Toop & Toop could achieve and contribute to the bigger picture.'

As a result, Toop & Toop has become an industry-leading real estate agency in South Australia and is recognised as one of the most innovative nationally.

Many of the initiatives that Anthony spearheaded are now considered standard industry practice. These include virtual inspections; internet and SMS-based marketing systems; free loan furniture and professional presentation; secure inspections; floodlit and pictorial display boards; a weekly property magazine; auction price guides; and colour press advertisements.

Toop & Toop was the first residential real estate company to achieve ISO9002 accreditation, has won a swag of national customer service awards and has been named Telstra South Australian Small Business of the Year.

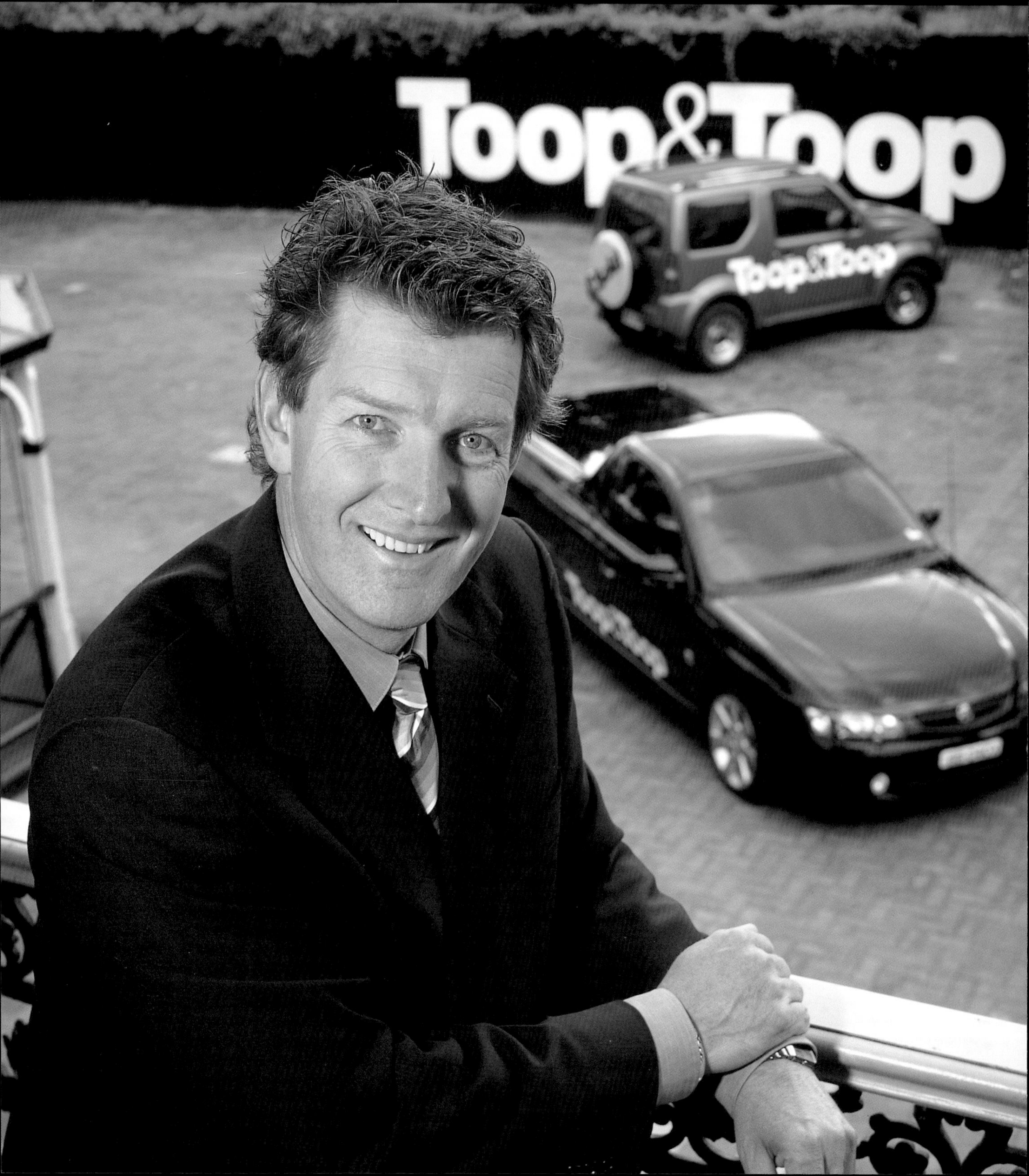
Toop&Toop
Toop&Toop

Anthony has actively and enthusiastically studied real estate best practice around the world. In the mid-1990s he visited the US and went to Orange County, a region experiencing a significant financial downturn, to learn about the initiatives real estate firms there were adopting in order to survive in such difficult times.

He has since made several more trips to the US, particularly focusing on Orange County (a relatively poor area) and Silicon Valley (a very wealthy part of California), to make comparisons on how the industry is run.

If it were not for our passion to be the best and drive change, we would not have achieved the success that we have. It's what pushes you through the pain barrier that you come up against time after time.

In those early days Anthony also got the chance to research best industry practice in Australia when a friend in Melbourne asked for assistance in selling his house. Anthony went to Melbourne and acted as a consultant, picking and interviewing 10 of the best real estate agents in the city at that time and learning everything that he could from them.

In subsequent years reconnaissance trips were also made to Perth and Sydney to study the practices and philosophies of the leading agents.

Now, agents from all over the world come to Adelaide to study the way Anthony does business and he is invited to speak at numerous industry conferences interstate and overseas.

Despite his obvious success, Anthony continues to look for ways to innovate, recognising this is imperative if Toop & Toop is to retain and grow its position as a market leader.

Rather than focusing just on other real estate firms, Anthony benchmarks the company against other innovative organisations in a wide variety of industries around the world. Regular overseas trips help him to keep abreast of the latest ideas, initiatives and technologies from other sectors that can be introduced into his business.

Anthony prefers the introduction of initiatives that continually reinforce Toop & Toop's position as 'the best'. He believes that if great ideas are best practice and properly applied, then the financial rewards will follow.

Company innovations in recent years have been driven by Anthony's awareness of the advancement of technology – including the maturing of the web, common use of SMS messaging and the proliferation of mobile phone users and electronic diaries – and the role it can play in assisting in marketing and selling properties.

'To continue to be successful in the future, real estate agents will have to look carefully at their business model. Costs are rising and margins are being squeezed. Future success will be about blending technology with existing personal skills to provide the very best customer service.

'But as with all types of innovation, measuring the success of technology is two-fold. You have to have the commitment to trust and believe in a new idea, but you also have to recognise when a new idea is not working and move on.

'Our reputation for customer service is unrivalled in the marketplace, so it is critical that we remain client focused and make long-term decisions that only enhance the reputation and quality of the service we offer.

'Being financially sound ensures that our vision of being the industry's best is not compromised by short-term monetary considerations. The development of new services and being the first in the market is often expensive.'

Toop & Toop handles annual property sales topping $600 million through its offices in Norwood, Glenelg, Golden Grove and Stirling.

However, achieving and sustaining a sound balance sheet can be difficult in a cyclical industry such as real estate, and with the general state of the Australian economy heavily impacting on the housing market and consumer confidence.

The company's 'buffers' against these unpredictable elements are its culture and its ability to service its clients well, with Anthony recognising the importance of nurturing consumer confidence and reliability in Toop & Toop's people, sales approach and results.

The organisation's culture is built on a strong work ethic and high expectations, with both staff and clients judged against a desirability and performance criteria.

'Quality people are attracted to our culture of innovation, but for many – both potential employees and clients – the constant change that comes from innovation can be intimidating.

'In everything we do we highlight to people the benefits that come from innovation, while ensuring that we are consistent and that we deliver on our commitments. That helps people to feel comfortable with the new initiatives that we are introducing, but it can take time.

'Our emphasis is on attracting and retaining desirable people who contribute to the team, and assisting these staff to achieve high performance. The fundamental characteristics need to be there from the outset though – you can't change people to make them more "desirable".'

Anthony foresees that with the use of technology people will be able to sell their properties within a few days if they are prepared to accept market price. While Anthony has developed and patented methods to instantly match buyer needs to property, he says that emotionally home sellers don't want a sale to look 'too easy' for the agent, as they associate the 'ease' with selling too cheaply.

To help overcome this barrier and achieve a shorter sales cycle, Anthony is also focusing on educating vendors about their expectations and their perception of real estate house prices.

'Today's expectations and needs were yesterday's innovations. The pace of change has increased – only the best operators are surviving and only the exceptional are growing.

'There are still a huge range of opportunities out there for us and for the industry as a whole, but we need to be open to them.

'I rely a lot on my intuition when developing new ideas – it's absolutely essential for our success as it helps us to create our vision. The vision becomes a plan, and the plan generates actions. Business coaching with The Executive Connection (TEC) has played a critical role as the business has grown.

'I think modern entrepreneurs have an entirely realistic view of the world but they see it through the eyes of the future. An entrepreneur is a visionary who has enormous passion for what they do.

'Passion and innovation are so closely linked – without passion we would have abandoned innovation long ago. On the flipside, without innovation, I would have lost the passion for what I do.

'The cost and pain of developing new products provides little return in the short or medium-term. If it were not for our passion to be the best and drive change, we would not have achieved the success that we have. It's what pushes you through the pain barrier that you come up against time after time.

'There's no doubt that it's far easier to emulate – but that's just not my style.'

Lessons Learnt:

* Always be prepared to try out new ideas and initiatives. If they don't work, start afresh and try something else.
* In order to be market driven you need to be receptive towards what is actually happening in the market. Be driven by the needs of customers and listen to what they want.
* Technology can provide your business with an edge, but it needs to be carefully blended with customer service to create greater efficiencies and service differentiation. Ensure you remain client-focused and don't introduce technology for technology's sake.

Advice to Others:

* Be passionate not only about your own business, but also about the industry in which you operate. Display passion in everything that you do and in your dealings with staff and clients and highlight the benefits of your innovations.

Sam Tucker

Run, run as fast as you can – but you'd be hard pressed to catch Sam Tucker in gingerbread sales.

Sam's company The Great Australian Gingerbread Company (TGAG) has about 90 per cent of the Australian market for character gingerbreads sold through retail stores.

It's a very different company to the struggling enterprise he bought in 1997 at the age of 22. At the time the Gingerbread Company was suffering heavy losses, but Sam – then operations manager for another bakery – recognised its potential, borrowed some money from his family, and bought into the wonderful world of novelty biscuits.

Within two years the company was making a profit. From a turnover of $160,000 when he bought it, the Gingerbread Company now has a turnover heading towards $2 million and dominates its sector nationally.

Sam's success has not been easy. The business came with baggage. His purchase locked him into some costly licensing and supply arrangements. Product was being supplied to retailers on a sale-or-return basis, with the Gingerbread Company having to wear all the costs of damaged product.

Hefty licence fees – including the right to manufacture biscuits shaped like characters from the popular TV show *The Simpsons* (Sam's biggest selling line at the time) – added to the firm's financial woes.

Point-of-sale merchandising was too expensive and distribution was a mess. Basically, the Gingerbread Company was unprofitable and Sam had to change things fast.

First, he let the expensive character licences lapse and began making a range of non-licensed gingerbread figures featuring new designs that quickly gained strong market acceptance. Meanwhile, he restructured the sales operation and found new and more energetic distributors in each state.

Sam was also able to secure a major supply agreement to Coles supermarkets, giving the products new markets and massive exposure to consumers.

By late 1999 the company was also experiencing supply and quality issues through its existing gingerbread suppliers. Manufacturing at the time was outsourced but Sam made the decision to bring baking in-house.

It was an expensive move requiring hundreds of thousands of dollars to be spent on machinery and premises. It did however enable Sam to improve the reliability of gingerbread supply and boost the quality of his product, once again lifting his sales as he won new contracts.

Also in 1999 Sam struck a deal with national distributor Food Service Solutions (FSS) to distribute his company's products. This provided the Gingerbread Company with truly national distribution for the first time, resulting in rapid sales growth and finally pulling the company into profitability.

But more challenges were around the corner. In 2001 FSS was in financial strife. Not wanting to lose his linchpin gingerbread distribution network and sensing an opportunity to expand his business horizons, Sam bought the struggling distributor.

It meant taking on significantly more debt but the acquisition was an inspired move.

FSS enjoyed exceptional relationships with the supermarkets, giving Sam national ranging status and opportunities with all supermarket chains, a major achievement for a small, niche manufacturer. Sam was now a wholesaler/distributor with more market clout and the ability to distribute products other than just his gingerbread. Since then, FSS has begun distributing additional products as diverse as chewing gum, sports drinks and fruit bars, and the range is expanding.

Being first to market and continuing to innovate ensures we maintain a competitive edge.

Eventually, with stronger financial returns under his belt, Sam was also able to re-enter the licensed product market, developing a range of icing-imaged biscuits where character figures such as Bart Simpson and Bob the Builder are printed onto an icing-coated gingerbread or chocolate biscuit base. The range, introduced in 2002, was instantly successful and won an award for Best New Retail Product in the Australian Fine Food Awards in 2002–2003.

The product is now being rolled out to the corporate market (gingerbread products with company logos) and schools (with the figures customised to wear different school uniforms).

Not all Sam's initiatives have been wildly successful. In 2001 the Gingerbread Company contracted with the Australian Football League (AFL) to produce gingerbread men emblazoned with the uniforms of 10 clubs. With millions of football fans around Australia this innovative product extension was expected to be a big winner but the products simply didn't sell and Sam was left with thousands of unwanted gingerbread footballers.

'It was a big eye opener that clearly identified where our target market was and where we should be aiming. Our target market for the gingerbread and chocolate figures was children and when we tried the AFL licence, which covers a broad market of people, it didn't work.

'These days we make sure our gingerbread and chocolate figures feature children's characters like The Simpsons, Care Bears, Ninja Turtles and other popular licences.'

Sam continues to expand his product range. Gingerbread is still the 'bread and butter' of the company, but he continually challenges the range and explores new ideas on the theme. The company has expanded into more chocolate-based products, a move that has proven quite successful.

Customer feedback is a great source for driving inspiration and helps Sam tailor his offering to maximise the returns for retailers. For instance, the Gingerbread Company has a broader range of products than its immediate competitors who produce only one or two characters and so do not easily win supermarket shelf space or repeat business.

Also, rather than provide retailers with a 24-pack entirely made up of the same character, Sam's team can hand-package four each of six characters into each display box, giving customers greater choice.

The Gingerbread Company's domination of the market means Sam has been able to secure additional licences for many of the most popular children's figures, creating a significant barrier for his competition.

'We are good at pre-empting customers and their needs and stimulating demand with new licences.

'Also, by keeping up-to-date with new technology we can produce top-quality graphics for the art on our product. Being first to market and continuing to innovate ensures we maintain a competitive edge.'

Along the journey, Sam completed his MBA after 12 years of full-time and part-time study. He is a strong believer in continuing education to boost his business skills and says 'you should never stop learning'.

While the company is in a strong position now, Sam admits that in the early days it was 'sink or swim'.

'I came in at the deep end initially with the business having debts and having to manage my way through those. Then I had our biggest distributor, Food Service Solutions, turn bad on us and that cost us a lot of money at the time and set our own growth back about a year.

'It certainly taught us that cash is king. Even if you are growing your business and you can see the benefit of continuing to boost trade, sometimes it can be better to slow down and concentrate on getting the money in the door first before taking the next step.

'With the Gingerbread Company, opportunities to acquire new equipment have not always presented themselves at the best times in terms of cashflow, but they have been opportunities that we could not afford to miss. Such acquisitions have therefore required an even greater emphasis on operating effectively and managing our working capital.'

Sam Tucker's entrepreneurial flair was evident from an early age, both at school and during his initial career in the hotel and hospitality sector.

'Teachers would comment that the way I arrived at the answers was very different to others, but I was still doing well so I knew that thinking in my own way wasn't a problem.

'When I started work in the hotel industry I'd often observe the way things were being done by colleagues and see that there were ways of doing things better. The mindset of challenging the way things were done and my frustration when they were not done as efficiently or effectively as possible was one of the reasons that I had the motivation to go out alone when the opportunity presented itself.'

As his two companies evolve, Sam says Food Service Solutions is now starting to overshadow The Great Australian Gingerbread Company in terms of turnover and potential for the future.

Future growth is being focused on sourcing, purchasing and supplying innovative products that have a sustainable competitive edge in growth categories in retail and food service industries.

Sam Tucker's vision is for The Great Australian Gingerbread Company to become the world's largest manufacturer and wholesaler of hand-decorated and edible image biscuits, while FSS evolves into a major national and multinational food distribution company.

When it comes to taking on the competition, Sam Tucker is one smart cookie.

Lessons Learnt:

* 'Hand-made' is not always a disadvantage in a mechanised age. The Great Australian Gingerbread Company wins new markets by being able to tailor its product offering, and the way products are packaged and presented.
* Wherever possible, lock up the licensing for your key products to help keep competitors at bay.
* Don't let expansion overtake cashflow. Expand strategically and carefully.

Advice to Others:

* Opportunity can come in all forms. The secret is to be ready to take advantage of a good opportunity when it comes along. By purchasing Food Service Solutions, Sam not only secured his long-term national distribution but also gave his company a new direction that now seems set to become the major part of his enterprise.
* Keep gaining experience and continue to educate yourself. These are the foundations for building your confidence to be a strong leader.

Richard Turner

Richard Turner has a habit of changing the rules in every industry in which he operates.

From food services and hospitality staffing to modelling – all have benefited from Richard's innovative approach to doing business.

As with many entrepreneurs, Richard's career has involved establishing, building and then selling a business to move on to his next challenge.

Richard's first exposure to the world of business was as a child watching his father grow his wholesale meat business to a turnover of $80 million-a-year. Richard went on to work in the family business, along with his two brothers Greg and Paul, drawing on his Bachelor of Business Administration to further develop and manage the company's IT system.

In their father's company, a small food services division had been established based on market research showing that total food service – the supply of virtually every food item to a restaurant or caterer – was a growing trend in both the US and Australia's eastern states.

In South Australia no such service existed, with restaurants and food outlets having to buy from a range of different suppliers.

Richard's father's business was eventually listed as a public company, before being sold into another large food group. The brothers purchased the food service arm from the new owners and set up Regency Food Services in 1987.

The company's first target customers were takeaway outlets – fish and chip shops and chicken shops – who carried a relatively small range of products and ingredients yet still required a number of suppliers. Now they could buy all those products from Regency Food Services.

The business started with five staff – Greg doing the buying and administration, a tele-sales person taking orders, a warehouse manager picking and packing the orders, and Richard and Paul delivering.

'Like any other entrepreneur starting a business, we were working absolutely ridiculous hours, from four in the morning to 10 at night,' Richard said. 'But the market latched onto the one-stop shop idea very quickly, coupled with our strong service attitude. We really promoted ourselves as a service company.

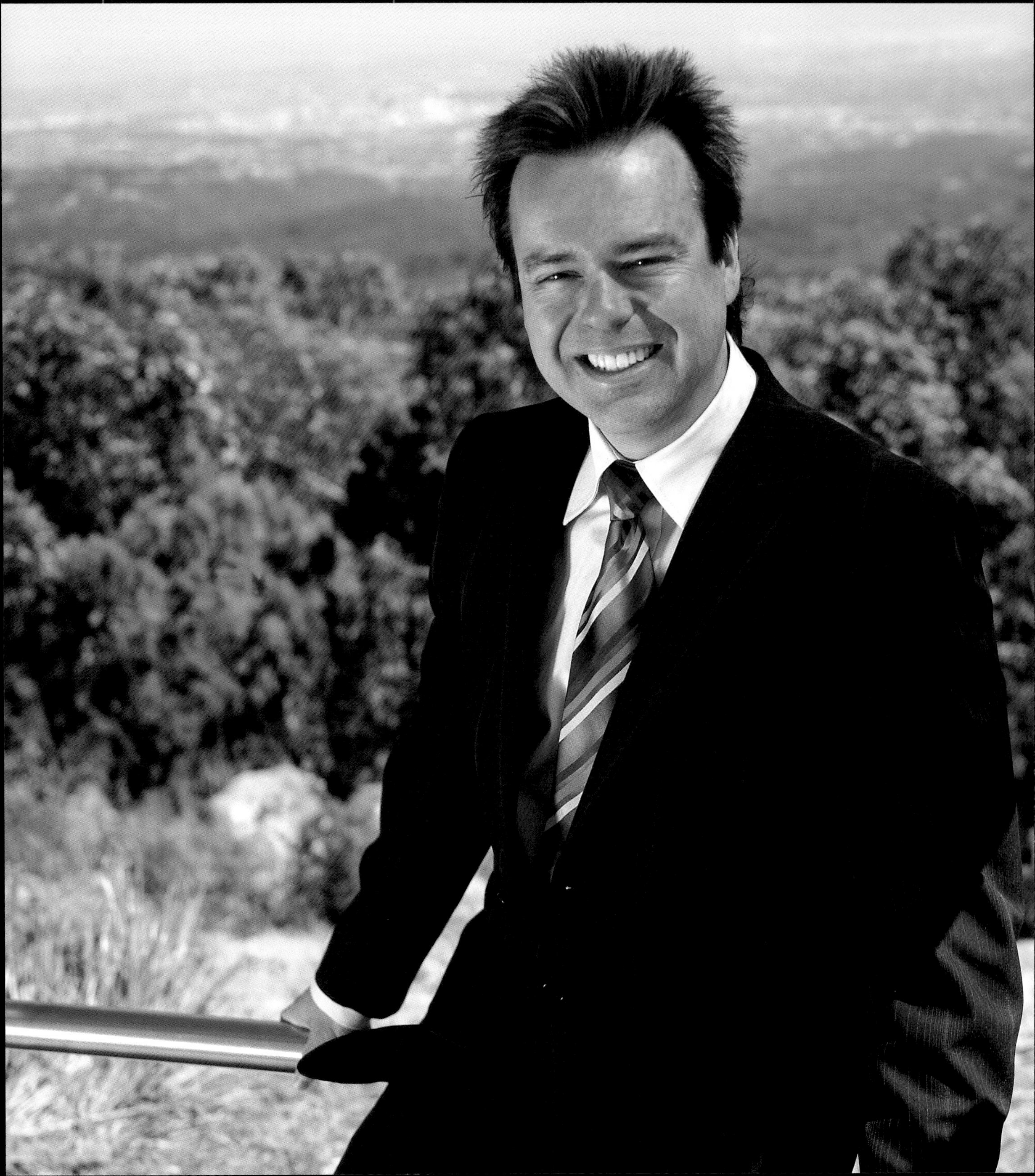

'Being young guys with our necks on the line and really keen on providing the best service we could, we were very different to your average truck driver. When we delivered the order, we knew what we were doing, we knew about the customer and the food they had ordered and often picked up errors and corrected them before the customer had realised.

'With my degree in business and marketing, I was able to talk to them about their business, things they could do to improve it, and could suggest the introduction of new lines, systems or marketing initiatives. Our service was definitely what set us apart from our competition.'

Regency Food Services then expanded its focus to include restaurants and hotels, enjoying further success in these markets.

A range of innovations drove growth. Regency invested heavily in computer systems to streamline the order and delivery process. It also became Australia's first 24-hour food service distribution company, with a fleet of refrigerated vehicles.

Regency's warehouse was continually expanded and modified to handle four temperature zones to store different types of products. Automated warehouse systems were introduced, reducing labour requirements and creating significant efficiencies in the loading docks.

Driving all these measures was a desire to understand customers and their needs. For instance, recognising that hospitality staff generally worked noon to midnight, Regency's tele-service staff were available from 8 am through to 10 pm, allowing chefs to place their orders after the dinner rush.

'All of these were huge moves at that time – and carried a great deal of risk. At the time we were still competing against backyard operators that were delivering cartons of frozen prawns off the back of tray top trucks.

'We wanted to create barriers to entering our industry. We adopted quality systems very early on, but with that comes the need for considerable investment. We certainly poured a lot of money into the company as we built it into the best and most efficient operation of its kind.'

> Our success was based on our ability to put systems in place that would guarantee consistency and predictability, so our customers knew exactly what they were getting, time after time. Consistency gives you the ability to charge a premium price.

The mid 1990s saw the explosion of the 'café scene' in Adelaide, with a resultant shortage of hospitality staff. Regency's customers kept asking Richard's sales reps if they knew of a chef or good waiting staff they could hire.

Recognising a business opportunity, Richard recruited a human resource consultant with a background in hospitality and launched Regency Staffing. Within a few years the business had a $3.5 million turnover and large national companies including Qantas and the Fosters Hotel Group among its clientele.

At the time, Richard was still involved with Regency Food Services, but in 1998 – with turnover nudging $30 million – an offer to purchase the company was made by a South African investment group.

Richard and Greg refused several approaches but after eventually receiving 'an offer we couldn't refuse', they sold Regency Food Services in 1999, enabling them both to move on and seek new challenges.

The sale allowed Richard to turn his full attention to Regency Staffing – and once again his innovative approach reshaped the recruitment sector.

Early in its development the company established one of Australia's first on-line recruitment websites. Available jobs were posted to a newsboard and people could respond by sending their resumes via email. This initiative was in place well before the sites that are now an integral part of the recruitment industry.

At that time the HR industry was rationalising quite quickly, with a handful of major companies dominating the sector. Regency Staffing was sold to a large firm keen to lead the hospitality staffing sector nationally.

Richard had little time to become bored though, having already co-founded another business with wife Debbie – Glitz Girls – in 2000. This business started as a retail operation for the sale of hairpieces, jewellery and accessories.

As a promotion to launch the brand at Adelaide's Le Mans race in 2000, 12 Glitz Girls models paraded around the track, decked out in the company's products. It was a great way to promote the Glitz Girls products – but people also enquired how they could hire the girls for their own company's promotions.

'Suddenly all these corporates were approaching us and asking where they could hire the Glitz Girls models. We recognised that there was an opportunity to start running our own promotional modelling agency.

'Before we embarked on the business we looked at the promo models that were already available in Adelaide. While they all looked good, most of them didn't know much about the product they were representing and had trouble even communicating, let alone being able to close a sale.

'We talked to some major clients who were using these models and found they were really disillusioned with what was available. We realised we could train our models in the basic principles of sales and marketing, and put a team out there who could really sell a product as well as look good.

'We thought that if we could recruit girls and guys who were attractive but also had brains we could teach them sales and marketing, and that would give us a real competitive edge in the market.'

Richard's theory proved correct and the Glitz Girls models – who could communicate the benefits of the products they were promoting – quickly doubled and tripled their clients' sales figures.

Following the success of Glitz Girls, Richard has recently focused his attention on a new venture – Zen Technologies (Power and Energy), a specialist company focusing on the commercialisation of energy saving appliances for the home and office.

Richard believes the foundation for all his business success has been consistency and determination.

'As far back as Regency Food Services, our success was based on our ability to put systems in place that would guarantee consistency and predictability, so our customers knew exactly what they were getting, time after time. Consistency gives you the ability to charge a premium price.

'But if you're good one day and bad the next, and still charge a premium price for your service, your customers won't come back. It all comes back to strong systems and training programs, and developing those disciplines throughout your business.'

In recent years and during his many business challenges, Richard has drawn great support from the Young Entrepreneurs Organisation (YEO), of which he was the South Australian Founding President in 1998.

'When I first learnt about YEO, I thought "Wow, I'm not alone". Very few of my friends had run a business, let alone a large business, and they always found it hard to relate to why I worked as hard as I did.

'The ability to be able to talk and network with people who are in business and share experiences has been enormously beneficial.

'So many people run a business in a very insulated environment and as soon as they join YEO and open up about their issues and problems, they suddenly find 30 or 40 other people who have had exactly the same experience. It's such an enlightening process to talk about business experiences and learn from them.'

Lessons Learnt:

* Change the rules. Changing the way your industry is run gives you a competitive advantage and allows you to 'own' the mantle of industry leader.
* Peer networking and learning is hugely important for entrepreneurs who can often feel isolated.
* Always look at your business from the customer's point of view and what will work best for them. This approach can help you shape the business from day one.

Advice to Others:

* Consistency is vital. Structured systems and processes are integral to ensuring that the customer always gets what they want.

David Urry

David Urry – through his company State Swim – has changed the shape of Australian swimming.

As Australia's leading swim school group, State Swim now conducts more private swimming lessons each week than any similar organisation in the country.

Ironically, when David started coaching swimming at the age of 19 in 1966, his learn-to-swim classes were merely a sideline to earn a buck so he could pursue his dream of coaching elite swimmers.

David began coaching in the outdoor pool of an Adelaide hotel. In return for tending the pool, the owner let David conduct his coaching program and swimming lessons.

It was a big success and in 1970 David had made enough money to construct a 25-metre indoor pool in the western Adelaide suburb of Seaton. David's reputation and facilities enabled him to attract a number of exceptional athletes to his coaching program and he eventually became the Australian National Men's Swimming Team Coach in 1974.

'We couldn't really develop the learn-to-swim side of things at Seaton because the pool was always clogged up with athletes, but I noticed that whenever there was space for swimming lessons we basically filled them. I saw the potential for greatly expanding the swimming school side of the business.'

Eventually he sold the Seaton pool to buy the larger and better equipped Clovercrest Swimming Pool, where he fine-tuned his blueprint for what he believed could become Australia's best swim school.

David took on a partner, Paul Mason, to help drive growth and State Swim was formally launched as the company's brand in 1991.

The group grew rapidly through a mixture of pool development, purchase and licensing. State Swim now includes swimming schools in Norwood, Golden Grove, Seaton, Unley, Mount Barker and Seaford in South Australia, as well as Whitford City, East Fremantle, Joondalup, Osborne Park and Canning Vale in Western Australia. Expansion into the eastern states is on the drawing board.

State Swim's model is simple. Each pupil is allocated a class grade on booking, according to age or previous swimming experience. Pupils are re-graded regularly and promoted from one grade to the next when the skills required for that level have been achieved. The grades range from Water Babies and Kindergarten, through to appropriately ocean-themed classes such as Starfish, Dolphins and Marlins.

State Swim also runs adult programs and swimming for fitness, as well as lap swimming, aqua-robics and an active teenage program.

Comprehensive systemisation is the backbone of State Swim's success. Every time a new pool joins the group the system becomes a template for that pool's operations. State Swim has also attracted excellent teachers and has in place an outstanding training system, with full-time training directors steering the development of new instructors.

Classes are small – sometimes only four to six children – which means more intensive tuition and greater focus on individual learning.

Also, the pool is kept at a constant warm temperature of 32 degrees. It can sometimes get a bit steamy for spectators, but the aim is to ensure maximum comfort for the people in the pool.

David Urry's over-arching philosophy is that 'swimming is an asset for life'.

'Everyone has a different perception of what it is to be able to swim. Does it mean you can swim from one side of your home pool to the other? Or does it mean that if your boat overturns in the ocean you can swim several kilometres to shore?

'Our philosophy is that every Australian child should be able to swim 400 metres freestyle non-stop by the time they leave primary school.'

Until State Swim, swimming lessons in Australia were generally provided by the education departments in each state and held mostly during the Christmas holidays. Classes were rarely held in heated facilities. Reluctant kids were dumped into freezing rivers, oceans or outdoor community pools and taught the basics by part-time trainers.

'Kids got a certain number of swimming lessons each year and some basic certificates, which really just recorded your attendance, not your ability. After a course of 10 lessons or so, the kids would stop. Why? Because the mindset of the parents was that you stop at the end of a course of lessons rather than keep going until they learn to swim properly.

'What we had to do was change people's perception of what it was to learn to swim. For instance, we have swimming certificates for kids who can swim 10 metres through to certificates for kids who can swim 1500 metres. The focus is now on ability and distance rather than a set number of lessons. That's better for the kids but it also helps give the parents more confidence that their children are getting the aquatic education they need.

'There's also the health benefit. Swimming has increasingly become accepted as a way of getting and staying fit – like running or going to the gym. Also, people can learn year-round in heated indoor facilities, which means they don't have to finish their swimming lessons just because the weather's getting colder.

'The system is obviously a good marketing tool because it keeps people in the program – but by the same token what health benefit is anyone going to get out of swimming just 10 metres?

'Before State Swim came along no one had ever run a swim school this way. Our whole company is wrapped around the belief that as they grow, children should make regular swimming tuition or aquatic tuition a part of their lifestyle. Gradually, the community has come to see this as a logical approach.'

David's philosophy is catching on. In the early days, the drop-off in swimmer numbers between summer and winter was about 40 per cent. Now it's only about 5 per cent.

The year-round nature of State Swim's operation has benefits for staff retention as well. Swim trainers can now be offered regular part-time work for the full year and comprehensive training to boost their skills.

'It's immensely satisfying to know that we have changed the industry so much from the days when it was really just a mums and dads cottage industry.

It's immensely satisfying to know that we have changed the industry so much from the days when it was really just a mums and dads cottage industry.

'When I went to the bank 25 years ago to finance a swimming school, they had difficulty seeing what I did as a business. We've helped lay the foundation for a new respectability in the corporate community for our type of business.'

David Urry's timing in the establishment of State Swim could not have been better. The company's development coincided with a gradual increase in the number of water-based leisure activities undertaken by the Australian public.

'When I was young you could go swimming or surfing and that was about it. The past 20 years has seen the development of aquatic experiences we never used to have – surfing and lifesaving not just as a sport, but as a recreation. Then there's the development of boogie boards, water theme parks, windsurfing and water-skiing.

'In the 1940s, 50s and 60s there wasn't a great need for people to swim unless they wanted to go into swimming as a sport. Now kids have pool parties and birthday parties around the pool.

'If your seven-year-old gets invited to a friend's pool party and can't swim he feels like a social outcast. Parents these days don't just want their kids to be competent but also to feel at home and comfortable in the pool. Now swimming is essential for kids' social development as well.'

David says State Swim's growth rocketed when he moved his office out of one of the State Swim buildings and leased a separate office.

'It really got me away from working in the business so I could concentrate on working on the business. I needed that physical change so I wasn't bogged down with the nitty-gritty of handling all the day-to-day elements of State Swim. I also learnt to delegate, which was important to the growth of the company.

'Once I'd handed over the running of the schools to Paul Mason and our managers I didn't want to be there treading on toes and nitpicking everything they did.'

David Urry has other entrepreneurial interests. His development group, Fortury, builds and owns many of the swimming pools in the State Swim group, along with other properties ranging from industrial parks to residential accommodation.

Several years ago he also founded Zedar Swimwear, built it into one of Australia's best-selling swimwear brands and then sold it.

Water may well be in David Urry's veins. His main passion outside work is yachting.

'When I got out of swimming coaching I needed some athletic or physical endeavour and I decided to get into sailing boats. I just love the water.'

Lessons Learnt:

* You can create your own market if you persist. The public perception of aquatic education is very different now to the days before David Urry started showing people that 'swimming is an asset for life'.
* Systemise whatever you can in your operation. It not only makes the day-to-day operations run more smoothly; it means you can quickly and easily replicate the business at other locations.
* Don't be afraid to switch from your core activity to take advantage of better opportunities. David's initial business was coaching elite swimmers but he soon recognised that learn-to-swim for the general public provided greater growth prospects for his business.

Advice to Others:

* Keep your bank in the picture – always. You have to develop a relationship of trust and partnership with your bank so that together you can make quick decisions to make the most of business opportunities as they arise.

Philip Vafiadis

Lovers of soft symphony music and those who like their rock'n'roll very loud – all are fans of Philip Vafiadis' life work.

Philip's company VAF Research is a specialist audio-visual manufacturer of world-class loudspeakers and designer of state-of-the-art home theatre systems.

An interest in electronics and audio equipment that developed in his teenage years has seen Philip design and manufacture speakers that *Rolling Stone* magazine has described as 'the ultimate in high fidelity performance, with the best bass in the world'.

It's a long way from the first set of loudspeakers Philip built from an electronics magazine design as an 18-year-old fresh out of high school. Deciding he could do better, his hobby led to the establishment of VAF Research.

Originally making high-quality, high-fidelity speakers for friends and a few specialist retailers, Philip used the money he made in the early days to satisfy his desire to travel the world.

Recognising the unique opportunity this provided to learn more about electronics and audio, Philip planned his travels so he could meet international leaders in their respective technical fields.

His experiences overseas fuelled his desire to return to Adelaide and become an Australian industry leader, building on the knowledge gained on his travels together with his own innovations.

In its first year of operation after Philip's return to Adelaide, VAF Research's turnover was just $20,000, with the company initially designing speakers primarily for other companies. The move to its own branded products came in the mid-1990s.

In recent years, VAF Research has achieved double-digit growth with annual sales now worth many millions of dollars.

VAF Research sells more quality loudspeaker systems each year than any other Australian company and employs 11 specialist staff with external contractors also supplying speaker cabinets and other materials.

Philip's motivation comes from inventing cutting edge technology and equipment for people's enjoyment.

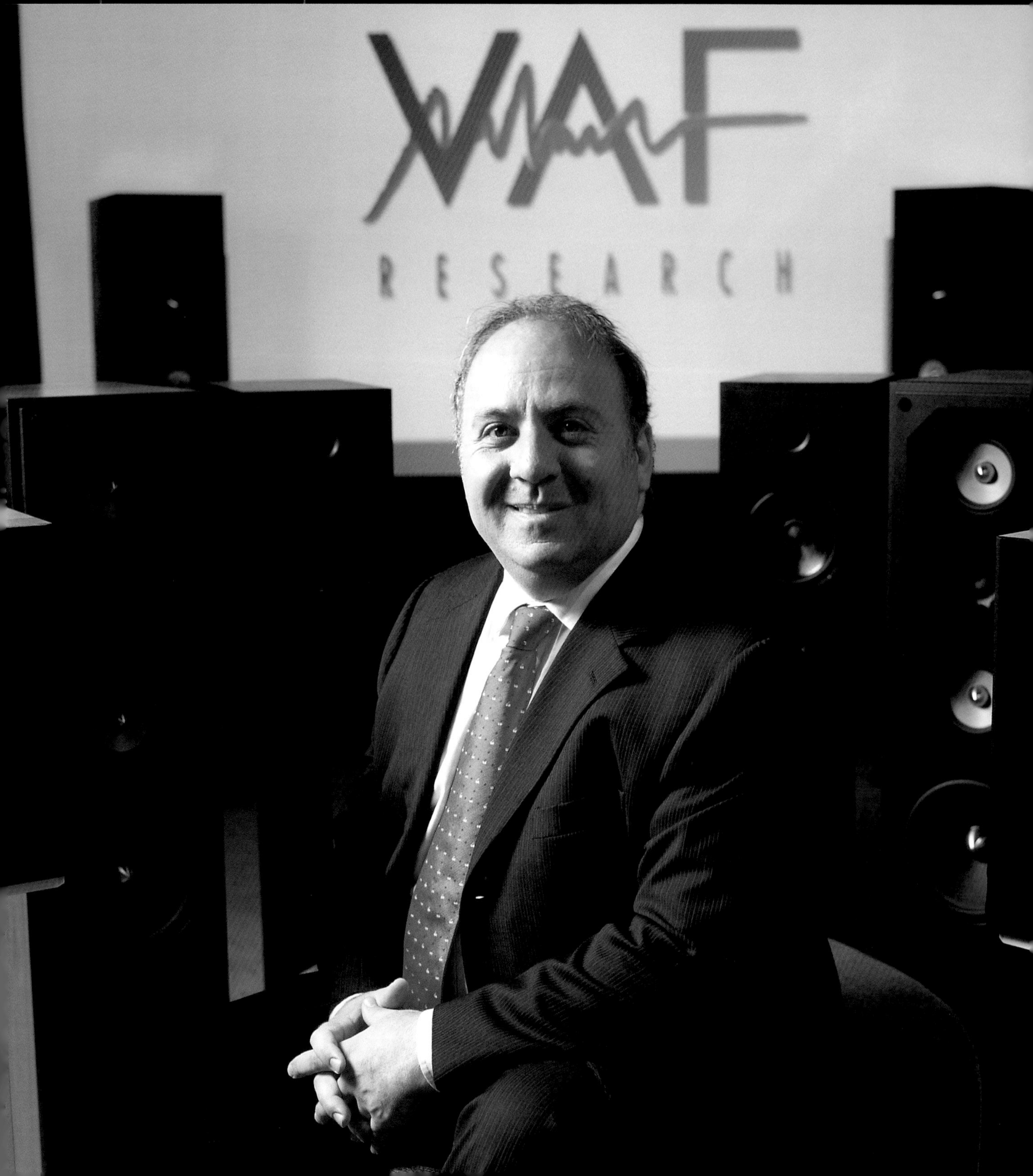
VAF
RESEARCH

'I enjoy running a business where we can be innovative, constantly learning and at the same time achieving global recognition for our quality of work.

'From the very outset, my aim was to develop speakers that were the most technically correct and delivered the most accurate sound possible.

'Human senses remain constant despite the changing technology surrounding them and our aim is to deliver the ultimate audio-visual experience for people.

'There's no doubt that we've gained an international reputation as an innovator and we're keen to build on that and to continue to differentiate ourselves from our competitors.'

For Philip, business and product excellence is not only about developing the best product; it is also about providing real value.

'There is an optimum solution for every problem and all problems are unique despite their common elements.

'One of our company values is that we give an absolute commitment that any products purchased from VAF provide maximum benefit to the user.

> We enjoy projects that have never been done before or are difficult to do. We have become involved in these leading edge commercial jobs because they're fun, they're on the edge and they help to keep us sharp.

'We pride ourselves on a clear reputation for helping customers not only understand what they actually do need, but at the same time eliminating the elements they don't need.

'For us, value means customers will always walk away with a purchase which provides the best outcomes and that the benefits will always outweigh the money invested in the product.

'It's also about simplicity of use, ensuring that the benefits of the product are easily accessible and that they can be simply integrated.

'While we are a very technically advanced company, the technology has to be used appropriately and meet the specific requirements of our users.'

The convergence across the information technology and audio-visual sectors has seen VAF Research move into new products including home theatre systems – one of the fastest areas of growth for the company.

With 80 per cent of global home entertainment spending on audio-visual theatre systems, it was a smart move for VAF Research.

In addition to the manufacture of some of Australia's most advanced loudspeakers, the company now supplies most electronic components such as DVD and CD players, Dolby digital home theatre receivers, audiophile-grade components and high-quality TV monitors and projectors.

The move followed Philip's recognition that while the 'tech heads' and audiophiles will always spend money on buying the most technically advanced speakers available, most consumers don't just want speakers, they want total home theatre systems.

These are the people who are less concerned with the technology and more interested in the functionality of a complete, simple audio-visual system.

In addition to its focus on home audio, VAF Research has built and installed technically advanced loudspeaker solutions for a wide variety of companies and organisations. Its electro-acoustic system for the new-look Adelaide Festival Theatre is still one of the largest and most sophisticated systems of its type in the world.

Other projects have been completed for the Adelaide Symphony Orchestra's Grainger Studio, the SA Museum and the Australian Science and Maths School. The ABC and Channel 9 are also among VAF's clients.

'We enjoy projects that have never been done before or are difficult to do. While our major market is home theatre and hi-fi, we have become involved in these leading edge commercial jobs because they're fun, they're on the edge and they help to keep us sharp.

'While the commercial market is much smaller than the home market, it is still part of our growth strategy to develop this side of the business. Most importantly however, commercial projects also provide an added perception of credibility and this flows back to our home consumer sales.'

VAF Research's move into these types of projects has also benefited from a blurring of the delineation between commercial and domestic systems. While up until recent years there was a stark difference between equipment used in commercial and domestic venues, increasingly similar technology is being used in both.

This has numerous cost benefits for a small company growing rapidly but still having to wrestle with constrained research and marketing budgets.

With considerable time and money having been spent on developing VAF Research's product range, Philip is keen to achieve the best possible mileage from each product.

Developing products that have applications across a number of market segments has provided the company with 'bang for its buck' and helped drive sales growth in a cost-effective way.

This has been enormously valuable for a company that has always invested a large amount of time and energy into research and development.

Many of VAF's team, including Philip, spend much of their time on R&D and a significant amount of the company's profits have been reinvested back into this side of the business.

For Philip, the company's strength in R&D – driven by a focus to be technically correct – separates the company from its competitors as it takes the 'technical high ground'.

The result is a company that is among the first to adopt new technology and will back its beliefs in technology and advancement.

Philip says future research and development is being broadened to focus on an enhanced understanding of technologies that will lead to new product developments.

This will be integral as VAF Research strives for a $15 million turnover through more concerted interstate and overseas expansion.

While the company has worked hard over the past 10 years to branch out from its core market in South Australia, local sales still account for 50 per cent of turnover. Interstate sales now make up 45 per cent with unsolicited international sales accounting for the remaining 5 per cent.

VAF Research has sold into overseas markets including North America, Europe, the United Kingdom, Ireland and Asia.

In most cases, interstate and international customers are purchasing VAF speakers based on reviews (such as that by *Rolling Stone* magazine), reputation and referral without seeing or hearing the product for themselves.

'There are plenty of competitors but most are just vying for market share, rather than offering quality brands. Given the strength of our brand and our fairly powerful point of difference, we think we are poised to make a real impact internationally.'

Lessons Learnt:

* Ensure that your company's products and services provide customers with real value. It's not just about achieving market share or giving people what they think they want – it's making sure that what you offer is actually valuable and will have a long life.

* Be receptive to projects that your company has never done before or that are difficult. Challenging projects can be fun and most importantly, they keep you focused. They also provide credibility and can offer the opportunity to explore new avenues for product development.

* Align product development to the strategic objectives of the company. In a small company, design flexible products that can be leveraged across multiple applications and distribution channels.

* Only do what you do best. If you can't or won't learn something so that you can do it best, then delegate it to someone else who can.

Advice to Others:

* Referral can be an extremely valuable yet inexpensive marketing tool. VAF Research has grown sales almost solely through reputation and referral – but you need to ensure a quality product or service to encourage favourable 'word-of-mouth' advertising.

* If your business is technology-based be careful that your products still meet the needs of your customers. Don't get so carried away with the technology that you become 'too clever' and lose sight of what it is that the customer wants.

Larissa Vakulina

Larissa Vakulina really doesn't know what all the fuss is about. Sure, she has won various entrepreneur and business awards, and her company Expo-Trade has been hailed in numerous media articles as a great South Australian success story.

It is clear though that Larissa is uncomfortable with all the attention. She sees herself as a reluctant businesswoman who has worked tirelessly to build a $12 million enterprise from a company she never wanted to launch in the first place.

After the break-up of the Soviet Union, Larissa moved to Adelaide with her family to start a new life. Unable to speak English and with her academic qualifications not recognised in Australia, she soon realised that establishing her own business was the only way she could avoid long-term unemployment.

She threw herself into learning English and studying for an MBA. Then, in 1999, she started Expo-Trade out of frustration and necessity, and to give herself a job.

Only a few years later, Expo-Trade has emerged as one of Australia's leading exporters to Russia. Along the way, Larissa Vakulina has become something of a business celebrity in South Australia. She was a state category winner and national finalist in both the 2002 Businesswoman of the Year and the 2003 Entrepreneur of the Year awards.

In 2003, Expo-Trade was named the third-fastest growing company in the country by *Business Review Weekly* magazine.

While Larissa finds the mantle of 'leading businesswoman' flattering, she says her career has been built on her survival instinct rather than a need to clamber up the ladder to success. She never set out to become a role model – just to make a living and give her children the best opportunities in life.

'I'm more of a creative person. I'm into fashion and interior design so Expo-Trade is not the business I would choose to be in. I basically couldn't find meaningful employment in Australia so this is what life forced me to do.

'Of course, I could find some sort of employment to make a living, but employment must be meaningful – it should be interesting and not boring.

'In times of desperation you analyse what you do best. The best thing I could do was use my knowledge of my country Russia and the contacts back there to create a business, and so Expo-Trade was born.'

Expo-Trade's growth has been rapid, largely due to Larissa's strong network of contacts in Russia and her outstanding knowledge of which Australian products will sell well there.

Larissa's tenacity has seen her spearhead trade into a region largely ignored by other Australian businesses because of what she says is their unreasonable fear of the Russian trade environment.

'It's a shame for Australia. The market is huge and basically other countries are very quickly making the most of that opportunity. Australia is losing this opportunity year after year because they fear a market they don't understand.'

This lack of understanding impacts directly on Expo-Trade's operations. Despite the company's outstanding success, Larissa says she has experienced tremendous difficulty garnering genuine support and building partnerships with the Australian financial and corporate community.

'It is interesting that the only thing limiting Expo-Trade's growth is our resources. We have to do it all ourselves from our own finances.

'At this stage we have virtually no external support. Government, banks, insurance companies – none of them understand trade with Russia and they are fearful of it, so we simply can't enlist their support. It's very disappointing.

'We have been going for more than five years and every year we try to obtain international credit insurance with the major worldwide credit insurance companies. We've been rejected a number of times. We apply constantly for credit lines with banks – not just domestic banks but the major international banks with a core business in international trade. We have been rejected by them too.

'Basically, they assess the risks involved in trading with Russia and just decide that the risk is so high that they're not interested.'

This means Larissa and her husband Andrey are effectively 'going it alone' – and despite enormous odds the company is doing very well.

The business now employs five people in Australia and has another three staff in its trade office in St Petersburg.

Each month Expo-Trade ships approximately 15 to 20 containers to Russia, packed with goods including frozen and chilled lamb, mutton, beef, veal and kangaroo for food, as well as sheep and lambskins for making warm clothing and lining for boots. Other diverse products range from wine to fertiliser, and even dairy products such as cheese and butter.

From its inception Expo-Trade's evolution has been a struggle. Sadly, many potential suppliers initially contacted by Larissa saw her as a 'woman with an accent', thought she was simply a time-waster and did not even explore the chance that she could create new markets for them.

'It wasn't just resistance; some of them did not even treat me as a real opportunity for them. Eventually I travelled around Australia for a few months talking to meat suppliers so they could meet with me personally and I could explain that I had a long-term strategy to supply this product to Russia.

'We started with just one or two containers from some suppliers and gradually over the years we have built up their trust. Now it's much easier because they know what products we need, how we work, and how we meet our responsibilities and obligations. They feel comfortable dealing with us.'

Larissa asked a lot of questions and soaked up as much information as she could about ways to improve her business.

I like to see good results but negative results are still results, so you should learn from them. Life is a never-ending learning process.

She found it an intriguing contradiction that despite Australian suppliers' nervousness about doing business with her they were still extremely friendly and open, offering plenty of advice and happy to help her learn the ropes.

Commodity trade is a tough business and margins can be thin but Larissa has positioned Expo-Trade to minimise risk. The company concentrates most of its efforts on sourcing and exporting essential products such as foodstuffs and sheepskins which have guaranteed end markets and sell quickly in Russia.

'Unlike branded products, essential products don't require an investment in promotion and advertising because they sell themselves in the right season. Meat sells because people need protein. Lambskins sell because they are needed for clothing in the winter months.

'Wine however is more of a luxury item and requires promotion, which is why it's not one of our major priorities. The distance doesn't help. It takes two months to get products to Russia by sea. The commodity products are sold immediately and we are paid. With wine it may take many more months to sell the product, which means we don't get paid for quite some time. We like to keep the payment cycle as short and fast as possible.'

Despite the numerous barriers she has encountered in building Expo-Trade, Larissa says she gains strength from focusing on the positive. She says it simply doesn't make any sense to be hobbled by negative things, preferring to treat any setbacks as learning experiences and move on.

'I like to see good results but negative results are still results, so you should learn from them. Life is a never-ending learning process.

'I am also very fortunate because I have a great professional team with me and I learn from them every day.'

Larissa says Expo-Trade is poised for even greater success in the coming years, but that the struggle is not over.

'We have had five years of very successful trading with a great track record, but we have still not achieved the trust of the Government, the institutions and the banks. I keep getting told that the company is still young. Maybe when we're 10 years old and a lot bigger people will look at the business differently.'

Until then, Larissa Vakulina will continue charting her own successful destiny.

Lessons Learnt:

* Great business opportunities can be found where others fear to tread. Take risks in exploring new markets.
* Be persistent. You can build a great company without the support of others. It may take a little longer but there is a certain strength and independence that comes from funding growth from your own resources.
* You can't escape negativity in business. Things go wrong from time to time and you will encounter barriers, but use these as learning experiences. Make sure you have positive people around you to support you and help build your confidence in times of difficulty.

Advice to Others:

* Don't try to do it yourself. If you lack certain skills or education in certain key areas of business, learn from those who know better, surround yourself with people who have those skills and, at the first opportunity, hire people with those skills to harness these capabilities within your business.

Jim Whiting

As the head of one of South Australia's largest construction companies, Jim Whiting recognises that for most people a major building project can be a traumatic experience.

His company, Badge Constructions, has created a thriving business out of taking the worries out of building projects for its many customers – primarily national food processors who invest millions of dollars in complex production facilities.

A strong focus on efficiency and effectiveness, in both communication and results, means Badge's customers benefit from a highly professional and experienced service.

Badge Constructions is South Australia's largest family-owned non-residential building company, with offices in Adelaide, Brisbane and Perth. Badge enjoys a turnover of about $100 million and employs more than 90 people.

By concentrating on building projects with a value of $5 million to $20 million, Badge has successfully completed projects throughout Australia and New Zealand ranging from commercial and industrial complexes to hotels and entertainment venues, schools, hospitals, aged care facilities, shopping centres and food processing plants.

Major buildings in Adelaide constructed by Badge include Stage 3 of the RAA building at Mile End; the University of SA Library; the Sports Centre at Prince Alfred College; the refurbishment of the Newton Shopping Centre; and the upgrade of the Sturt Street Primary School.

Badge Constructions has differentiated itself from competitors by specialising in the design and construction of all types of food processing buildings.

The company's many repeat food industry clients – more than 50 per cent of the company's work is repeat business – include Springs Smoked Salmon, Aldinga Turkeys and chicken industry giant Inghams.

'Our success to date has largely come from focusing on servicing the niche market of constructing buildings for the food industry, and we're committed to continuing to concentrate on this in the future.

'We haven't simply provided a product in the form of a building, but have taken the process one step further by providing our clients with a complete design and construction service.

'The commercial, industrial and food processing areas in which we operate are quite complex. For many clients the whole construction process can loom as something quite traumatic.

'In these circumstances, people are primarily looking for the job to be completed professionally, efficiently and effectively, and that's what we concentrate on delivering.

'If you do that, other things like relationships will follow, and from that will flow repeat business.

'Our company motto is: "Efficient results through effective communication".

'Our competitors might claim to be cheaper than us, but we promote ourselves on our professional attitude. While most of the parameters for projects on which we work are predetermined, such as the cost or the length of construction time, it's our job to provide the best building service possible.

'The modern building industry is very different to what it was even just a few years ago. It's about service. We don't just lay bricks; we are professionals who go about the business of building.'

Constantly changing regulations, technology and product development within the food processing industry have been a key driver in Badge's steady growth, with clients needing new, altered or upgraded facilities on a regular basis.

'Food processing is extremely complicated and these facilities are some of the most difficult buildings to construct. They're a lot of work.

'We're not just constructing a building and a production line. We're also involved with providing the services associated with these processing systems.

'A good example is a $30 million factory we did in Brisbane. It didn't just need hot and cold water; it needed chlorinated cold water, unchlorinated cold water, high-pressure hot water and high-pressure cold water – and that was just the water!

'It needed oil, gas, cooking oil, refrigeration and very complex electrical, right through to vacuum transport systems. Some of these facilities are more complex than a hospital and it's complicated work bringing it all together.'

Many of Badge's clients operate nationally and internationally, fuelling the company's expansion into Queensland, Western Australia and New Zealand.

In 2000, Badge Constructions drew on its considerable expertise and formed a second company, Food Processing Design (FPD), to design and construct food processing facilities. This also freed up more resources within Badge to service the needs of other industry clients.

Badge Constructions was established in 1983 by seven employees of the former Cowells Group, which was involved in materials supply and construction. Cowells had been taken over by another large company in the early 1980s and as a result the seven decided to go out on their own, forming Badge Constructions.

Four of the original shareholders left the company in 1985, leaving Jim and two others as equal shareholders.

In 1988 Jim, by this stage the company's Managing Director, and a family company comprising his seven brothers acquired the interests of the remaining two shareholders, placing the company entirely in the hands of the Whiting family.

While Jim was thrilled to be able to run Badge Constructions as a family business, the next five years proved extremely difficult.

In 1986, Badge had purchased Kingswood Aluminium, a window and façade fabrication business. The Whiting family assumed ownership of Kingswood as part of the Badge takeover in 1988.

It was soon discovered that the purchase of Kingswood Aluminium had been a mistake, with Badge paying too much for the goodwill and redundant stock that was part of the business. Kingswood's continued operating losses were being covered by the trading profits made by Badge Constructions.

The company was also trying to recover from the substantial payout to the former shareholders, which had been largely funded by debt at a time when interest rates were in the high teens.

Despite Kingswood Aluminium's problems, it was a major player in the Adelaide construction market and it was decided that the best option was to sell a stake in the company to another business which could profit by supplying into the company.

Fifty per cent of the company was sold to Adelaide's major glass company, with the associated injection of funds relieving the burden from Badge.

Although it took several years, Kingswood Aluminium is now dominant in its industry, and profitable and very successful in its own right.

I've been in the construction industry for 25 years and I believe that being consistent and being persistent are not just essential to success, they are the only way you'll ensure your survival.

Free from the financial pressures associated with Kingswood and with a growing reputation for its expertise in food processing facility construction, Badge Constructions has gone from strength to strength.

One of the greatest challenges for Jim now is to ensure that Badge Constructions continues to have access to the resources, expertise and capacity that have resulted in the company's success to date, to ensure it can continue servicing its ever-growing client base.

'Our growth to date has been organic rather than contrived and has been driven by developing our own resources, rather than hiring them in. That won't change in the future.

'Many of our employees are long-standing members of our team and have extensive knowledge and expertise that has greatly benefited our clients.

'We already have very good systems in place, I'm sure our systems are just as good as anyone's in South Australia, and these will come to the fore even more as we grow.

'While we spend a lot of money on systems, we want to be on the leading edge, not the bleeding edge, so it is done in a very hands-on manner.'

Jim is adamant that Badge's professionalism in servicing its clients and the principles of partnering and best practice will continue to differentiate the company from others in the industry.

'I've been in the construction industry for 25 years and I believe that being consistent and being persistent are not just essential to success, they are the only way you'll ensure your survival.

'Being consistent means concentrating on what you do best, where you make your money. If you've got spare money buy a toy like an expensive car if you want, but don't make the mistake of buying another business that's outside your core expertise.

'You also need to be persistent because no matter how successful you are, at some stage something will come along that knocks you around. You have to be able to weather that.

'Badge Constructions has certainly learnt both these lessons throughout its history and the results speak for themselves.'

Lessons Learnt:

* Create a niche for yourself in your chosen industry. If you don't have a point of difference and a specific target client base you're not even in the game. Set yourself apart from your competitors.
* Don't just offer a product; provide a service. Value-adding by providing services that your clients require will help to develop ongoing relationships, generate return business and protect your business from the dangerous practice of having to win work on price.
* Stick to what you know, as success in one industry won't automatically guarantee similar results in another. Concentrate on what makes the money for you and if you get sick of that, get out altogether and do something else. Don't try to be a master of more than one thing at a time.

Advice to Others:

* Communication and results go hand-in-hand and both should be efficient and effective. If you continually provide these with the utmost professionalism, your business will automatically succeed.

Shane Yeend

Shane Yeend has been able to do what most entrepreneurs can only dream of – pioneer a whole new consumer category.

As founder of one of the world's leading entertainment companies, Imagination Entertainment, Shane has driven the development of interactive television and now has his sights set on DVD games – already emerging as 'the next big thing'.

From his days running a wedding video business at the age of 15 and travelling the world as an award-winning cinematographer, Shane has built a $150 million-a-year entertainment empire.

His company creates and distributes games and other forms of entertainment globally and has partnered with some of the world's board game giants.

Shane began in the entertainment industry in the mid-1990s with his involvement in interactive TV programs, where viewers use 0055 phone numbers and websites to vote, chat online or provide feedback.

He entered into a joint venture with television production group Beyond International, and produced a weekly program for Coca-Cola which included phone-ins and merchandise retailing.

I'm not awed by too many people now. I have learnt that the best way to get things done is to just ring the right people on the phone and seek their involvement.

He then produced Australia's first interactive program, Pepsi Max, where viewers could go to the program's website and talk online with the show's host and other audience members.

Shane was soon making more money from the phone calls and websites than from the production fees.

'We were pioneers in understanding the emotional drivers of the viewing audience and changing the content of television to make it interactive for the audience,' Shane said.

'Our aim was to work out how to make more money from relationships with the audience. This was in the mid-1990s, well before anyone else started really doing this stuff.'

Shane's exploration and reinvention of traditional media set him off on another path. He realised that the most popular interactive games were those played on radio – such as Battle of the Sexes.

As a generic radio contest copied from station to station, Battle of the Sexes was not licensed or trademarked. Shane began by securing the trademark for the concepts outside radio, while building them into strong cross-media interactive games.

It was a turning point for Imagination. Shane took the popular radio trivia concept and turned it first into a board game, then sold it to Channel 10 as a television game show. Battle of the Sexes became the country's number one website and then a mobile phone game.

'It was a pioneering time. We were working to create a concept that could work across all platforms so the sum was greater than all of the parts, all fuelling each other.

'Our main focus was still TV production at the time and really the Battle of the Sexes concept was a hobby for me; something I was doing as a sideline.

'I ended up ringing the buyer for Kmart. It was crazy stuff because it's almost impossible to get to see the buyers for these organisations, especially when they don't know you.

'But I just rang him up and wouldn't take no for an answer. I said I'd be over to see him at 2 pm the next day, and jumped on a plane with the concept board game under my arm. I walked out of his office with an order for 10,000 units.

'Within the first year it was the highest selling board game in Australia, outselling Monopoly. I had to quickly work out a way to produce and supply four semi-trailer loads of these games.'

Over the next few years Shane went on to produce many TV programs including E! Entertainment (a weekly entertainment news program), Big Brother specials and dating program Match TV.

A $4.5 million capital raising was carried out in 2000, with high-profile investors such as Frank Lowy, John Singleton and Jack Cowin. An Australian Stock Exchange listing was planned, with the company expected to be capitalised between $80 and $100 million. But then came the 'tech wreck', scuttling the listing plans.

Shane admits that after the dot com crash he experienced his 'darkest hour'. With only three weeks of cash left, he had to sack 32 people in one day.

'It was a very stressful time – really horrible. I guess I just never wanted to let our investors down.

'There have been some deep, dark times where it looked like things wouldn't work out but we just pushed on and kept on going. In some of those dark hours, cash flow meant everything. We had to watch every dollar as we rebuilt from scratch.

'Fortunately I have been able to pick up a company that I knew only had three weeks of life left in it, restructure it and deliver growth on growth as we have built a new global consumer category.'

This revival was achieved through the development of the Imagination Games division of the company, which since 2001 has developed and distributed more than 15 successful board games around the world, including games for The Wiggles, Simpsons, Friends and Hi5.

Much of Shane's energy is now focused on taking the board game concept one stage further by adding the magic of television through the development of interactive DVD games, thus combining the company's two core competencies.

There is enormous upside in the concept. Unlike Playstation or Nintendo formats, DVD games can be cheaply manufactured and sold, and the market already has the equipment to play the games – the home DVD player.

Around 150 million homes around the world currently have a DVD player and this figure is expected to quadruple by 2009.

'DVD interactive games are really taking off now. I spent three years in a row trying to convince retailers that this was going to be the next great thing. Many of them didn't believe it. Now it's just exploding, and we are perfectly positioned to take advantage of that growth in the market.'

Imagination Entertainment controls all elements of the game development process, from concept through to creation, distribution and sale.

'If we come up with a new game concept, our speed to market is incredible because we control all the required elements needed to get it on the shelves. I can have a new game ready for shipping in two months.

'For one of the larger multinational organisations it may take them two years to get a concept onto the shelves. That gives us the jump on them every time.'

That's why the global games giant Hasbro has partnered with Imagination in Europe. Hasbro is one of the world's largest producers of board games. The relationship is helping Shane build his own company's image after he negotiated a no-cost co-branding deal whereby the Imagination name is now printed on the box of each game sold.

DVD games already represent about 10 per cent of total board game sales in the US, equating to approximately $US100 million a year. This figure is expected to rapidly grow in the coming years.

Achieving such enormous success has provided Shane with renewed faith in his own abilities.

'Early in my business career, I believed I was not the smart guy, so I had a lot of other people around me telling me how to do things. Many of them were consultants who thought they were going to make millions out of my companies with stock options and that sort of thing. They just had no street knowledge about running a business like mine.

'At the end of the day, I should have believed more in my own ability. That's certainly the case now. I have learnt a great deal over the years, and I now take much more control over steering Imagination's destiny.

'I remember way back when I was pitching TV shows I used to sit there quietly and not say much. Over time I just got more confidence – and now I don't like taking no for an answer.

'I'm not awed by too many people now. I have learnt that the best way to get things done is to just ring the right people on the phone and seek their involvement.

'These days there are not many people in Hollywood or around the world that I can't get on the phone. I was recently talking to actor Johnny Depp's people about him doing a project with us, and I signed socialite Paris Hilton to get involved in another project.

'I've got the contact book from hell – but I'm not scared of anyone and I don't have trouble asking for their help.

'I'm probably seen as "that guy who keeps ringing" and some people will take the call or meet with me just to find out what I want and why I'm so persistent. At the end of the day you will get a meeting once, but if you are not smart and inspiring they won't waste their time again. That will be the last chance you get.

'Luckily I'm a great negotiator and I can close deals. I just don't give up.'

Lessons Learnt:

* Get on a plane and start selling your idea – and don't stop. You never know who will say yes to your concept.
* Seek advice from others in areas that you're not an expert, but don't underestimate your own abilities and have the confidence to steer the business in the direction you think is best.
* If you love what you are doing and really believe in it, that will get you through those really tough times when you just want to give up.

Advice to Others:

* Don't be afraid to pick up the phone and ask people you admire for help. Don't waste their time, but if you've got a real problem or a real solution, you can get the right people on the phone.

Ian Young

Ian Young has learnt from experience that while having your own high-profile brand might be good for the ego, it's not the only way to business success.

His company, Mexican Express, has made a name for itself by becoming a valued supplier to other companies, rather than focusing on the more popular option of only developing and promoting its own products.

While the company has had its own branded products in the past, and still has a couple, its main focus these days is the supply of cheese and tomato-based products to major national food producers.

As the name suggests, Mexican Express's journey began in the Mexican food business.

Ian came to South Australia from Victoria in the late 1980s to become a director with a small Mexican restaurant chain that was considering the possibility of franchising.

In order to achieve consistency across the three restaurants, a central kitchen was established to produce much of the food used in the various dishes. The kitchen also started manufacturing products for others and the operation at that stage was named Mexican Express.

Several years later the various directors of the restaurant group parted ways, leaving Ian with the Mexican Express business.

In the mid 1990s executive chef and catering services manager Steve Pitman bought into the business, becoming Ian's partner.

Ian admits that in the early days, Mexican Express was involved in a wide variety of initiatives as a matter of necessity.

'What we haven't done isn't worth knowing about. I joke to people that we've travelled a rocky road, rather than a growth path.'

The initial focus was almost entirely on Mexican food, with the company producing its own food lines as well as wholesaling some products such as corn chips. National distribution was through a chain of privately owned distributors in each state, with Mexican Express establishing a presence interstate before it began selling in South Australia.

EXPRESS
MEXICAN EXPRESS
Nachos to Go
EXPRESS
Nachos to Go
Nachos to Go

Problems with some of the interstate companies meant that Mexican Express had to use a large food service distributor that wasn't comfortable with the company's speciality products. It was proving increasingly difficult for the company to distribute product nationally without Ian or Steve needing to be physically interstate on an almost daily basis.

While the company operated out of a simple factory facility, it had always been very aware of product quality and testing, and manufactured its product well within legislative requirements.

However, tightening food production legislation meant that the company needed to upgrade its facilities and an existing facility at Dudley Park was purchased from another food producer. Contract manufacturing jobs were taken on to help supplement revenue.

Contract manufacturing became even more important to the business when it decided to no longer wholesale products because of the high levels of inventory, and associated costs, that it had to carry. The move provided long-term benefit to the business, but it saw the company's turnover immediately drop by 50 per cent.

One thing I've learnt is that you've got to have your ego in the right spot otherwise you'll go broke.

As the contract manufacturing side of the business began to grow, Mexican Express undertook two strategic culls of its client list. The first step was to discontinue the very small jobs that it was doing that produced minimal return for considerable effort.

'Later, we stopped manufacturing for those medium-sized contracts that were unkind to our machinery, too labour intensive or required manufacturing that we just didn't want to do.

'While we had built up the contract manufacturing side of the business, we knew we had to cull what wasn't going to take us where we wanted to go long-term.

'I've lost count of how many times we've hit turnover of $3 million and then pulled back from there because of something we've decided to do for the long-term benefit of the business. However, we've had to do it and it's provided a good foundation for the future.'

One of the more expensive experiments for Ian was trying to develop his own retail food brand, by taking his food service products and packaging them into take-home Mexican food kits.

Initial discussions with a major retailer were held in January 2000 and by May the kits were on the shelves of 422 supermarkets nationally. In hindsight, Ian concedes the process was probably rushed and that some of the products should have been redeveloped for the retail market.

While the product was well received, the initial retail margin of $13.99 was too high and later the retailer dropped the price to $9.99, damaging the credibility of the brand. Small volumes of orders meant that distribution and packaging didn't have the required critical mass, becoming increasingly expensive.

The product was reluctantly withdrawn two years later.

Mexican Express does still have a few branded retail products, including its Nachos To Go and Dip Kits, which sell in Australia as well as Japan, Singapore and the Pacific Islands.

However, its core product range is now salsa sauces, cheese sauces, squeeze top cheese sauces, pre-cooked Mexican products, pre-cooked pasta sauces and seasonings.

Production is about 800 tonnes of product a year – about half of which is cheese products, 40 per cent tomato based and the remaining 10 per cent miscellaneous products.

'In 2002, from our strategic planning session, it was decided to concentrate on our three volume areas – cheese-based sauces, tomato-based sauces and unit packs.

'Rather than being everything to everybody we thought it best that our traditional Mexican food systems and products that we were known for were refocused under the Rosita's brand, taking us into a far superior sales and distribution market.

'Our focus now is on supporting and aligning ourselves with other brands and carving ourselves out a core segment of the Mexican heat-and-eat convenience food market which allows us to fulfil our unit pack aspirations.

'For example, Devondale is the largest cheese and butter manufacturer in Australia, but they don't make liquid cheese for food service, so we've aligned ourselves with that brand.

'We had our own brand of squeeze bottle cheese sauce, building on the success of our nachos cheese, which we developed for the service station hot dog market. It's now co-branded with Devondale and is one of our biggest selling products.

'Rosita's make corn chips and flour tortillas, but not salsas, so we have co-branded products with them.

'Devondale is a huge brand. If you put a good product in a Devondale pack it will sell. If you put a good product in an unknown pack, say like Mexican Express, nobody cares.

'I think that one thing I've learnt is that you've got to have your ego in the right spot otherwise you'll go broke.

'If you look at food retail these days it's dominated by huge manufacturers. For companies like ours, it's about finding the right partners and making sure that we're all working together towards the best outcome.'

Ian attributes the success of this partnership approach to 'the right strategic fit'.

'You've got to find something to bring to the table that the other company really needs.

'Every product has its features and benefits. You've got to be able promote your product offer, but don't change it.

'Be flexible and move with the times, but you can't say to a big company, "I'm going to do this for you this week, but something different next week and something else again the week after".

'It will usually take years to get a product up and running and selling well, so if you're going to change your mind, make it every four years or so – otherwise you're going to confuse your customers.'

Despite considering itself more a manufacturer of dairy products than Mexican food, there are no plans to move away from the Mexican Express name.

'I've lost count of the number of times that we've thought about whether we should change our company name, but our view has been that other people really don't care about our name. If we're supporting other brands, the last thing we want to do is be competing with them.

'So our name remains Mexican Express and the people who need to know us understand who we are and what we do.'

Lessons Learnt:

* Accept that your original plans may well change along the way. While it's good to have an idea of how you want the business to look in the future, accept that opportunities or challenges may take you in a different direction.
* Great companies don't have to be founded on their own brand. Your business may end up being more successful by partnering with others and becoming a valuable supplier or support to them.
* Don't be frightened to cull, or at least evaluate, your customer or client list from time to time. As your business grows and evolves it may well be that some of your existing customers aren't the best fit for your product or service.

Advice to Others:

* If you are partnering with others, particularly large companies, make sure you're consistent. It can take a massive time and financial commitment to get a product up and running and while you need to be flexible, your customers need to know that your product offering to them won't change.

Jim Zavos

For Jim Zavos, founder of EzyDVD, success hasn't always been easy. He's the first to admit that mistakes have been made along the way.

Fortunately for Jim those errors were made early on in life, providing the business lessons that have enabled him to create his thriving and ever-growing DVD retail company.

Working in his parents' fish and chip shop, as well as a paper round while still at school, gave Jim his first taste of running a business.

'It was through that experience that I became business savvy at a very young age. When I could see the benefits that owning a business brought to my family, I knew I wanted to be in business for myself.'

With this goal firmly set in his mind, Jim left Morialta High School in Year 9 to work full-time at Kmart.

His first business wasn't too far away – in 1982 he established a video store at the age of 18.

Jim was one of only a few people in Adelaide who owned a video player but was frustrated with the product and service on offer at his local video store. Thinking he could do it better, he established Redwood Video Hire.

It was one of the first video stores in Adelaide at a time when not many people owned a video player. Such was the 'privilege' of being able to watch videos that stores such as Jim's charged for membership.

Success in this venture saw Jim immerse himself in a series of family-owned businesses including delicatessens, pizza bars and supermarkets.

Gaining confidence with the success of each venture and feeling that he was 'invincible', he became involved with running a restaurant in his early 20s. It wasn't a pleasant experience for the young entrepreneur.

A lack of knowledge about the restaurant business saw him get his fingers badly burnt. It was only with the assistance of his family, a hard work ethic – learnt from his Greek immigrant parents – and persistence that he avoided bankruptcy.

'That was my entrepreneurial training – working in those many different businesses. I made a lot of mistakes and I learnt from these. I strongly believe that in order to be successful you have to make mistakes along the way.

'I'm a shrewder business person for those experiences, but I am grateful that I made my mistakes earlier rather than later, as I didn't have as many responsibilities when I was younger and I was able to tough it out.

'When you are running a business the size EzyDVD is now, you can't afford to make too many mistakes.'

Having nearly lost everything he had worked so hard to achieve, Jim decided to stick to what he knew best – video retailing.

'It was my passion, my life and something I knew I did really well.'

You either want to go out there and make it happen or you don't. I think it's in your blood and I had that desire as a young kid.

Jim still had the original video store and soon expanded this to a group of six stores as part of the burgeoning Video Ezy franchise.

People regularly hired videos but the quality of the product and its tendency to quickly deteriorate through use meant people generally didn't collect them.

Then, in 1996, Jim read about the development and pending introduction of the DVD (Digital Versatile Disc) and recognised that being able to access movies in a format that was practically indestructible would be an instant success with the consumer.

He kept a close eye on the release of the DVD in the US and used his honeymoon as an opportunity to take a study tour there. The trip confirmed Jim's belief that DVDs would be a huge success and offered tremendous business opportunities.

In 1999 Jim invested $3000 to develop a website – www.ezydvd.com.au – pioneering the introduction of DVDs into Australia. It was originally available to customers of his six video stores, allowing them to buy DVDs online and make bookings for rentals. Only 12 titles were available for purchase in those early days.

'In retrospect, and against today's standards, the website was extremely basic with very few features and very little functionality. Fortunately it was the start of the internet era so there was very little expectation from visitors to the website.'

Despite the basic nature of the website it quickly became popular with customers and others, confirming Jim's belief that DVDs would be enormously successful. He sold his video stores within months of starting the website to focus on expanding the on-line business.

By 2001 the EzyDVD business was booming and the website was considered the only serious destination for the on-line purchase of DVDs in Australia. However, many consumers had concerns about security and remained reluctant to submit their credit card details on-line.

There was growing demand for 'over the counter' sales and Jim realised that a network of specialist retail stores would be viable. The first EzyDVD retail store was opened in Regent Arcade, in the Adelaide CBD, in April 2001. Emulating the success of the website, the store was hugely popular from the first day.

By the end of that year, EzyDVD had an on-line business and three specialist retail stores that were rapidly developing a thriving market. The business was not only extremely successful with customers, it was winning the confidence and support of the major movie studios, ensuring Jim had easy access to the fast growing number of titles becoming available on DVD.

Recognising there was still so much potential in EzyDVD but constrained by availability of funds to keep opening stores, the decision was made to move into franchising.

In October 2002 the first franchisee store, in Sydney, was opened and by the end of that year, 10 retail stores were trading.

There are now about 40 EzyDVD stores spread across all Australian mainland states. The stores are predominantly located in high-traffic, high-profile shopping centres and major developers now actively seek to include an EzyDVD store in their centres.

EzyDVD is the only national retailer that sells only DVDs, stocking more than 9000 titles. The website continues to be extremely popular – it receives thousands of orders daily and is considered the number one e-commerce store in Australia.

By 2003 the explosion in the popularity of DVDs meant the Australian market was worth $800 million and mass market retailers such as Kmart, Target and Big W were dominant despite the success of EzyDVD.

'I could see that the market was only going to keep on growing and that if we were going to keep pace with that growth that we would need a partner to help us with our operations.

'I had traditionally run smaller family businesses for more than 20 years and knew that we had to do something different to take us to the next level.'

Australian Stock Exchange-listed company Brazin Ltd, which owns the Sanity and Virgin music chains of around 300 stores in Australia, was also having difficulty competing with the discount chains on DVDs.

Jim approached them regarding a joint venture and they subsequently purchased 50 per cent of EzyDVD in October 2003, providing Jim with $1.5 million in cash and $4.8 million worth of Brazin shares.

The move was the catalyst for continued rapid expansion. The company recently clocked up $100 million in annual sales, representing 10 per cent of the national DVD market.

The company's goal is to have 100 stores operating by Christmas 2005. The longer-term business plan will include stores in regional areas, a move that could easily take the number of locations to well in excess of 150.

For Jim, his 'leap-frog' approach to creating businesses and then moving on or rapidly expanding them has rewarded him handsomely. In 2004 he was named in *Business Review Weekly*'s 'Young Rich' list with a fortune of $15 million.

Along the way he has also won a swag of local and national awards for entrepreneurship and business innovation.

'Entrepreneurship is about looking for that next opportunity and then seizing on it. It might be that there's a shop for lease next door to where you are already running a business – and it can grow from something as simple as that.

'It's about building on the success that you've already achieved for yourself.

'While I really enjoyed those early days, I became bored with the smaller businesses as there really wasn't much opportunity to grow further.

'Each business that I've operated has been bigger than the one before it. I knew that if I wanted to make it big I had to keep starting new businesses or find ways of rapidly growing those businesses that I already had.

'You either want to go out there and make it happen or you don't. I think it's in your blood and I had that desire as a young kid.'

Lessons Learnt:

* Start early. If you're working hard in a business environment from an early age, this provides you with many years of experience while you are still relatively young. This can give you 'the jump' on those who come to business later in life.
* Accept that you will make mistakes. The trick is to make these at a time when they will have minimal impact on your long-term success.
* Stick to what you know and don't be fooled into thinking that success in one venture will automatically translate to another.

Advice to Others:

* You won't make the big league if you're standing still. Always be on the lookout to capitalise on your achievements to date and to take yourself to the next level.